THE GET A JOB WORKSHOP

How to Find Your Way to a Creative Career in Advertising, Branding, Collateral, Digital, Experiential, & More

Laurence Minsky - Executive Editor
Bruce Bendinger - Publisher

With contributions from 33 people who want to help you succeed

The Get a Job Workshop
How to Find Your Way to a Creative Career
in Advertising, Branding, Collateral, Digital, Experiential & More

© 2013 The Copy Workshop
All Rights Reserved. Published 2013.
Printed in the United States of America
22 21 20 19 18 17 16 15 14 13   1 2 3 4 5

ISBN: 978-1-887229-47-0

Published by The Copy Workshop
A division of Bruce Bendinger Creative Communications, Inc.
2144 N. Hudson • Chicago, IL 60614
773-871-1179 • www.adbuzz.com

Cover Design: Kristi Pagoulatos, Associate Creative Director, commonground Marketing

This book is dedicated to your first professional paycheck.

The Next Level

Let's start with a story.

It's the beginning of college baseball season.

A young pitcher is getting hit hard and often.

After two ugly innings, the coach comes out for a chat.

"Coach," says the young pitcher, "I don't get it. In high school I struck out eight of every nine guys."

The coach smiles and pats the pitcher on the shoulder. "Don't worry son. That ninth guy? They're all here."

Hold that thought.

You may already be one of the best in your class, maybe one of the best in your school. You may be in a great college program, and you're probably working hard so that you can do well in the world outside.

That's great. Only now think of all those people in all those other programs for whom that is also true. Do you have what it takes? Do they? Probably.

But the whole point of this book – a collection of good advice from some of the very best people out there – is that, good as you are, hard as you're working, you still have to dial it up.

You have to get to "The Next Level." Get it?

It's simple and it's complicated. You need to develop your skills further. That's simple. Sort of. And you need to enlarge your understanding of all the opportunities in today's evolving marketplace. That's complicated. Very.

And as you develop your own career strategy, you need the know-how (and the know-who) to help you make the right connections – the ones that lead to the job that's right for you.

Now you understand what this book is all about.

And the people who are going to help you?

They're all here.

Welcome to the Workshop

I know what you're thinking.

Is this book really going to help me get a job?

The short answer is "yes."

The longer answer is contained in the pages of this book.

And the even longer answer will be contained in all the work that you are going to do to make it happen. Because, as Frank Blossom of The Polishing Center observes, *"It's a job to get a job."*

Frank is one of the many contributors to this book, and that's just one of the useful insights we've pulled together.

It's a job getting a job, and it's an even bigger job building a career.

After all, as Jobs Propulsion Labs Founder and contributor to this book Bart Cleveland reminds us, your first few jobs will help determine the quality of your later ones, despite what you picked up from reading F. Scott Fitzgerald.

And to be a success in your early jobs – as well as your long-term career – you actually need to master the skills (and manage the process) in three key areas:

First, your search: This book casts a wider net on the ever expanding – and fast growing – world of creative marketing and advertising. It's the first book that we know of that shows you a wider range of creative career choices—important, because a wider choice means you have a better chance of finding the best fit.

Just one request: Please set aside those pre-conceived notions that come from too many episodes of Mad Men and open yourself up to the real world of opportunity.

Second, your portfolio: What was once a pretty standard collection of stuff in a black zipper case has turned into an area as dynamic as the Internet itself. No longer can you get away with a "book" consisting of three campaigns – a campaign for a durable, one for a service, and a final one for a packaged good – each with three ads. Now it takes much more thought, planning, and creativity.

Finally, your reputation: That collection of tangibles and intangibles that will influence everything from the initial "you've got the job" decision to the ability to build a successful long-term career.

Before you dig in to the rest of the book, let's look at these three areas, starting with your search and ending with your reputation.

To start, you need to understand the creative marketplace. A marketplace that is continually evolving. You need to know:

- What do you want, and why do you want it?
- And what will a prospective employer get from you, and why will they get it?

This will help you understand where you fit. Which might not be as obvious as you first thought.

Which brings up the second, although intertwined, key area: Your ability to go to market.

Before you can have a reputation (at least a positive one in the industry), you'll need a portfolio – something that hints at your abilities if you're just starting out and one that clearly shows it if you are already working – and someone will need to "buy" it.

This requires you to market yourself.

In other words, you also need to be able to explain yourself and sell yourself during the interview.

It also requires that your portfolio is current with (not just that your work is up-to-date, but also that your portfolio reflects) or exceeds current expectations. After all, what's required in them – outside of smart thinking – is changing every day.

Finally, your reputation on the job – as an intern, full-timer, or freelancer – is clearly tied to your abilities, and, if you are currently a student, they are being developed right now. But that is not enough.

As ad legend Lee Clow said in my first book, the now semi-classic *How to Succeed in Advertising When All You Have Is Talent,* you need to think of your first few jobs as a continuation of your education – and even that is not enough.

You need to invest in developing your skills on your own, so when a boss gives you a new assignment, you can hit it out of the park.

And keep in mind that even a few jobs in, your learning doesn't stop. And it never should if you want to keep up with the pace of change within the industry.

---

* If you're so compelled to check it out, I recommend the Second Edition published by The Copy Workshop in 2007.

What's more, your reputation is clearly connected to how well you manage it. To quote ad legend Nancy Rice – again from my first book (sorry) – "Make sure you merchandise yourself early in your career. If you don't do this for yourself as well as you do it for your clients, your career isn't going to go far."

Some of you may intuitively have all the answers.

But most of you will need to work through all of the questions. That means this is a workbook where you're actually going to have to do some work. But we've made that hard work as enjoyable as we know how – with interesting essays as well as illuminating activities – all designed to help you launch a successful creative career.

To accomplish this task, we have brought together a team of experts who really will help you do your job.

Many of them have written their own books, teach in "post-graduate" portfolio programs, are on the faculty at leading colleges and universities and understand your needs in the classroom, or they're practitioners who have some useful perspectives on generally ignored corners of the job market – really great opportunities that you might not have considered – and they all want you to succeed.

Each and every one of them is an educator at heart. Each offers great insights that you can use right now and long into your career!

They've all been very generous with their time and advice, and I'd like to give them an extra thank you here. We'll save the group hug for later – *after* you get the job. And we bet you will get that job – if you do the work.

Once you learn from their insights, take advantage of their advice, and see your results, I bet you'll want to thank them, too!

So here's to success.

Read on!

Contents

Section III: Going to Market

Section IV: On the Job

Section I:
Overview

"You need to know how to sell yourself,"
> Alison Sullivan, Photo Researcher and Photographer's Agent

Welcome to the section specifically designed to help you get ready for the job of getting a job. That means you need to get to "the next level."

- First, we'll tell you a few things about the growing range of opportunities you can find out there. "Six Words."
- Next, Rick Mathieson is going to introduce you to "Generation Wow" and help you get a feel for what it's going to take.
- That growing range also includes increased diversity. Aubrey Walker, Creative Director at Commonground provides some valuable insight in "Why?"
- Ever hear of a book called *Hey Whipple, Squeeze This*? You need to read it. But while you're waiting for it to arrive from Amazon, author Luke Sullivan gives you food for thought in "Dynamite Stored Here." Think of it as an appetizer.
- This first section finishes up with "Career Gear," a brief summary of what you need to be packing to get that job.

OK, let's go.

Six Words

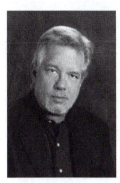

Bruce Bendinger
The Copy Workshop

The job market has changed. So, if you're reading a career book that was first written ten, or twenty, or thirty years ago, you're kind of not getting fresh information. Things have changed. Big time.

For example, if your career guide only guides you to advertising, or design, or PR, you're missing some of the most interesting pieces of the puzzle.

Let's see how quickly and simply Bruce can explain what's going on.

Think you can remember six words? OK.

Understand the six simple words and their slightly more complicated implications and you'll start to have a handle on the opportunities that are out there. No kidding.

Understand those six words and you'll have a clue about who might want to hire you, what it is they might want you to do, and how success will be measured in the 21st Century. Fasten your seat belts.

Advertising. MarCom. StratCom. Paid. Owned. Earned.

Those six words sum up the evolution of the Media Marketplace and the exciting growth in new career opportunities – at the same time many old business models lost steam. Let's look at what's going on.

Advertising. MarCom. StratCom.

First, let's understand these three words. It started with *advertising* (you know what that is), but it has grown into something more.

The seed of advertising has grown into a multi-functional something we call *MarCom* – Marketing Communications. It's a whole range of marketing activities – and most of them are hiring.

Now we're also seeing that's even broader in scope – *StratCom* – Strategic Communication. This is also communication with a purpose.

MarCom = Marketing Communications

First, let's make a quick alphabetical list of MarCom activities:

- **Advertising.** Ad agencies used to do most of this – now ads are also created by design firms, media companies, and digital providers.
- **Branding & Design.** The traditional design firm, which did things like logos, letterheads, and package and store design, now works on a whole range of marketing communications activities. Design and design thinking have become more and more important as a way to handle the growing range of communication "touch points."
- **Direct Marketing.** This is a discipline that combines database expertise (the list of targets), sales promotion thinking (the incentive that will get us to respond), and creative writing (the design and creation of the message that serves it up).
- **Event/Experiential Marketing.** We've all been to concerts, festivals, and street fairs. Spring break is another example. Here, marketers look to get our involvement as we experience an enjoyable event. Posters, hats, T-shirts, and free samples are the things you see. There's a lot more that goes on behind the scenes.
- **New Media.** It might not be new to you, but that's what we call it. This refers to the whole range of digitally delivered communications. Digital? We can dig it. The growth of the Internet and all the related activities is what many of us call New Media. As you might imagine, in this area, the job market is exploding.
- **Public Relations.** Here, companies look to get their messages into the old-fashioned media, the kind we read and watch. Done well, publicity is very cost effective; if you have a knack for that kind of writing and thinking, you can do well.
- **Sales Promotion.** Here, marketers use incentives to influence our behavior. The creative message is usually wrapped around the incentive (Win/Free/Save) to get us to buy.

And there are other combined forms of MarCom – for example …

- **Sports Marketing** – this is an exciting combination of all these things – Sales Promotion (think of the special events and giveaways), Public Relations (press conferences and press releases), Direct Marketing (that's how they sell Season Tickets), and New Media (naturally, you want a website for the fans).

See? The marketing marketplace has opened up a ton of opportunities for those who like to communicate with a purpose. And that's not the only aspect of sports marketing to consider. Many companies and promotional agencies have sports-related marketing activities (e.g. beverage and fast food marketers). On that side of the game, sports marketing ranges from sponsored shirts for the local ball team to global sponsorship of the Olympics.

And that's not the only kind of purposeful communication.

StratCom = Strategic Communications

StratCom is also communication with a purpose. While building business through marketing is a big important purpose, two other important reasons to communicate are also a part of our lives – *Inform* and *Entertain.*

All the different types of strategic communications have one, two, or three of these objectives. Sell. Inform. Entertain. Sometimes it's only one. Sometimes it's all three.

When you look at the range of creative communications jobs in our 21st Century economy, that pretty much sums up the range of tasks that can make for a pretty interesting career. Here's a quick list of some careers attached to the Inform and Entertain parts of the StratCom world.

Information: News – whether the newspaper, broadcast, or your own blog, as a society we value good information on what's happening right now. It isn't just news, *education* is an important part of the information business – we need to know about better health and better ways to learn all the things there are to know. If you have the skills to make learning interesting, that could be an exciting opportunity.

Entertainment: Here's another word to remember – *Content.* That's what some of us call the communication that fills all those media channels – movies, TV shows, articles, and more. It's songs, poems, and comedy routines. Music videos, reality shows, movies, and sitcoms.

Put them all together and you're beginning to understand the playing field for those who are thinking about a career in communication. This book is going to focus on the advertising and MarCom parts of that playing field, but realize that jobs can grow in interesting new directions and, more and more, cross the borders of the various disciplines.

For example ... Years ago, a young advertising copywriter wrote a very entertaining commercial for Nike – it featured the basketball star Michael Jordan and the cartoon character Bugs Bunny. The commercial was so successful that the ad writer became a screenwriter, helping to write the movie *Space Jam*. Maybe you saw it when you were younger.

Or how about *Home Alone*? John Hughes, who wrote a lot of the movies you may have enjoyed, started out as an advertising copywriter.

So, your first job could be a first step in a career path that takes you in all kinds of interesting directions. And, of course, it depends on what you're good at and what interests you.

We all have to start somewhere. But today, there are more and more exciting opportunities related to where you might end up.

For example, you might start with a career in health care marketing, helping to introduce important new medicines, and then finding yourself writing health information designed to help mothers with nutrition or seniors with the consequences of diabetes – you won't be selling anything, but you'll be doing an important job – that's StratCom – strategic communication.

OK, got it? *Advertising. MarCom. StratCom.*

Now let's talk about those other three words.

Paid. Owned. Earned.

OK. This section is short, but once you truly understand it, it should make your head explode. (If your head doesn't explode, read it again.)

Companies, and other groups, like non-profits and government organizations, have a lot of ways to communicate – a lot of channels.

Once, when the media world was advertising dominant, we focused mainly on channels that were *paid* communications – things like newspaper and magazine ads, billboards, and commercials for TV and radio.

All of that is still big business.

But now that playing field has grown as well. Seen something you liked on YouTube? Maybe you were at a street fair and picked up a brochure that interested you, or you were shopping and picked up a magazine and found that it was published by a drug store or some hip marketer like Red Bull.

That brochure and that sponsored magazine are something we call *owned* media. The marketer owns it (the regular magazine, where you pay for an ad is *paid* media – got it?).

Now how about that pop-up concert you saw on your way to class.

It might have been created by a marketer, then picked up by the news, and that coverage by the news is what we call *earned* media.

This is the BNG – Big New Game – and content creators for Big Smart Brands are changing it Big Time.

And here's another word – *negotiated*. Often times you can trade out space in the media you own, such as on your website or packaging or in your restaurant or store, for the equivalent space (i.e. equivalent number of exposures) in media somebody else owns, such as an amusement park.

Two More Words... StratCon and Shared.

As you can tell, the playing field is changing under our feet.

And, as this book was being assembled, we sensed two more words entering into your vocabulary.

StratCon – Strategic Conversation.

One-way communication models pretty much defined 20th Century communication. People now have the power to interact with virtually every message. And that has created a new advertising communication model based on a part of traditional human behavior: Conversation – where there is a back-and-forth dialogue between you (or your brand) and someone else.

Once, technology only allowed for one-way communication – whether printed on newspapers or broadcast on television.

But now, the audience has the power to respond and interact.

Now, unlike free-wheeling conversation late at night with friends, this is most often managed conversation. But it is conversation nonetheless.

The most obvious manifestation is what we call social media.

So as you think about strategies for Advertising, MarCom, and StratCom (with an "m"), you might also need to start thinking about StratCon – with an "n" – strategic conversation.

Shared.

This is another word to describe what we call Social Media. It's interactive. It's – to some degree – a conversation. But let's face it, you usually have a strategic objective. And it's changing even as you read this. The clear lines of commerce – who pays, who buys – start to blur, and it's clearly still in a state of evolution.

Six Little Words: One Big World

OK, it's time to stretch your mind to understand how big and growing and changing that world is.

TV commercials that turn into movies.

Careers that start in one place and grow into another place entirely.

This is the playing field you are entering. Try to understand the range that's available to you – and how fast it's all changing. Then focus in on the fields that are the best match for your strengths and your interests.

Got it? Good.

Now let's review what we just talked about.

Work Steps

Throughout this book, we'll be offering some additional thoughts on additional work you can do to get better, get smarter, or get ready. Get it?

The work steps themselves might not be all that profound, but, just like sit-ups, spending time doing them can help you shape up.

1.   **Review.** After you read each of these articles, think about what they just told you. Each of the people in this book has something useful to say. What was it? Learning to take in new information and have it stick is a critical skill. Practice it.

2.   **Write down the six words.** Seriously. Write them down. Now what we'd like you to do is write your own definition next to each. But we'll settle for your spending a bit of time thinking about them.

3.   **List the MarCom variations.** This one's serious. Any more come to mind?

4.   **Pick one.** Select a type of MarCom that interests you. And …

5.   **Look for examples.** Make this something you think about as you make your way through your day. Look around. Make a mental note each time you see an example – and think about what it is and who might have been paid for doing it.

More Resources:

First, some materials from *The Copy Workshop Workbook*.

- Go to adbuzz.com – click on CAFÉ.
- Download **The MarCom Matrix Worksheet**.

- Download the pdf section from the book – pages 110 to 134 – it's a great introduction. It should be labeled **The MarCom Matrix**. Better yet, buy the book. It just so happens that adbuzz.com has a bookstore, and you can get 20% off. (By the way, we'll be recommending a lot of books in this book. Now you know what to put on your gift list.)

Bruce Bendinger will be showing up here and there throughout this book. No escape. He's the publisher, so we guess he can pretty much do what he wants. Some have observed that Bruce seems to have an exploding resume. In his twenties, he won awards and became the youngest-ever VP Creative Director at Leo Burnett. In his thirties, he had a music company, did consulting for ad agencies and for companies ranging from Apple Computer to a President of the United States. He produced music with rock and roll legends and had a few more corner office creative jobs. He was even a CMO (Chief Marketing Officer) for one of those dotcoms. Then, onto more creative consulting, and publishing books like The Copy Workshop Workbook, Hitting the Sweet Spot, The Book of Gossage, Advertising & The Business of Brands, *and* How to Put Your Book Together and Get a Job in Advertising. *As you might imagine, he has a lot to say about the business, and since he's the publisher, we don't quite know how to stop him. FYI, Bruce does not watch* Mad Men *but tells us he's due to show up in two more seasons – wearing bell bottoms.*

Welcome to 'Generation Wow'

Rick Mathieson
Award-winning Writer, Author, and Creative Strategist

What does it take to make it today?

Here, a top MarCom professional offers us his take on the world where you're going to be looking for a job. This is the same advice Rick offers to executives on many of the world's top brands.

It's an exciting snapshot of today's noisy marketplace, where products and services will either be found – or ignored. The right creative solution can make all the difference.

Take the time to understand what Rick is saying. Some of it may feel a bit "over your head."

That just means you need to read it again – so you can grab onto his insights and put them to work for you.

A Philosophical Approach to Staying ahead of the Change Curve

Call it the digital generation.

The websites are so 20th century generation.

The iPhone-toting, Facebook-hopping, Angry Bird-fragging, Twitter-tapping, I-want-what-I-want, when-where-and-how-I-want-it generation.

In an age of mobile apps, augmented reality, viral videos and emerging forms of social media, the digital revolution is having a seismic impact on marketers the world over.

Whether your target audience is 18-years-old or 80, traditional television spots and even expansive online campaigns are no longer even remotely enough. Today, your audience is simply and relentlessly rejecting media – and brand marketers – that fail to connect with their interests and their increasingly interconnected digital lifestyles.

So what are marketers to do? How do you create the kind of experiences needed to engage consumers in an increasingly fragmented media universe?

How do you identify and capitalize on the right mix of digital channels and interactions that will build awareness and demand for your offerings – before your audience hits the snooze button?

In short: How do you stay ahead of the change curve?

Whether you're a seasoned industry veteran or a promising new entrant, it's about far more than (just) tracking the latest technologies and trends – it's almost impossible (and maybe even unnecessary) to do so.

What most marketers (including many young ones) lack are the right tools – the philosophical framework – to create the kinds of experiences consumers demand, whether it's through the digital platforms we know and use today or ones we haven't even dreamed of yet.

In my book, *The On-Demand Brand*, I interview many of today's most innovative marketers about what has worked in digital, what hasn't – and why. What emerges is a set of rules that any new marketer would be well advised to follow. Here are a few of the most important.

Keep them in mind as you begin your career.

Insight Comes before Inspiration

At advertising agencies across the land, if you've heard it once, you've heard it a million times. Let's do "x" – insert your own trendy marketing buzzword here. Not because it has any relevance to target consumers – who don't, despite all the hype, necessarily want to seek out ways to engage with your brand.

Rather, it's because "x" is the sexy digital watchword of the day, and every agency needs to be doing it – whatever "it" is – before the agency's coolness credentials are questioned.

It's just as bad, or worse, among the ranks of brand marketers – especially large, established brands.

Who hasn't heard this uttered at least once from a high-level executive's mouth: "We need a mobile (or social, or viral, or some other "x") strategy. Never mind that these are channels, not strategies, and it's akin to someone proclaiming, "We need a TV commercial strategy," or, "We need a brochure strategy."

The truth of the matter is, it doesn't matter what you know, or what you think you know, about digital.

Most successful digital initiatives typically don't start with an amazing idea for a cool new experience or a "me too" approach to major trends.

Instead, they start with consumer insights culled from painstaking research into who your customers are, what they're all about, how they interact with consumer technologies, and what they want from the brands they know and trust.

Dove, for instance, conducted a 10-country study of 3,200 girls and women aged 18 to 64 to better understand their satisfaction with their own looks. What resulted was the massively successful Campaign for Real Beauty, which used channels like social media, mobile, and digital outdoor signage to encourage women to define their own sense of beauty – and helped increase Dove sales by 10% worldwide.

Dove could have just run the standard issue ad campaign. Instead, by truly understanding their customer, they were able to start a movement.

Don't Just Join the Conversation – Spark It

When it comes to social media, I'm not sure what kind of crack we've all been smoking. Who says every brand has got to have its own Facebook page? Who says people want to have a personal relationship with your brand – much less hang out with people who do?

Despite all the hype we hear today, social media will go through the hype cycle of great expectations before falling to earth just a bit.

At this writing anyway, Forrester Research is finding that the percentage of online Americans who actually use social media may at least be temporarily flattening or even declining just a bit.

Regardless of how the popular social networks we know today evolve, or which new ones emerge, look for some advertisers to start tapping into a growing anti- anti-social media dynamic that's brewing in the marketplace.

Over the next few years, consumers will start being as authentic in their online relationships as they are in their offline relationships. And brands will realize that we're past the point of thinking of social media as a cool way to connect with consumers. Instead, they will come to view social media as a means by which brands can enable consumers to connect with one another.

One needs look no further than Johnson & Johnson's BabyCenter.com, to find a great example. The site is so popular with mothers seeking advice and camaraderie that it attracts 78% of online women in the US with children under two.

Or consider Vail Resorts, a chain of ski resorts that has extended this equation, moving beyond connecting consumers in the same old lame desktop Internet experience – out into the physical world.

With Vail's Epic Mix mobile app, friends can see exactly where their peeps are on the slopes; earn points and badges that can be redeemed back at the lodge; post automated status updates to Facebook and Twitter about their activities; and review and compare their performances with others.

Look for this trend to become far more common as social media continues to evolve.

Products Are the New Services

You may not recognize it by taste alone, but Coors Light isn't just a beer anymore.

It's a portfolio of Facebook apps that enable you to access maps that direct your "brew crew" to nearby bars.

For that matter, Chantix isn't just a smoking-cessation drug anymore, either. It's a service that connects you with a personalized website and easy-to-use tools to track your progress, as well as access to support groups and on-call coaches who can help you squelch your addiction.

Even your Special K cereal is far more than a lowly bowl of cornflakes these days. It's an online weight management service and social network called "The Special K Challenge," where you can share your frustrations and triumphs with others, and customize a meal plan that is, not coincidentally, built around Special K products ranging from Cinnamon Pecan Special K Cereal to Pink Lemonade Special K20 protein water mix.

The point? In the digital age, differentiation may come less from the quality with which your products are manufactured and more from the on-demand digital services they deliver to your customers.

The Nike+ running system, which enables you to track your running performance through your iPod, helped Nike's share of the running show category skyrocket from 48% to 61% in just three years.

Whatever the product you're marketing, always look for ways to expand that product into a service to deliver added value to customers and to help your offering stand apart in an increasingly crowded marketplace.

It's Good to Play Games with Your Customers

It won't come as any surprise to young professionals that for consumers of a certain age, there's no better way to engage them than to play with them – in the form of branded games.

In fact, according to studies, consumers will spend an average of 12 minutes with branded games – far longer than they're likely to spend with most forms of marketing communication.

Whether you're talking about a print ad that lets you play an augmented reality driving game featuring a VW Jetta or a Concentration-style game promoting the latest features of Microsoft Office, games can make sense for any brand, in any category, whether you're talking B2C or B2B.

And some are doing some serious bank with all this fun and games.

When Burger King launched a line of X-Box games featuring its creepy King character, it ended up selling three million copies, to the tune of $11 million in revenue.

And when they gave the games away at participating restaurants as promotional items, burger sales shot up 10%.

This trend will only grow – in new and unexpected ways – in coming years.

Mobile Is Where It's At

Mobile isn't (just) about advertising sent to consumers via phones and tablets. It's also – more importantly – the ultimate response mechanism or activation mechanism for traditional print, television, direct, outdoor, and radio advertising.

When women's wear brand Bravissimo ran a TV spot asking viewers to visit a website, call an 800 number, or send a text message, text messaging turned out to be by far the most popular response mechanism, accounting for 43% of all responses.

Factor in mobile apps like Foursquare and Shopkick, as well as offerings like Kraft's iFood Assistant meal planning tool, and suddenly what was once purely promotional now offers utility for consumers on the move.

The importance of all this cannot be underemphasized. No matter how the notion of a mobile "app" evolves – from native apps to web apps to who knows what else – mobile will ultimately define the brand experience for many companies.

That's true whether someone uses what we presently call an "app" – like the one that enables you to point your phone at a color to see the closest matching Benjamin Moore paint, along with a map to the nearest retail location carrying it – to the most utilitarian.

Nationwide Insurance's iPhone app, for instance, carries all your insurance information and, in the event of an accident, enables you to collect the other party's information and send it directly to Nationwide. Press a button, and police are dispatched. Press another, and a repair truck is on its way. You can even capture photos and videos of the crash scene to send directly to the company.

In essence, this app becomes the brand. The only other time you're likely to interact with your insurance carrier is when you are buying your policy. This becomes the brand experience at the exact moment you want and need the brand most.

Factor in the way mobile will begin to dramatically enhance the in-store shopping experience, and we will surely be looking at a radical redefinition of what we call "mobile marketing" – and, by the way, what we call "retailing" – for a new generation of shoppers.

And all of this is just the beginning.

Welcome to 2054

The examples I've mentioned here only hint at what will come to be during your careers.

Over the mid-term, we may experience a phase reminiscent of the marketing-centric world imagined by Steven Spielberg in his visionary 2002 film, *Minority Report.*

In my first book, *Branding Unbound,* I interview scenario planner Peter Schwartz, the futurist Steven Spielberg hired to define the consumer-driven world of 2054.

In reality, what Schwartz described was so fantastic that he and his team actually scaled things back – from 2054 to the year 2020.

Whether things work out that way remains to be seen. But in some respects, I think the film represents the logical progression of advertising, at least for a period.

Commerce may (or may not) be driven by retina scans. But we are looking at a world where advertising will increasingly call out to us on a first name basis, based on our identities, our preferences, our advertising response behaviors, our past purchase histories, and more.

That's already happening with mobile marketing today, with location-based marketing and technologies like Near Field Communications (NFC) – and has been happening on the old school Internet for over a decade.

But there is an element to the movie that I think most people missed, and I think really illustrates the possible mid-term future of advertising.

If you watch closely, you'll realize the main character, played by Tom Cruise, lives in a suburb where there is absolutely no advertising.

What you have is a stratified society where the wealthy control their communications environments – through technologies and/or just political pull – and the middle- and lower classes are advertised to, pardon the pun, ad nauseam. I think this is a fair representation of the situation the industry and our culture is speeding toward already today, online and off.

New tools will help people of means block intrusive advertising and enable them to instantly call up offers based on their needs and preferences, when and where they want them – free of obtrusive overtures. Everyone else: Look out.

Without regulation and common sense, I think this is a likely scenario, at least in the mid-term.

You and your generation will help define marketing's future - and whether it resembles Spielberg's dystopian vision, or something exciting, fun and rewarding for consumers and brands alike.

Bernbach Is Dead

Whatever the future holds, recognize one thing as you begin your career: As revolutionary as it once was, the old Bernbach model – putting a writer together with an art director and going from there – is as anachronistic as TV's *Mad Men*.

Today, ad agencies are really software companies – experience companies – built around media of all sorts.

Make no mistake: There are no longer "old media" or "new media." There are just "media" – and it's your job to figure out the right mix of media and experiences to connect with consumers and move your business (or your client's business) forward.

That takes putting developers, programmers, media planners, account executives, art directors, copywriters, and others in the same room, working together to push through new limits to create the kinds of innovative experiences that make consumers go "WOW!"

The most successful marketers of your generation will think bigger, bolder, and far more bodaciously about creating consumer experiences enabled and empowered by amazing new digital technologies.

It's what makes this the most exciting time ever to be entering the industry. For the first time ever, if you can dream it, you can quite literally do it.

And you'll have a whole lot of fun along the way.

Work Steps:

Rick Mathieson gave us some thoughts to "keep in mind."

Before we go onto the next chapter, let's think about them and see how they can help us sharpen our thinking for today's job market.

1. **Find your answer.** What does he mean by "Insight Comes Before Inspiration?" As you review your work, what insights inspired your creative solutions?

2. **Find your answer (again).** OK, what the heck does "products are the new services" mean? Hint: you want to expand the conceptual footprint of the brand you are working on. How will you do that? The author cites some examples. Can you name any examples? Does your current portfolio have any examples?

3. **Spark the conversation – don't just join it.** Actually, this is good advice for our lives as well as our career. How do we get an interesting conversation going? (This is a skill you can practice pretty much all the time.) Here's a way to exercise that skill: When you meet someone, how quickly can you discover and then generate conversation around that person's favorite topic?

4. **Play games with your customers.** Gaming is big and getting bigger. Here's a game. Invent a game for each brand in your portfolio.

5. **Make it mobile.** Do your concepts "travel" well? How are you mobilizing the concepts in your portfolio?

— — — — — —

Rick Mathieson *is a leading voice on marketing in the digital age.*

An award-winning writer, author, speaker, and frequent media commentator, Mathieson helps brands understand and capitalize on new digital platforms as part of integrated communications initiatives.

Heralded as a strategic marketing expert by Harvard Business School's Working Knowledge, *Mathieson's insights have been featured in* ADWEEK, Advertising Age, Wired, Forbes, *and on* MSNBC, CBS Radio *and* NPR.

His book Branding Unbound *has ranked as the world's #1 best-selling book on mobile marketing. And it has been hailed as a visionary and indispensable guide to the mobile revolution.*

And his most recent, The On-Demand Brand, *was a #1 Amazon "Hot New Release," and has ranked among Amazon's Top 10 books on advertising. Spanning social media, branded entertainment, mobile marketing, and more, the book has been described as "required reading for the digital age" for its strategic approach to delivering blockbuster brand experiences through digital innovation.*

Over the last few years, he has briefed executives from FedEx, Virgin America, Bloomingdales, Procter & Gamble, Yahoo, Kraft Foods, MasterCard, Hard Rock Café, Accenture and many other organizations on the trends in digital marketing and emerging media platforms.

A veteran of the advertising industry, Mathieson has been recognized with over a hundred regional, national and international creative awards for work produced for a veritable "Who's Who" of global brand names, including HP, T-Mobile, and TiVo.

He can be reached via his website at RickMathieson.com

Why?

Aubrey Walker III
Creative Director, Commonground

Once upon a time, the faces you'd see in advertising were mostly male and 100% white. Advertising was a "WASP" business. That stands for White Anglo-Saxon Protestant. The mere thought of Jewish copywriters or Italian art directors was fairly revolutionary in the Mad Men *world of advertising back in the day.*

That was then, this is now.

Today, the United States of America – once a country of Northern European population and values – is now a world country with a multiracial President, growing diversity in its population, and increasingly connected to a global marketplace.

Today, creative career opportunities are evolving with our changing world. Here is a view on that world from one of those working to change it – one ad at a time.

Timing is everything. As I was about to write about the lack of African Americans in advertising, I was hit with a conversation in my counterpart's office about why we do what we do? It stopped me in my tracks and made me rethink why. Why do we take so much interest in advertising products that many or most of us don't or never will need?

Well, first, I believe it's to be a part of something "bigger" than us as individuals. And as much confidence as it takes to be a rock star creative, there's actually something bigger than you. And that's watching your spot air on Monday Night Football. What bigger power is there than to stop millions of people and make them listen to your voice? We all get caught up in believing that what we create defines us, and that's partially true, but in order to become part of something bigger, you have to be bigger than advertising and the work we create. How do we do that is the question. I won't pretend to have the answer, so I'll let you ponder on that.

I believe a good number of us, mostly creative, take interest in advertising because we need an outlet to express what's in our brains. Not to mention, the pay isn't bad. But I'm sure most of us would love to open our own clothing/lifestyle brands, production companies, or rent a loft in Brooklyn and sell our paintings. But the fact is advertising can afford you to do those things. With the same furor we have for creating ads, use that to build YOUR brand. At the end of the day, that's the only brand that matters.

_____ (← insert name)

And maybe we do what we do because we love it. I love it. I've loved it since I was a kid. I loved billboards. I took pictures of billboards. I loved reading the back of products and packages when I was supposed to be taking a shower. I loved creating flyers for my band. And, more than anything, I loved Adidas and how they used RUN-DMC as a launching pad for their shell toes. Genius! It was 1986's version of guerilla-marketing 101. And as I got older, I loved to create different voices and took pride in writing novels from different perspectives. Men, women with twins, angry teenagers.

I once had an ECD tell me that Advertising isn't art; it's business.

Part of that is true, but as a creative, if you take that approach, you'll be driven by money, not creativity. And that's what separates incredible innovative agencies from below average shops – Money vs. Passion.

When you truly believe in your clients and your clients believe in you, it creates harmony, and art comes out of harmony. Don't ever stop creating art because that's the stuff that people/peers remember. By the way, that ECD is out of the business because of their drive and greed of money.

If you take anything away from this, remember these three things.

- Passion > Money
- Agencies buy into your personal brand
- At the end of the day, African-American, White, Asian, Latino, it doesn't matter. We're all creative; we're all human. We all want the same things out of advertising, and that's a VOICE.

Work Steps

Aubrey raises some good points.

Let's talk about them before we move on. Answering these questions now will help you during your job interviews.

1. **Explain why you want to do this.** Let's give it a little thought. If you have some easy to access motivations and some good reasons for going on this road, good for you. If you're in the, "I don't know, it just seemed cool," or, "I kinda liked watching *Mad Men*," frame of mind, we might casually suggest you give it a little more thought. As the pig said to the chicken, "It's the difference between ham and eggs. For you, eggs is involvement. For me, ham is commitment."

2. **Describe why you feel it's important that you do this.** We hate to get all profound on you so early in this book, but this is no small matter. Here's the deal, and we don't know why it's true, but it sort of is. "If you don't care a lot, it usually turns out that you're not really much good at it. But… and here's the beauty part. If you care too much, it makes you crazy!" So, what do you think about that?

3. **Are you going to be OK with real results as opposed to "dreams come true"?** Hey, even if we can't play in the NBA, we can still enjoy the game. Do you have a direction you'll be happy with, and, even if you don't play in the majors, will you still enjoy playing the game? We recommend a "yes" answer, but you need to think about it.

— — — — — —

Aubrey Walker is Commonground's Creative Director known for making everyone who works around him better. Prior to becoming an integral part of CG leadership, Aubrey served as Associate Creative Director for GlobalHue where he developed award-winning TV, radio, digital, experiential, and print for GM Jeep, Jeep Grand Cherokee, the Call of Duty Jeep launch, Chrysler 300, Chrysler 200, and the Chrysler Town & Country relaunch. Prior, Aubrey worked for the True Agency where he created award-winning TV, radio, digital, experiential, and print for GM Nissan and Infiniti Day. Before joining True, he worked as Associate Creative Director for Carol H. Williams where he developed TV, radio, digital, and print for the Nissan African American business. Aubrey also executed award-winning, African American targeted TV, radio, digital, and print for Toyota and Lexus at Burrell Communications.

Dynamite Stored Here – Danger Explosives Danger

Luke Sullivan*
Author, Advertising Dept. Chair, SCAD

Luke Sullivan is the author of Hey Whipple, Squeeze This, *one of the most influential books for young creatives going into advertising. He is now Chair of the Ad Department at SCAD – Savannah College of Art and Design. Here, he shares with you some fresh observations on how our world has changed and the role advertising can play to change it for the better.*

What follows is one of the single most interesting passages I've read in my 50-some years of reading. It's from a marvelous book called *1939: The Lost World of The Fair*, by David Gerlernter.

It paints a picture of an America that no longer exists.

"Question: What is wrong with this picture? [Rhetorical; there was no actual picture in the book.] It appeared in a 1939 survey of New York City: A construction site with pedestrians walking past in front, leafy trees and apartment buildings to the rear. Painted on the fence around part of the work site are the words 'DYNAMITE STORED HERE – DANGER EXPLOSIVES DANGER.' It is a tall, solid board fence. But there is no barbed wire, no policeman; Women and children [walk] by a fenced-off magazine of high explosives," the caption reads.

I find this observation amazing.

To think that there was actually a time when you could safely store dynamite in an unprotected shack in New York City; and to feel so certain of the character of your fellow Americans that a simple danger sign would be sufficient to keep people away. It's hard to believe such a world ever existed,

---

* I got some much-needed advice on this essay from the delightful and brainy Nicole McKinney here at GSD&M.

but clearly there was some social force in play that kept this dynamite safe. This force, Gerlernter proposes, was the fact that in 1939 "people lived in an 'Ought' culture."

Such a marvelous insight, and all gleaned from one photograph in a yellowing magazine – America as an "Ought culture." We ought to eat our vegetables. We ought to doff our hats in the presence of ladies. We ought to report neighbors who we suspect of communism.

Later on Gerlernter expands the definition to what I'd describe as "Authority culture." In fact, it's arguable the entire period from the '30s through the early '60s was all Authority culture. Citizens trusted authority entirely, wherever it was – in a corporation, in a policeman's uniform, or just the voice over the radio. ("Hold on, ladies and gents! I've just received this important telegram!")

For purposes of discussion, I tender here a few advertisements typical of the times, copied from my collection of old magazines. I regard advertisements like these as windows into the soul of the times; emotional Polaroids of ancient evenings; the zeitgeist in rotogravure.

THE BIGGEST IS THE MOST GLAMOROUS, TOO!

ALL-NEW PLYMOUTH '55

Note how Plymouth baldly states – with neither hesitation nor proof – that big-ass cars are glamorous. Saying it's so, makes it so. General Electric decides for us that spring has a new color. And don't get me started on this ad for Gaylord shaving supplies. I will, however, also note that illustration seemed to be the preferred visual style of the '40s through the '60s. Screw photography; illustrations let advertisers show life the way they wanted it to

be and showing it so, of course, made it so. All three also feature exclamation points. Hey, when you're an authority, you shout your orders.

Simply running an ad in a magazine made you an authority. ("See, honey, it's printed right here. In a magazine!") A cigarette ad could claim there wasn't "a cough in a car load." The government could deny radioactive iodine 131 was in the nation's milk supply. Facts didn't count. Authority did.

Pick up an old magazine sometime and see if you don't agree; almost every ad and every article feels like a pronouncement from an authority.

Sometime in the mid-'50s, however, this omnipresent voice of authority started to lose its credibility. How this came to be is perhaps a story for another day, but it happened. Somewhere in the cultural whirlwind of the times (the dethroning of McCarthyism, the quiz show scandals, the arms build-up), Americans developed the ability to be skeptical; to doubt; to question authority.

For my generation, I'll wager many of us date the last days of unquestioned authority with the Vietnam war – its final public humiliation, the resignation of Dick Nixon. America finally had evidence – on tape even – that authority could be more than just wrong, it could be corrupt.

From Authority to Authenticity

Let's turn the yellowed magazine page now to the year 2010.

Imagine we were to run that Plymouth ad in next week's *Time* magazine. I'll bet that even if we updated the ad's look and feel, its presumptuous tone ("Big is glamorous, dammit!") would still make today's readers snicker at its authoritarian cluelessness. We simply wouldn't get away with it today. It is a different America now.

We've become a nation of eye-rollers and skeptics. We scarcely believe anything we hear in the media any more, and marketers can't make things true simply by saying they're true.

So, what I'm wondering today is this: where people once looked to authority to tell them what was true and wasn't true, perhaps what people look for today is authenticity.

Merriam-Webster says something is authentic when it actually is what it's claimed to be. Which makes authenticity in advertising an especially tricky proposition given that advertising is at its heart self-promotion and driven by an agenda. And yet while Americans today are suspicious of anyone with an agenda, being authentic doesn't always require the absence of an agenda, only transparency about it.

Admitting that your commercial is a paid message with an agenda is one way to disarm distrust. Under-promising and over-delivering is another. Even self-deprecation can help establish authenticity; VW's "It's ugly but it gets you there" being perhaps the most memorable example.

If you have a complaint, call the president of Avis. His number is CH 8-9150.

There isn't a single secretary to protect him. He answers the phone himself.

He's a nut about keeping in touch. He believes it's one of the big advantages of a small company.

You know who is responsible for what. There's nobody to pass the buck to.

One of the frustrations of complaining to a big company is finding someone to blame.

Well, our president feels responsible for the whole kit and caboodle. He has us working like crazy to keep our super-torque Fords super. But he knows there will be an occasional dirty ashtray or temperamental wiper.

If you find one, call our president collect.

He won't be thrilled to hear from you, but he'll get you some action.

DDB's early Avis work was similarly authentic whether it was admitting to shortcomings ("We're only #2.") or giving customers with complaints the CEO's actual phone number.

In my opinion, Canadian Club's masterful print series is an excellent modern example of an advertiser leveraging reality, warts-and-all, to sell its wares. An unapologetic statement of "Damn right your Dad drank it" coupled with images of '70s dads (somehow still cool in their bad haircuts and paneled basements) leveraged authenticity instead of authority.

So too does a marvelous campaign for Miller High Life, in which the beer truck delivery guy takes back cases of his beer from snooty people who aren't truly appreciating the Miller High Life. Grumbling on his way out the door of some hoity-toity joint ("$11.95 for a hamburger? Y'all must be crazy."), he is himself a spokesman for authenticity.

But even with these good examples of authentic messaging, it's now time to question the supremacy of the format itself – that of paid messaging. It worked fine in the '50s when TV was new and citizens were happy to listen to the man tell them Anacin worked fast-fast-fast.

But everything is different in 2010. As Ed Boches said, "In an age when the manufacturer, publisher, broadcaster, and programmer have lost power to the consumer, reader, viewer, and user, … the power of controlled messages has lost its impact."

Authenticity Is the Walk, Not the Talk

It may be getting to the point now where marketers can't make anything happen by employing messaging alone, no matter how authentic. Doc Searles, co-author of *The Cluetrain Manifesto*, agrees, stating that a brand isn't what a brand says but what it does. What all this suggests is that perhaps the best way to influence behavior and opinion in the year 2010 is to do things as well as just say them.

Where it once served our clients to make "claims" on their behalf, it may be better now to do things that are less claim-based and more action-based, or reality-based, or more experiential – to demonstrate in the ad itself a brand's promise or a product's benefit.

For example, a print ad promising that VW is a fun brand, well, that's nice. But bringing this claim to life with a subway stairwell of working piano keys was more powerful in a number of ways. Instead of making some happy claim about an emotion, it created the emotion right there on the stairs. And of course there's the P.R. talk value of such an interesting execution.

I'm reminded also of Denny's offer to America: a free breakfast during a recession. This is an event as much as it is paid messaging, and America took them up on it. Also from Goodby came the Hyundai Assurance Program, which allowed customers who bought a new Hyundai to return it if they lost their job within the year. These are not ads so much as they are events. They are not "claims;" they're actions.

In the end, these musings suggest several possibilities.

- Marketers cannot simply list a product's benefits and tell customers why they should want it. It doesn't work very well anymore.
- Persuading a nation of eye-rollers requires a message, tone, or platform that is authentic.
- No matter how authentic your message, you cannot become X by saying you are X. You must actually be X. So, after you figure out what your brand needs to say, figure out what it needs to do.
- Same thing with customers: after you figure out what you want customers to think, what is it you want them to do?
- Similarly, don't try to tell customers how they're going to feel. Help them actually experience the emotion.

The bottom line:

Brand actions speak louder than words.

Brand experiences speak louder than ads.

Walk beats talk.

Big Philosophical Closing

My college psychology professor once wrote on the board, "Ontogeny recapitulates phylogeny." It means the life of the individual organism is often reflected in the life of the species.

I confess I see in my own life a similar pattern of authority-to-authenticity. As a child, I blindly ascribed authority to many things (first was my parents; second, the Beatles) and in so doing came to know the world. But as I grew up, black-and-white authority became nuanced with the greys of authenticity.

Perhaps the nation grew up the same way.

We don't need Dad-Brands anymore, wagging their fingers at us with nothing by way of proof beyond "Because I said so."

Work Steps

Luke has given us some important things to think about. Let's do that and start by asking some tough questions about ourselves and our work.

1. **What makes our work (and ourselves) authentic?** Did we get all the way into the essence – or are we dancing on a slick surface? Have we found an authentic expression that engages people with a lot on their minds, or is it one more something that looks like all the other somethings?

2. **What do you believe?** We're going to stay on Luke's point for a bit. Is there some way we can make that a part of our voice and the way we look at the economic world? Can we make a profit by adding genuine value? Let's think about that.

3. **How do we go from messages to actions and experience?** Actions speak louder than words. How can we evolve our words into more authentic brand experiences? Maybe we can't rebuild a subway stairway – but, on a smaller scale, maybe we can do something. Let's look around our own locality. Do we see something new we can do?

4. **OK, if it's not a "Dad Brand" what kind of brand is it?** If we're not telling people to do something, how do we help them come to feel that this is something they want to do? Something they want to have as a part of their life.

— — — — —

After 30 years in the advertising business, author **Luke Sullivan** *is now chair of the advertising department at the Savannah College of Art and Design. He's also the author of the popular advertising book* Hey Whipple, Squeeze This: A Guide to Creating Great Advertising, *the blog heywhipple.com, as well as a new book:* Thirty Rooms To Hide In: Insanity, Addiction, and Rock 'n' Roll in the Shadow of the Mayo Clinic. *His new book releases in fall of 2012. Sullivan now lives in Savannah with his family. He reports that he "enjoys the indoors" and likes to spend a lot of his time there.*

Career Gear

Wendy Lalli, 21st Century Career Coach with **Bruce Bendinger**

You're not just looking for a job – you're starting a career.

So, what are you packing? Career Coach Wendy Lalli and Copy Workshop guru Bruce Bendinger team up to give you a brief look at the kind of equipment you're going to need to climb onto that first rung of the ladder of success.

Ready. Set. Pack.

First, This Is a MarCom Job

That's one of the six words you need to know. Remember?

There's a reason career coaches like to use marketing references – "target market," "personal brand," "sales strategy," etc. – in all those self-help books you have sitting on your bookshelf.

The simple fact is, taking "The Brand Called You" into the job market is pretty much the same as marketing anything else. It just doesn't feel that way.

So let's try to remove as much emotion as possible and take a clear-eyed view of what you need. Let's take a quick look at …

Your Brand Story

Hello. I've just met you. Who are you?

What do you want to be doing? What makes you special?

Can you tell me without it sounding stupid or like you're bragging?

Be able to tell it straight – like in an interview – and then have a more entertaining version for people you meet in a casual social situation.

Can you handle that first thirty seconds?

How about that "elevator pitch?"

And let's not forget those visual first impressions.

Your brand needs to be packaged well. Sure, it's just on the surface – but it counts. What do people see when they meet you for the first time?

Remember, how you look is as much a part of your brand as a logo is for a product. A cutting-edge graphic designer will certainly be packaged differently from someone who works for an accounting firm, but whatever is appropriate, you need to be projecting a first-rate version.

Hold that thought.

OK, we're just getting started.

Now it's time to think about …

Your Resumé

You've already got one, right?

We're guessing that you've had one for a while, and, as you've evolved from baby-sitting and yard chores to whatever you're doing now, it has gone through a number of drafts. Well … has it?

You may even have more than one resumé – the one for the restaurant job may look a bit different from the one for the web strategist job.

When career coaches talk about resumés, they describe them as "an ad about you." That's a good description as long as you understand one basic principal of advertising – ads are written for a specific target audience in a language they understand. The purpose of an ad is to tell the target market why buying the product will benefit them. The same applies to resumés.

Like ads, they should be tailored to a particular audience with specific needs and preferences.

So, as you re-write that resumé, don't just think about you, think about the person reading it – and what they might be needing.

Moving right along, it's time to think about …

Your Go-To-Market Strategy

What do you want to be doing? Where do you want to be doing it?

Are there steps along the way to get there?

Even if you don't know your ultimate destination, you need to aim for some entry points. Throughout this book, we'll be introducing you to a variety of industries that might be interested in your talents.

As you begin to focus on where you want to go, your strategy will start to develop.

Simply put, your strategy encompasses what you want to accomplish, how you want to accomplish it in general, and the specific actions you'll take.

Marketing people will call that Objective, Strategy, and Tactics.

You might call it How I'm Going to Get a Job.

Your Target – a key part of your Objective is the Who – your Target Market. We've tried to introduce you to a wider range of possibilities. Each of those possibilities is a possible target.

The better you can focus on one and match your talents with their needs, the better your "hit rate" will be.

Your Strategy – in general, it's to develop a portfolio that makes your Target want to hire you.

Your Tactics – you will be looking for effective ways to make Your Target aware of you and have them connect with/look at …

Your Portfolio

Different industries look for different things. What should be in your portfolio? The Promotional Portfolio, Sports Marketing, Web Design, Fashion … each of these business areas will be looking for something a bit different.

Your portfolio should – to the best of your ability – reflect the area you're aiming for. Certainly, there's a limit to how tightly we can choose, but the better you aim, the closer you'll be to hitting your target.

You need to have both a printed and an online version. Got it?

Bottom line, if your portfolio is good enough, and the right match, eventually you'll get a job. Some of the next things we'll talk about are Career Gear that will enhance your chances.

So the next gear we need to grind is …

Your "O.P."

OK, we just made that up, nobody else calls it your "O.P." Yet.

It stands for your "Online Presence." It may be as basic as your social media – Facebook and some LinkedIn connections – or it may be a dedicated website or your own YouTube channel.

In today's digital working world, this is one more requirement – and you need to make your "O.P." compatible with your career goals.

If you have a retro hair metal band on the side as well as a nice design portfolio – no problem. Just be sure it's clear to potential employers that your focus is on your career.

The world we live in isn't just digital. And, more to the point, additional creative dimension is something that will serve to put you and your creative talent in a better light.

But the digital world can do some pretty nice things to build your "OP." So make a list of the ways you can, appropriately, shine a digital spotlight on who you are and what you're doing.

- **The Basics:** Do you have an appropriate e-mail address? Is your Facebook page appropriate? Check those photos. Are you on LinkedIn? What happens when you get Googled?
- **Sites, Blogs, Postings, and more:** OK, do you have your own website? If so, is it impressive? If not, why not? If you're a writer, do you have anything "blogworthy" anywhere? If not, think about it. If you're an art director or designer, do we see some great visual skills demonstrated? And does YouTube feature anything worthwhile that you had something to do with?
- **The Next Level:** More and more, the people who will be looking to hire you will be looking to add more digital skills. What are your online skills, and how are they demonstrated? Again, give it some thought. The online environment will be ever-changing. We won't pretend to have completely up-to-date advice for you – getting to the cutting edge – that's your job.

Moving right along, as we said, the world we live in isn't just digital. There's that real world out there – you know, the one that's full of pockets, people, and mailboxes that have actual mail.

So, your next gear involves thinking about ...

Personal Brand Contact Points

Know what a "Brand Contact Point" is?

It's pretty much anyplace or moment that your audience comes in touch with a brand. If it's toothpaste, it's on the shelf at the store, in your medicine cabinet, and maybe a small size that goes in your travel kit. Wait – maybe a sample at the dentist and some advertising. You get the idea.

But it's not toothpaste, it's you. Where and how do we connect with you?

For a start, it can be as simple as a business card with some useful information. It may be a mini-portfolio. You should have a pdf.

It should reflect that "Brand Called You." And it should be consistent from one touchpoint to the next.

Here's a thought.

"3-Ups"

Personally, I like to print up something I call "3-ups." They're tall, skinny, light cardboard note cards that fit nicely in a #10 envelope.

Bruce has a few of them – there's a design that has a drawing of a musical note in a martini glass at the top of the card.

It says "Note Card." Duh.

You can use them to

Here are three of Bruce's 3-ups. One for notes, one for his publishing, and one for a non-profit – The Czech Legion Project.

accompany clippings, quick hellos, congrats, or maybe a CD of some music you just produced.

They're cheap and easy to make. Here's how.

Develop your own design, something that is an appropriate reflection of what you do, and put three of them in a row along the top of an 8.5"x 11" layout – horizontal.

Then, take that layout to any copy shop – tell them you want 20 printed on fairly heavy card stock – and then cut into three pieces.

Just like that, you'll have 60 unique personalized note cards. (20 x 3 = 60)

No need to write a whole letter worth of stuff – just scribble a note (with a nice writing instrument and your best handwriting) and there you go. A card no one else but you can claim and an easy, quick way to keep in front of the people you want to remember you.

You Deserve a Promotion

Why not look for creative opportunities to use your abilities at the same time you promote yourself.

The world is full of them.

Lowell Thompson saw an opportunity with Martin Luther King's birthday.

He designed a King Day card. Hey, why not?

And quick as a trip to the print shop, you have a great new product from Lowell Thompson Creates.

See where we're headed with this? You may want to design a great poster for your band – even if you don't have a gig yet. Maybe a post card? How about a greeting card – or something else you can put in the mail? A great party invitation? An invitation to lunch? How about an invitation to look at a great portfolio – and you'll bring coffee and bagels. Whatever.

You're smart. You're creative. You get the idea.

So … get your brain in gear.

In Conclusion
Brand Story. Resumé. Market Strategy. Portfolio. Online Presence. Brand Contact Points.

A successful personal job strategy will have something going on at each level.

And, no surprise, the better you do on each of these, the better you'll be at getting your career in gear.

Work Steps

OK, you're going to be working on these Work Steps for … well, pretty much your entire career.

But we're guessing you're only getting started. You've probably got a resumé, the beginnings of a portfolio, and some thoughts still in formation.

That's fine. But now let's focus on getting a bit more organized …

1. **Start some folders.** You'll probably want some physical, hard-copy folders as well. You can either have one called **Career Gear** or as many as seven. For Printed Portfolio and Online Portfolio, you might be outgrowing that right away – but you still want to use the folder for ideas and examples. Remember, you're still on the learning curve. Be a sponge. Soak it up.
2. **Start filling the folders.** Articles. Notes you made on a napkin while having coffee. Class notes. You have a lot to think about and writing it down and printing it out are good ways to start filling both your head and those folders with good thinking. What's your **Market Strategy**? What **Brand Contact Points** make sense for you?
3. **Design a 3-up.** How do you want to make an impact with real mail?
4. **Keep it up.** At first, those folders are going to be a bit empty. There's a challenge. See how you can fill those folders (and your fine creative

mind) with more information.

5. **Create in 140 characters.** Turn 'em into tweets – your Resumé, your Brand Story, your latest great thoughts.

6. **Set some deadlines.** All of us work better when we have firm goals – even if they're only our own personal goals. Set some for yourself. Practice your **Brand Story** on a friend. Update that **Resumé**. Write down that **Market Strategy**. Improve your **Online Presence**. Lots to do, isn't there? How about a monthly review?

— — — — — —

Wendy Lalli *helps clients increase sales, build reputations, and get jobs. In the process of developing her own award-winning career as a copywriter, direct response strategist, and digital marketing expert, she discovered she had a talent for mentoring others. With that realization, her own career took on a new dimension. Her career advice column, "Dear Lalli," became a regular feature in 25 newspapers. Her articles on job search and career development have appeared frequently in both newspapers and various trade publications. Currently, she teaches copywriting at one college, a course on how to market yourself at another, and continues as the principal of Wendy Lalli, Ltd.*

Section II:
The Creative Marketplace

"Create a personal project that you have no intention of putting in your portfolio. This will help create balance and keep your energy up,"
Angela Martin, Certified Career Coach, Defining Success Coaching

Get ready to expand your horizons.

Today's creative marketplace is an expanding and dynamic place.

It's a fast-changing world, and this section will help you wrap your mind around all the new jobs opening up while many older business models are shrinking.

You may find yourself introduced to creative business areas that are new to you. Good. Or you might find that an area you had once discounted is actually a specialty you want to pursue. Better yet.

We want you to understand how much variety there is in today's creative marketplace – which increases the chances that there's a fit just right for you.

So hang on, here's what we're going to do in this section:

First, we have three articles on "Finding Your Place."

- One. Executive Editor Larry and Publisher Bruce provide you a list, pretty much in alphabetical order, of the growing range of creative careers you might want to think about.
- Two. From the surprisingly happening city of Grand Rapids, Frank Blossom of Grand Valley State and The Polishing Center, offers some thoughts on expanding the geographical range of your search.
- Three. Our international correspondent Katarzyna Dragovic sends us her message from across the sea. Katya runs a portfolio school in Poland. She wants you to know about some of the successful "Get a Job" strategies happening on her side of the Atlantic. (She also invites you to stop by for a visit if you happen to be in the neighborhood.)

Next, we'll provide you with some discussion of core *skills* needed for just about every one of these career opportunities – understanding brands and visualizing.

- Robin Landa, author of *Take a Line for a Walk* and other excellent books on design, discusses some of the brand-related skills we all need.

- And the legendary Stan Richards offers some initial career advice for visualizers thinking about both art direction and design.

Then, we want to start telling you more about various career areas. Some of these may not be at all right for you, but, then again, you just might want to stretch your horizons a bit. We reached out to bring quite a range of talents into this next section with the express purpose of expanding both your mind and your horizons.

- Kelley Fead opens your eyes to the ABCs of B-to-B. That means "Business to Business," and there are a lot of jobs connected to it.

- We all know that the healthcare industry is growing. Find out more from Robin Shapiro and her prescription for a healthy career (and a healthy salary) in health and medical marketing.

- Remember those McDonald's Happy Meals? Colleen Fahey, who helped make them happen, introduces you to the basics of Sales Promotion.

- Sales Promotion has grown into a lot of exciting new areas. Bill Rosen helps point you in the right direction for these new opportunities.

- We all know that every agency is digital. So why should one consider working at an agency specializing in digital? Ethan Smith has the answer.

- Are you experienced? There's another growth area called "experiential." Erik McKinney takes you for a test drive.

- Did you know that a lot of companies offer creative opportunities on the inside? Well, instead of being on the outside looking in, Tom McManus shows you what happens "in-house."

- Diversity can be more than a company policy – sometimes it's a marketing strategy! Here Mike Williams introduces you to some good news about those growing opportunities.

- Who makes sure all of this stuff gets done? Mary Ryan Djurovic offers her creative career secrets in "I'm a Project Director."

- So what's next? And what is that large scarf doing wrapped around that water tower? It's the Wexley School for Girls in action. One more example of creatives creating careers where none existed before.

Ready? You better be.

Finding Your Place - Part I:
Creative Careers for the 21st Century

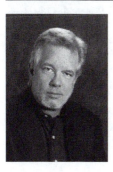

Bruce Bendinger
Publisher
Laurence Minsky
Executive Editor &
Associate Professor,
Marketing
Communications Dept.,
Columbia College

Okay, gang, this is THE BIG TRUTH – the creative marketplace has expanded – some say exploded – into a much wider variety of industries and skill sets.

*Add the relatively new reality of digital – which is changing **absolutely everything**, and you've got a lot to choose from.*

With that in mind, Bruce and Larry teamed up to provide a quick alphabetical summary of some of the kinds of jobs that are out there.

It's fairly complete, but with the way things are changing, who knows.

A Is for...

Advertising – This is where most people start when they think about creative careers. Most of us are familiar with advertising (after all, we've been seeing it for as long as we can remember), and we know a little bit more about how it gets created from TV shows like *Mad Men* (and *Bewitched* re-runs), ad executives in movies, maybe someone your family knows who works in advertising or marketing, and, for many of you, an advertising program at your school. All these things have made it a common career destination. And, the fact is, it's a great starting point. When you create advertising, you learn how to communicate strategically, and you learn about how businesses work. Throughout this book, you'll find people and programs to introduce you to how to prepare for getting a job in advertising. But it's just a starting point. Just like it's the first entry in this list, you'll find that the basic skills of advertising actually have a number of interesting variations. And, as some of the traditional advertising models have decreased, other newer and more specialized ways of communicating have emerged.

Agricultural – There's a lot going on "down on the farm." If you already have some familiarity with this important part of American business, you already know that there are a lot of companies that market to them. These firms produce everything from heavy farm equipment, to seeds, to animal health, to all of the chemicals, fertilizers, and herbicides many farmers use. And there are lots of specialized agencies working in this area. If agriculture interests you, track them down. They'll be interested in talking with you, letting you know what they're looking for, and providing you with other connections in the field.

Brand Marketing – These are essentially media agnostic agencies that create integrated campaigns; they do everything from digital and direct to shopper marketing and experiential events. Even collateral. The bigger brand-marketing firms are usually partnered and/or owned by a mainline agency. Many smaller brand-marketing firms are that way because they take all of the assignments from their typically smaller-size clients.

Branding – Many places that used to call themselves design firms now call themselves branding firms. They did logos and books filled with "graphic standards," showing how to use that logo in everything from signage to matchbook covers. Today, these firms deal with an even deeper range of issues for companies – helping their clients tell their "brand" story – and they have evolved into firms that do "branding." They perform a wide range of creative tasks – some staying fairly close to that of the original design firm, and others developing websites, broadcast, experiential, signage, packaging, and more. If you're already involved in some form of design, you should see how these firms have evolved. Look in the resources section for books on branding and design.

Branded Content – See Creative Content

Broadcast Production – If you want to get into making films, commercials, music videos, and all the other things you can do these days – often downloaded onto YouTube – this is an area that might interest you. In fact, if this is a career area for you, we'll bet you're already interested and shooting and editing – even if it's only weddings and birthday parties. You may want to be the one involved in actually producing the video material, you may want to write it, you may want to learn to do the editing or special effects, or you may want to do it all. Today, with Apple platform editing programs like Final Cut and the other professional tools, there are lots of opportunities. A quick warning – it can be kind of crowded (but expanding due to the Web becoming a video-based medium), and it's often easier to find ways to spend money than it is to make money. But whatever creative career path you choose, sooner or later you'll probably be dealing with broadcast production – so learn what you can.

Business-to-Business – For the most part, you've grown up seeing consumer advertising. Well, businesses do a lot of advertising and marketing, too. They create trade ads, build booths for trade shows, and write articles for trade magazines. They create websites, apps, and a whole range of programs designed to help them do a good job making a persuasive connection with their own specialized audience. Somebody has to create those materials. In fact, a lot of people do this kind of work. You might want to find out about it.

Catalogues, Circulars, Brochures … Collectively, We Call It *Collateral* – The communications that marketers create aren't just advertising. There are lots of other kinds of content that need to be created. Just about every business wants some sort of brochure, and they usually want the same information on their website. If they have a lot of items, they'll usually need a catalogue – most probably web-based, but some use print or both. Sometimes it's simple technical writing, and sometimes it's a lot more. All those brochures, catalogs, and other selling materials are often referred to as *collateral*. Somebody has to create those materials. Who knows? It might be you. Why not start collecting some examples that you think are really good?

Corporate Communications – Most big companies do a whole range of communications aimed at their *internal* audience – like newsletters, training programs, and communications on their own intranet. It's not just the company newsletter – there is often video production and big meetings that use the latest A/V technology.

Creative Content – Who writes magazine articles or the scripts for those documentaries about business? How about that magazine you picked up at the drug store – the one that is under their brand name? More and more companies are creating and publishing "owned content." Some call it part of their "Public Relations" efforts; some call it part of their "StratComm" efforts; some call it "Creative Content," and still some call it "Branded Content." We call it a great way to build a career.

Creative Services – Companies that do a lot of marketing produce a lot of material. All of the collateral. All of the in-store posters. Sometimes even the broadcast advertising is produced "in-house." Retailers (like Target and Apple and Starbucks and The Gap), fashion companies who want to keep their designs secret, and just about every restaurant and beverage company that creates a poster, a menu, or a neon sign has a department that is generally called "Creative Services." It's another place to look for a job that might not have occurred to you. To start, look to the larger marketers with home offices near you.

Design aka **Graphic Design** – Some, today, call it "branding," and some still call it "graphic design." Whatever they call it, the job is to manage the critical visual part of a marketer's business. Some companies – like retailers – have a lot of this creative work that needs to be done – after all, they have to fill a whole store with signs and specials. That's a lot of work. Other marketers have a pretty long list of smaller, but just as important, jobs that need doing. If you're studying design, you need to understand the whole range of jobs that need doing – not only in dedicated design firms but in the graphics or "creative services" department of a larger marketer.

Digital – See "Interactive."

Direct - aka Direct Mail, Direct Marketing, Direct Response – Basically, companies involved in "direct," work to generate a measurable response from a database – a list of people that usually share some sort of characteristic, whether it is the same hobby, the same lifestyle, or the same Zip code. In all of these fields, the core dynamics are similar – list/offer/message. First, what's the list of prospects? Second, what offer are you making to provide an incentive for action? A special deal, free shipping, or an attractive item they pretty much can't find anywhere else. Finally, what's the message? It could be a letter, catalog copy, something on the outside of the envelope, or all of the above. As our electronic life grows, more and more of the work in direct is shifting from your mailbox to your e-mail and Facebook, but the basic principles are still the same. If you're good at thinking this way, and creating messages that get results, you might want to see what the world of direct has to offer.

Entertainment Marketing –There are many firms and freelancers specializing in the marketing of entertainment properties – from movies and music to games and more. Likewise, many consumer brands and some B-to-B companies use entertainment properties to help market their products and services through sponsorships and co-marketing programs, and again there are agencies that specialize in this area, too. And all of them hire copywriters, art directors, and other creative marketing specialists. See Sports Marketing for more information.

Events – Whether you have been to a small street fair or a major festival, you should know that there are companies that specialize in making them run right and other companies that help marketers participate. You've probably walked past a booth, maybe you've picked up a sample or a T-shirt; you might have noticed all of the signs with marketing messages. Events have become a big business, and, guess what, there are companies that help make it happen – companies that might need your skills. To find out more, read the next section – "Experiential."

Experiential – Many used to call it Event Marketing – now, with a wider range of services, it is called "Experiential." Because, when you think about it, you're offering an experience. It might be a big experience like a major concert, or it might be a small one like a vending machine that, rather than coins, requires you to smile to receive an ice cream cone or free ice skating at an outdoor rink ... in July ... in Las Vegas. You might get a sample – a water bottle or T-shirt – or just a picture of you engaged in the activity to put up on Facebook. And you might be asked to leave your name, so the sponsoring company can work to build a fuller relationship with you. And keep in mind that Experiential Marketing is more than just creating events. Some people in experiential agencies argue that it's anything that gets the target to "experience" something, even via a print ad. So it is really more of an approach to creating communications rather than merely a "tactic" of holding an event.

Field Marketing – It's more marketing than creative, but one of the better ways to get into the business of promoting brands is by going to work for one in "the field." What kind of brands? Virtually every fast food franchise has a Field Marketing staff – McDonald's has many, small chains have just a few, the beverage companies – beer and soda – have staffs of people who work to see that their beer brands have everything from neon signs in the window to a booth at the street fair. Soft drink companies do the same with their marketing, as do other marketers, such as Frito-Lay. How creative are those careers? Well, probably not as much as if you were working on the brand at one of the advertising or sales promotion agencies, but there are still a lot of fun, exciting, and creative opportunities kicking around.

Financial – These firms need annual reports, cover sheets full of legal disclaimers, and articles for the investment community. They even need print advertising and websites, perhaps a TV spot or two for a business channel. Plus, much more. If you have the head for this kind of thing, you might be surprised at all the writing that people need to go along with the numbers.

Interactive – Some people see interactive and web design as being the same. But interactive is really much more. It's getting people to literally interact with the communication and can include banner ads and in-game advertising or even physical environments through outdoor boards or other installations. Meanwhile, many websites are really more like old-fashioned print brochures and catalogs that have been put online (but with, perhaps, a search component).

Media Sales – Sales? Maybe so. In the smaller entry-level areas, like radio and cable, you're often involved in the creation and production of the actual advertising. If you're outgoing, can handle a lot of rejection (something just about every creative career gets a lot of), and enjoy helping people by selling them something that can help them, this might be an interesting avenue. There are lots of local media outlets in every market – radio, cable TV, and your local TV station, as well as your local newspaper, and, probably, some alternative print vehicles. City magazines in larger markets are another example. Want to know more? You might grab a copy of *Make the Sale. How to Sell Media with Marketing.* You can get it for 20% off at www.adbuzz.com.

Medical – Health Care – Pharmaceutical – This is a huge area of the economy, and they're not just sitting around waiting for sick people to show up. Hospitals in your area have marketing efforts, pharmaceutical companies have programs to introduce and manage the sales of their products targeting doctors and hospitals, and there are all manner of other companies involved, from local community groups, non-profits, and practitioners, to clinics, individual doctors, dentists, chiropractors, podiatrists, and more. They all need some sort of creative material to "recruit" new patients and help maintain their practice. There are many companies in this field, and if this area interests you, you may be surprised at where you will find healthy opportunity.

Mobile – Figure out this area and you'll probably have a nice ride for the next twenty years of your career. It's that simple.

New Media – This one is changing even as we're writing it. All the new ways of communicating – it used to be Websites, e-mails, blogs, Twitter, Facebook, but these are now all established. So what is the new media of the future? We'll find out when we get there.

Online Marketing – Banner ads, video, and any other marketing communication activity carried out online. See Mobile, see Web Design, see Business-to-Business, see Direct, see Interactive, see the center of most future integrated marketing campaigns.

Project Management – You might think that the only creative thing you can do is create something – with writing or design. But you may find that helping to manage a project that creates an event or a program can be creative and satisfying in its own right. This book considers certain kinds of project management to be uniquely satisfying and important creative careers. In our view, project managers are a critical part of the creative team that gets it done.

Public Relations & Publicity – Are you a PR major? Then you already know a lot more than we can put in these short paragraphs. If you're not a PR major, you need to know that whatever you do, you'll be more successful if the world finds out about it. How do they do that? With public relations and publicity. As you create various pieces of content, think about how that content will be of interest to the media in general and, specifically, to some media channel. If you can become better at thinking about a publicity component for your creative programs, you'll be more successful, and if you partner up with someone else who is good at that kind of thinking, better yet. In general, you need to think about how your creative project will be newsworthy to some media channel. Start thinking that way, and everything you do will be more successful.

Recruitment – You're looking for a job. So are a lot of people and so are a lot of companies. So it might be no surprise that running effective recruitment advertising is a good-sized business all by itself. You'll still produce ads, websites, and more. Possibly even television. The difference? Recruitment agencies call the people in the HR Department their client instead of the people in the client's Marketing Department.

Sales Promotion – How can you use incentives to promote a sale? Or, as some say, "what's the bribe?" There are many creative ways to say, "Win. Free. Save." And, in fact, you will find that this area is one of the biggest and most important parts of marketing. Plus, it offers great, highly creative career opportunities. So study up. But even if you don't plan to go into sales promotion, you should at least know the basics. After all, somewhere along the line, you will be called upon to craft a campaign featuring an offer, and here is where you will learn how to do it effectively. But also keep in mind that sales promotion has also changed. In many ways, it's a key part of Experiential. In other ways, parts of it evolved into Shopper Marketing.

Shopper Marketing – Built on the recognition that the consumer and the purchaser of a product are not necessarily the same person, shopper marketing works to understand how people behave in the retail setting – both brick and mortar as well as online – and then develop communications – everything from packaging to POP and, yes, mobile – that gets the shopper to purchase their products. In many ways, this is the new world of sales promotion. But in this world, it's not just about "Win. Free. Save." It's also about retail real estate – "negotiated" media – creating unique experiences, and truly adding value beyond the discount. No wonder it is the fastest growing discipline within marketing communication.

Social Media – Yes, you can build a viable career focusing on creating for Twitter, Facebook, Pinterest, and networks that have not even been launched yet. After all, if it helps further your client's brand, it will help further your career.

Sports Marketing – As we noted in an earlier piece (in "Six Words"), this is an area that combines many MarCom disciplines: Digital, Public Relations, Sales Promotion, Direct (you have to sell those season tickets), CRM (have to keep those season ticket holders satisfied), Promotional Products, and lots more. If you're interested in this area, you might start by tracking down the Sports Information Department at your school. More and more schools are adding sports marketing courses. Finally, the teams in your area, major league and minor league, are always looking for interns. Track 'em down and see if you can score an internship. (And don't forget that for Sports Marketing, like Entertainment Marketing, there's another side of the equation – the use of sports properties for the marketing of consumer and some B2B brands, giving you lots more opportunities. In fact, most major brands have sports relationships that need to be managed, and most that do take interns. Check them out and you might be on your way to great career in sports.)

Video Production – See "Broadcast Production" and keep in mind that not all commercials today are being "broadcast;" some of them are being "narrowcast" to key targets. Additionally, while they are called "commercials" when broadcast on television, they are called "video" when distributed over ad networks online.

Web Design – Websites. Everybody needs them—from corporate sites that are mostly brochures on the Web to promotional sites to those that convey an experience. Even if you're an old-fashioned writer doing books, poems, and articles, your writing will now be published electronically. You're best strategy? Learn to build a basic website – or build a fancy one. If you can master the variety of skills necessary to do them well – both the technical skills and the marketing and conceptual skills – there is lots of work in this area. And here's more good news – the people who teach this tend to be in touch with where the entry-level jobs are in your market.

Work Steps.

We bet you know a lot more than you did when you started this article. Now let's figure out what we're going to do about it.

1. **List your areas of interest.** Right now, which two or three areas interested you the most?

2. **Identify your best bets.** Given your current skills and interest – assuming you'll keep improving – where do you think you have the best chance of getting hired?

3. **Collect collateral.** OK, time to start another new file folder. Call it **Collateral**. Call it **Stuff I Like**. Call it Whatever You Want. But start saving things that you think are examples of good work. Brochures. Ads in newspapers and magazines. Print-outs of nice online work. In the old days, we called it a Scrap file. You need to become more of a sponge (without the square pants). You also need to start an electronic file folder. They can be URLs, screen grabs, whatever. The point is, you need to become a bigger and better consumer of good work.

4. **Educate yourself.** Was there an area where you'd like to learn more? Now you've got a good reason to "go Googling." See what you can dig up.

Finding Your Place - Part II:
It's Everywhere. And It's Good for You.

Frank Blossom
Affiliate Professor, Grand Valley State
& Coach, The Polishing Center

Direct from Grand Rapids, Michigan, Frank Blossom describes how you can start your personal Get A Job program from anywhere – the top floor of a Manhattan high rise or a basement apartment in Manhattan, Kansas.

Today, great agencies, creative departments, marketing firms, and job opportunities are happening wherever smart thinkers can get on the grid.

This chapter describes the geo-democratization of the ad industry. Take a read through it, and maybe you'll see some new places to start your career path.

Remember, nothing is holding you back – including your location.

You may have the perception that you have to go to a big city – one where there's a major advertising market – to get a big time job in the advertising business. Not any more.

The power centers of the ad business and jobs in advertising are no longer restricted to big cities. Just as mass media has fragmented, so have the masses of advertising agencies and ad jobs.

In past years (the Mad Men Era) the ad business was centered in NYC, Chicago, and LA. Many of the big companies and big advertisers were headquartered there. So agencies located close to the clients and grew with them. Nearly 50% of all advertising billings were once located in NYC alone.

Smaller cities did not have much advertising mass and, therefore, not many job opportunities.

Today, the advertising business is thriving anywhere smart, creative, engaging ad people are. It's not about big cities. It's about big thinking. It's not the size of the agency. It's the size of the thinking. And anywhere big thinkers can power up a computer can be an advertising power base.

Because clients (advertisers) will go to where the best advertising thinking is for their products, no matter if it's Manhattan, New York or Manhattan, Kansas.

So big advertisers followed the big thinkers. Now NYC, Chicago, and LA are still big advertising markets. But smart advertising is coming out of big thinking ad agencies in Portland, Seattle, San Francisco, Austin, Dallas, Boulder, Milwaukee, Minneapolis, Richmond, Miami, Boston, Detroit, Atlanta, and many more.

On the Grid—In the Game

Technology, the Internet, and unlimited digital connectivity make it possible to make great advertising and transmit it anywhere. Copywriters, art directors, designers, creative directors, media planners, account planners, researchers, account executives/project managers can work from anywhere and everywhere they can connect to the Internet.

Sometimes, smart ad ideas come from a basement bedroom of a teenager. Nick Haley, an 18-year-old English student and Apple iPod Touch devotee, created his own commercial for the iPod Touch on his MacBook and posted it on You Tube. http://www.youtube.com/watch?v=KKQUZPqDZb0

Marketing people from Apple saw the spot and had their ad agency, TBWA/Chiat /Day contact Nick to bring him to LA and co-produce a broadcast-ready version of his spot. Nick's spot then ran on national TV in the US, Japan, and Europe. His story was reported in the *New York Times* advertising section as well as numerous blogs and websites. Not bad for a teenager and his laptop.

What Does This Mean for You?

Smart can be anywhere. And you can be smart from anywhere.

Not just big cities and big markets. And this is good for you, since most colleges are not in big cities. You can start preparing, start researching, and start interviewing for your next job from anywhere, too. So don't wait. Your competition for that job isn't waiting.

So if you are living in Manhattan Beach, CA or going to school at Manhattan College, it doesn't matter. Think big, bold ideas. Put them out there and get ad agencies and advertisers following you.

Today, beautiful places to live can also be beautiful places to work. Like CP+B in Boulder, CO. Or the Martin agency in Richmond, VA.

Besides technology driving new job opportunities there are two more factors working in your favor. New media and new clients.

Big Results from Smaller Markets

Grand Rapids, MI is home to Grand Valley State University, which has been ranked among the top 10 advertising programs in the country and also home to The Polishing Center, a small, but powerful portfolio, interviewing, and networking program.

Neither is well known outside of West Michigan, yet young creatives and account executives from these two programs are working in ad agencies, big and small, around the world. Top agencies like Wieden & Kennedy, CP+B, Saatchi and Saatchi, Boone Oakley, Team Detroit, and 17 Triggers in Thailand. Plus cool companies like, The Onion.

Check them out:
www.thepolishingcenter.com,
http://www.gvsu.edu/soc/advertising-public-relations-major-47.htm

More New Media

The advertising business is dynamic – active and always changing. New media channels are being created weekly. The driving force has always been creating meaningful content. But now we have many more new media channels that need content and research and media planning and strategy.

Somewhere in a garage in Cupertino, CA or a dorm room in Boston, MA, the next big media channel is emerging. And more new communication channels means more new job opportunities. And the big advantage that you have is that you are highly skilled in these new communications like Facebook, Twitter, Foursquare, YouTube, blogs, and whatever the next big thing is going to be. Two of the hottest new job categories for college grads today, Digital strategist and Digital Media Analyst, did not exist a couple of years ago.

Who is better prepared to help guide and manage these new media than those who are already steeped in them? Ad agencies and in-house marketing departments know this. They are hiring young creatives and young marketers like you to help them create content, plan, strategize, and execute the new media. So wise up and study up on it. Learn the marketing side of the new media not just the social side.

More New Clients

The technology changes and cultural changes in communication are making it easier and less expensive for small retailers (on line and off), Internet start-ups, and entrepreneurs of all shapes and sizes to create and distribute advertising with the same quality and professionalism as major marketers. Everybody can play in the same advertising sand box. Small marketers can act like mega marketers. Everybody can look like the big boys and girls. And this creates more job opportunities for you.

Because every business, big and small, is also in the marketing business. If not, they'll be out of business soon. More marketing means more advertising, more PR, more communications, and more new media, and all of that means more job opportunities.

So let's review:

- Major advertising and content creation is happening everywhere, literally from rooftop apartments to mountaintops
- Technology is creating new media/communication channels
- More clients are creating a need for more advertising
- Technology is reducing the costs of creating advertising

More new people are needed to meet the changing demands of the advertising business. And it doesn't matter if you are from a big university or small college, megatropolis or little town. It's the size of your thinking that matters. And this means you.

Start investigating the place and people that excite you, that you dream about. Where do you want to be for the next 5 years?

Work Steps:

1. **Make a list.** On this list, write down the characteristics of cities and communities where you'd like to be a part. It might be family and friends. It might be a cultural and music scene. Great outdoor recreation. The key - identify what you think is important to you. Then, start to identify the places that meet those characteristics.

2. **Read all about it.** Now it's time to find out more about these places. Might be time for another folder – or at least a list of links.

3. **Identify the growing agencies.** Now it's time to find out about the companies in those markets that might be hiring. Many are obviously agencies with recent wins. But look beyond them, too. You might be surprised at what you discover.

4. **Plan a visit.** If it's not your hometown, looks like it's time to see what that place might look like. You might camp on the outskirts, go to a music festival, or sleep on a cousin's couch. Hey, you're creative. You can do this.

— — — — — —

Frank Blossom is the strategic director of Frank Communications, founder of the Polishing Center, director and head referee of The Yardsticks – College Creative Competition & Critique, and an Affiliate Professor in the School of Communications at Grand Valley State University. He splits his time between consulting and marketing communications and preparing students for the ad industry. He has worked in advertising for more than thirty years with a broad range of both agency and account experience at Leo Burnett, D'Arcy, Noble, and regional ad agencies. In addition, Frank has served on District AAF Board of Directors in Missouri and Michigan, and judged numerous international, national, and regional advertising competitions. And won a bunch himself. In 2010, Frank's accomplishments were recognized with The Silver Medal—the American Advertising Federation's highest honor.

The Polishing Center (http://www.polishingcenter.com/) is a post grad program to help aspiring young creatives and account execs get into the ad business. And it does; Polishing Center alum are working at Burnett, Saatchi & Saatchi, CP+B, McCann Erickson, Doner, Team Detroit, T3, and dozens of regional shops from New York to Miami to Seattle to Thailand.

The Yardsticks (http://www.theyardsticks.com/) is an annual creative competition for college students in Grand Rapids, MI.

YARDSTICKS

COLLEGE CREATIVE COMPETITION & CRITIQUES

SPONSORED BY THE POLISHING CENTER

Finding Your Place - Part III:
Where in the World

Katarzyna Dragovic
former Creative Director, now Owner, Szkoła Mistrzów Reklamy, Warsaw, Poland

Not only are the horizons for creative careers expanding into many new areas of marketing communications, they're expanding into many new markets. Now we find young men and women preparing for creative careers around the world. With that in mind, we asked Katya, Katarzyna Dragovic, head of Poland's creative career school, to show us how people are getting a job in her market. Dzięki, Katya.

Hello from Poland. This is Katarzyna Dragovic. I run the ad school Szkoła Mistrzów Reklamy here in Warsaw.

We train young creative talents for jobs here in Poland. And even with all the economic problems that are here, just like there are in the United States, there are jobs for talented people who know where to look. And even more than that – with the economic crisis and the necessity to cut expenses, agencies tend to get rid of the seniors with huge salaries and look for young talents, because someone has to do the job!

Here are some of the jobs that recent graduates of our program found in Poland: junior copywriter at Leo Burnett, junior copywriter at Euro RSCG, junior art director at Saatchi&Saatchi, junior copywriter at Publicis, junior copywriter at JWT, junior art director at McCann-Erickson, a team at Y&R – just to name a few, because our graduates are in nearly every agency in Poland.

And here are some examples of the student work that helped them

find those jobs – I've translated a few, but, as you can see, good communication often transcends language. As our world and our markets become more global and connected, that's something we should all keep in mind.

As you begin your journey into the world of work, remember that there is talent everywhere and there are opportunities everywhere.

But in every market, one of the most difficult jobs will be finding that job – particularly that first job.

You need to remember that the people who really need you, the ones that are very busy and need help – are often too busy to look for you – so you have to go look for them. I think this is true everywhere.

So – as we say in Poland "powodzenia" which means "good luck." We wish you all good fortune, but in today's creative job market – good work, hard work, and thinking about the person who needs you ... these, I think, are the things that will help to improve your luck.

I will tell you three completely different stories about my students.

One day I told Kuba, an art director, that a Polish owned, very creative agency was looking for an art director. So he took his portfolio and went for an interview. The owners (and creative directors at the same time) were impressed with what they saw: "Man, for a copywriter, you have quite a good portfolio. Have you really executed all these works yourself?" – they asked. Kuba was shocked: "But ... I'm an art director! ..." Now they were shocked: "But we need a copywriter... we have too many art directors." There was a long, uncomfortable silence. Suddenly Kuba got an illumination: "What if I come in team with a copywriter?" he asked and saw a sign of interest in their eyes. "Is he also looking for a job?" they asked. Kuba decidedly confirmed, although he didn't have the faintest idea if Bartek, the guy he was thinking about, also our graduate, was looking for a job. He bluffed. The guys said: "Ok, let's see his book." Next week Kuba and Bartek showed up in the agency and ... got a job as a team. And they are still working together as one of the most talented teams in Poland.

This little story shows you have to be prepared for the unexpected!

Another story shows how being different and bold pays.

Maciek couldn't get a job for quite a long time. One day he heard the agency he's always dreamed about was looking for a copywriter. Unfortunately, for a senior, while Maciek, of course, was a junior without any experience. So he thought that perhaps he could become a senior only for the sake of the interview. When Maciek entered the agency, the creative director saw... a senior. Maciek glued a huge, grey moustache under his nose! Everybody in the agency was laughing for the whole day. He was hired. The search for a senior went on, though.

And the third story, about Kamil. He believed in his success so much that as a student he used to send his work for international contests, such as D&AD, The One Show, Golden Drum, etc. He paid entry fees himself. At some of them he got awards, at some was shortlisted, but as a result, when he graduated, he was already a successful ad man. More successful than most of the regulars already working in agencies. No wonder he didn't have problems with getting a job at Leo Burnett.

This story shows that sometimes it's good to be proactive.

These success stories are, I think, very similar everywhere.

And, when you come to Europe for a nice vacation – or, better yet, a business trip, be sure and come see all the exciting new things we are doing here in our little corner of the world.

Or better still – send your portfolio to a few agencies in Warsaw. We don't have many multicultural teams here, and they are always more than welcome, as people from different countries bring different points of view, different experiences, and different thinking, which is what advertising is about. There are people from other countries almost in every agency. Of course there are some formalities to be set, but if you are talented and persistent, getting a job here is not impossible. So, if you are ready for a European adventure, think about it.

Work Steps:

Once, agencies around the world looked at the award books in the United States. Now it's a worldwide market for creative.

1. **Find some international award books.** Can you tell what the creative idea is without reading the translation?
2. **Track down a copy of *Archive Magazine*.** Again, can you tell what the selling idea is without translation?
3. **Pick a country.** Now go to Google and type in the name of that country and the words "advertising awards." See what happens.
4. **Bonus:** If you're fluent in a second language or have other cultural connections, why not find out more about that advertising market? You never know what you might discover.

— — — — — —

Katarzyna Dragovic is the Founder and Creative Director, of Szkoła Mistrzów Reklamy, in Warsaw (This translates to Champions School of Advertising). It is the only Polish portfolio program. She has been an advertising professional in Poland since 1993 and is the winner of many Polish and international advertising awards.

The Creative Imperative: Big Ideas and Brand Storytelling

Robin Landa
Distinguished Professor, Robert Busch School of Design, Kean University

In a creative career, you almost need to develop new brain cells. Almost. The good news is you probably have the brain cells already, but you may need to give them a whole new kind of exercise.

Here, design author and industrial strength creative person Robin Landa opens the door to the exercise room for those brain cells. Want to know more? Buy one of her excellent books.

What if you could become invisible at will? Imagine an apple skin covered with hair. What if all foods tasted the same? What if no one ever died? Imagine the fusion of a tennis ball and a croissant. What if there were no eggs? Right now, if you could dream up three *What if* scenarios, you would have a good shot at a career in a creative profession.

Or try this. Conceive a way to make *any* brand social. For the moment, forget creative briefs or strategy statements. Can you think of two ways to engage people more than once with a brand or organization on Facebook or Twitter?

Prefer branding to advertising? Name two new ways to enable a wine neophyte to successfully pair wine with food. Or conceive a plan to make select service hotel customer experiences memorable. Imagine a completely novel way to present breakfast cereal—a new kind of package design, completely fresh graphics, and an atypical cereal brand name. Now think of a totally fresh approach for toothpaste or banking or wireless communications.

Big ideas and real deliverables are it. Unlike repairing potholes or lifting heavy boxes, what graphic designers, brand designers, art directors, copywriters, and strategic planners do has far less to do with labor and more to do with diligent creativity. As a junior entering the visual communication profession, the non-negotiable requirements are critical and creative thinking because you're not going to be able to acquire those skills on the job. You have to walk in knowing how to construct creative ideas and turn them into relevant, engaging visual/verbal solutions.

An ad or a branding idea is the creative conceptual solution to a marketing problem—a strategic formulated concept. Required is the ability to come up with an idea, cogently state the idea, and then evaluate it. To think strategically, you have to be a sound critical thinker. Here's where the ability to analyze, identify and address key issues, conceive concepts within a strategic framework, communicate effectively, and evaluate for relevance all come in pretty handy.

Imaginative designers and writers can form creative images and word relationships, relying on associative thinking (recognizing commonalities, common attributes); metaphorical thinking (identifying similarities between seemingly unrelated things); and, elaboration and modification (working out details, being able to propose alterations, and create iterations).

If all that weren't enough, you have to give interesting form to synergistic visual/verbal relationships—as well as be a transmedia storyteller. Think whole brand story, whether you are telling a story through a logo or a social media game. Think of what each specific media channel can do and use that media to full advantage to create a smooth, integrated media story. Henry Jenkins coined the term "transmedia storytelling," which represents a "process where integral elements of a fiction get dispersed systematically across multiple delivery channels for the purpose of creating a unified and coordinated entertainment experience. Ideally, each medium makes it own unique contribution to the unfolding of the story."

Yes, you have to be a storyteller. Remember, at the outset I said, "Big ideas." Small ideas aren't based on brand stories. Big ideas are. Dove has a story to tell. Nike has a story. Apple has a story. The American Red Cross has a story. But don't worry.

In advertising and branding you don't conceive the brand story alone. You collaborate. In an advertising agency, a conventional creative team is a duo comprised of an art director and a copywriter. A creative director or associate creative director, who makes the final creative decisions about the idea, approach, and art direction, supervises the creative team and copywriting. Some agencies prefer unconventional creative teams or brand teams with several other members, which might include a strategic planner, account manager, tech expert, interactive designer (if appropriate), and a marketing expert, among others. Together they work on strategic conceptual development.

After generating ideas, the art director is responsible for the art direction (overall look and feel, visual style, selection of photographer or illustrator) and design. The copywriter is responsible for the writing. Junior art directors and copywriters generate solutions across media, working to engage people with brands through storytelling and design, whether the solution is for broadcast channels, desktop web, mobile web, unconventional or social media. When a creative team works well, the division of labor might overlap. Any good art director should be able to write copy, and any good copywriter should be able to think visually.

Besides the traditional creative team of art director and copywriter, or the unconventional multi-member team, advertising and branding depend upon other professionals, including media planners, marketing managers, programmers, and interactive designers or agencies when dealing with screen-based media, unconventional marketing agencies, commercial directors, producers, talent (actor, musicians, photographers, illustrators), casting directors, location scouts, social anthropologists, among others.

Graphic designers who work for a brand consultancy focus on brand strategy, brand design across media, and brand creation/innovation. An entry-level portfolio should reflect a deep understanding of brand storytelling, brand strategy, audience, creative concept generation, cultural insights, transmedia brand design, including engaging campaigns for brands or groups (organizations, non-profits, companies, charities).

One's work should reflect an understanding of the connections between people and brands or groups. That's one place where storytelling comes in— stories connect people to brands.

A junior graphic designer working for a branding firm will receive briefs and direction from a design director or creative director and may be part of a brand team, working with strategists, innovation specialists, social scientists (psychologists, anthropologists), tech professionals, market researchers, trends analysts, customer experience experts, among others.

A brand designer may tackle such projects as brand architecture, brand strategy and positioning, branded environments, green branding, identity, internal branding, naming, package design, brand creation, brand innovation, and digital and social media branding.

Graphic designers employed by ad agencies work on a variety of projects. Ad agency clients may have problems, such as corporate communications, that are solved by graphic designers from the ad agency rather than by a graphic design firm. A good agency will deploy the appropriate team for the right outcome, thus they may need a graphic designer.

Graphic designers solve a variety of visual communication problems, from promotional design to information design to editorial design to identity design. Some graphic designers or design studios specialize in one of these disciplines. Some design across disciplines. An entry-level portfolio should demonstrate creative concept development, strategic thinking, interesting visualization and composition, admirable typography, and a working knowledge of software and various media channels. Graphic designers create for print and screen in a variety of formats, for example: logos, posters, book covers, magazine interiors, websites, corporate communications, icons, wayfinding systems, brochures, apps, and much more.

Most often, a graphic designer is supervised by a design director and works alone at his or her computer, collaborating with an illustrator, writer, other kind of designer, tech specialist, interior designer, architect, or other kind of creative or technology professional, when necessary. There are two main differences between the roles of graphic designers and junior art directors. Junior art directors almost always are partnered with copywriter for concept generation. Solutions created for an ad agency focus on heavy promotional content across media channels, from TV to social media.

All creatives and strategists working in advertising and branding must understand people well enough to create solutions that are inviting, engaging, and *participatory*.

If you can think critically and creatively, you might be able to conceive big ideas that invite consumers to participate, that consumers care about. You might be able to conceive brand stories with experiences that are worth having and sharing. If you work on being a brand storyteller you might be able to imagine stories that strike a chord with people, that are capable of living and thriving across platforms, with a bit of the story told through each media channel.

All visual communicators must be creative. Beyond getting an undergrad or grad degree, how do you become creative enough to build a portfolio that is worthy of landing a creative job? Think with a pencil (or stylus) in your hand. When your ideas involve brain, eyes, and hand—moving from mind and eyes to hand to paper, your creativity is made visible. You visualize your thinking. The more you do of this, the more fertile and flexible your thinking becomes. Without a doubt, there is an accumulative benefit. The more you conceive and sketch, the more your thinking evolves, thus so do the images you conceive and make. The processes of sketching, visual thinking, observing, extracting, and making connections—all stimulate creativity. Sketching is a whole brain activity. Involved are the areas of the brain governing vision (huge areas of the brain), motor system (planning and executing movement), thinking, and processing. Recently, it has been shown that based on what you do daily, the brain constantly rewires itself.

If you're an aspiring copywriter or strategic planner, remember Winnie-the-Pooh's counsel, "Think, think, think." Couple that with John Keats' observation:

"How happy is such a voyage of concentration, what delicious diligent Indolence!"

Think, concentrate, write, play exquisite corpse. Read a great book. Look out the window. Think with a pen in your hand. Sketch if you want to. Concentrate. Think. Read. Have fun doing creative exercises, and then, write some more.

Whether you want to design transmedia campaigns or logos, write copy or plan strategy, you'll be thinking for a living, so exercise your creative muscles. Merge two unrelated objects to form a new whole. Letter your name by only drawing the negative shapes. Turn an inkblot stain into something else. Change one characteristic (texture, pattern, shape, color, etc.) of an existent thing to make us see it anew. Take a line for a walk.

Work Steps:

1. **Take a line for a walk.** That's the title of one of Robin's books. Take a look at some of your latest work. What happens when you "walk it" to the next step of the journey?

2. **Switch sides.** If you're a visualizer, write down in one to seven words an entertaining description of your latest visual. If you're a

writer, look at your latest cool words and figure out the visual. Even if you can't draw, turn some of those words into a picture.

3. **Tell a story.** Look for opportunities. Improve your storytelling skills. Think about what it takes to become a *transmedia storyteller*. What tools do you think you'll need to do that?

4. **Find the Big Idea?** What's the story? Let's hang on this just a little longer. Robin makes a very, very important point. One thing that makes ideas Big Ideas is that they are big enough to contain stories. So let's look at our work and think about the stories it might contain – or inspire.

Robin Landa is the author of Take A Line For A Walk: A Creativity Journal, Advertising By Design, 2nd ed., Graphic Design Solutions, 5th ed., Designing Brand Experiences, *and many other books about creativity, advertising, and design. She is the creative director of her own firm, robinlanda.com, and Distinguished Professor in the Robert Busch School of Design at Kean University.*

Advertising or Design?

Stan Richards
Principal, The Richards Group

Here, Stan offers some useful perspective on the differences – and similarities – between advertising and design. We felt that this was an important topic as many young men and women starting out aren't quite sure which they are.

Certainly, to some extent, if you're visually talented, you're a bit of both. But if you can identify your strengths early on, it's a real advantage. From How to Succeed in Advertising When All You Have is Talent. *Used with permission.*

Where do you best fit: in an ad agency or a design organization? While many art directors and even writers may be able to fit into both, the beginner who knows where his or her strengths are has an advantage.

Let's have Richards shed some light on this topic.

"The basic difference between the design organization and the ad agency is that design work is done on a project basis," he says. "Even if the organization designed an annual report for a client for 20 consecutive years, it's still a project. We do his annual report, and at the end of it, he gets a great annual report, we send a bill, and that's the end of it.

"With an ad agency, it's a total relationship. Concerns go beyond the advertising. The agency works to help improve the sales organization. Or understand the products and services enough to recommend enhancements. That way, creative people can have a profound influence on a client's business.

"I think designers are pretty much the way they always have been with the exception of the fact that they all have had to learn to deal with the graphic world. Obviously designers in the design organization need superb design skills. Most good designers have a sense of how to string words together to support an idea.

"In the case of writers, someone who can write an annual report, slide presentation, or a film may not necessarily have the skills to write an ad. It's a matter of style. It has always been a lot easier for me to write ten pages than to entertain, excite, and explain in a seven-word headline. Consequently, a writer in our design organization may be excellent in writing long assignments but may never have written a headline in his or her life.

"This person who is likely to wind up writing annual reports is more interested in journalism or in writing the great American novel. He or she may love to read English prose or write three-page letters to erudite friends.

"Within the advertising agency, I look for great conceptual skills. A successful art director needs the right combination of verbal/visual skills. They have to be able to write headlines as well as conceive an ad or TV spot visually. The people I hire in my design organization will have superior design skills but won't necessarily be able to sit down and write a headline. Several of our people are able to work in both areas comfortably.

"With everybody working in teams now in advertising, which wasn't the case 15, 20 years ago, it is very difficult to determine who came up with the concept. Did it come from the art directors, or did it come from the writer? Or was it somehow magically born from both of them?

"One of the interesting things that happens in advertising is that once you've been in the industry for a while, you cease to be either art director or writer. You become both. In advertising, if you're an art director, you're as comfortable writing as a writer is. If you're a writer, you're as comfortable with art direction. Both people are usually on a shoot, so they both have a high degree of television experience. A lot has blurred between a writer and an art director, although both hold a different title, so there's something separating the two. The further in the development of the business the people are, the more blurred the demarcation becomes."

Work Steps:

These work steps are for the visually inclined.

There are others that emphasize things that writers need.

And, as Stan Richards noted, the lines are blurring, and good people are a bit of all those things. Still, focus can be a real advantage early in your career.

So let's look in the mirror.

1. **Designer or Art Director?** Let's ask the first question. Which do you think you are? And what does that mean to you? If you had to

choose between making it look better or making it sell better, which would you choose? Be honest.

2. **Art Director or Designer?** What kind of work turns you on? In what areas would you like to improve? These are hints you should pay attention to.

3. **Determine your strengths?** Finally, what tasks are you best at right now? Where do you need to do some more work? What comes easiest? What is a bit less comfortable? We're not saying take the easy road, but we are saying you need to understand your strengths, and, at least at the beginning of your career, before your talents are fully developed, you need to make the most of them.

━ ━ ━ ━ ━ ━

The Richards Group is America's largest independent agency.

They are consistently ranked among the nation's most creative.

They have achieved both positions by an abiding belief in the power of integration. They have several agency functions that extend well beyond advertising.

Stan Richards, *the founder, lists himself as Principal. Some of us think that should read Principle. He enforces a dedication to high standards that is reflected in all of the 600+ employees. The Richards Group began as a design firm – and Stan was a designer with a larger vision.*

He founded The Richards Group after graduating from Pratt Institute in New York.

He's been AdWeek's *"Top Creative" four times, one of the* Wall Street Journal's *"Giants of Our Time," and even an* Inc. Magazine *"Entrepreneur of the Year." The Dallas Society of Visual Communications named him "the single individual who has made the most significant contribution to the advancement of creative standards in the SouthWestern United States."*

The Peaceable Kingdom

Building a company without factionalism, fiefdoms, fear and other staples of modern business.

Stan Richards *with* David Culp

Tough. Smart. Top notch.

When he has something to say… listen.

Calling All Renaissance People! B-to-B Wants You!

Kelley Fead
Creative Director and Partner at Slack and Company in Chicago.

B-to-B means Business to Business – and it's a big business, where companies advertise to other specialized companies – their customers. Here's a look under the hood at one of the engines that drives this amazing economy – and some of the interesting work that gets done keeping that engine running. Thanks, Kelley!

You tug a Diet Coke out of the cooler at a 7-Eleven. Your friend who's lazing in your Honda outside texts your iPhone: "Get Doritos." Yeah, yeah. You grab everything, swipe your Citibank card and head back to the car, transaction completed and your consciousness full of all those consumer brand experiences.

Hidden beneath the surface of your consumer moment (*The Matrix* is appropriate here) is another whole level of brands and transactions: the world of business-to-business. As in businesses marketing to other businesses. That Diet Coke needed aspartame sweetener and caramel color, the aluminum in the can, the machinery to bottle it, and trucks to take your frosty quencher to your 7-Eleven. The Doritos needed the finger-licking nacho cheese powder – probably made up of six ingredients itself – and corn and ovens and bags with bright graphics and more trucks. And someone had to negotiate with 7-Eleven Corporate to get X bags of Doritos in Y flavors there. The iPhone? Don't get me started on all the transactions in that one.

In fact, the U.S. government says that the business economy represents most of our gross domestic product. And take a look at the Interbrand Best Global Brands 2010. Coca-Cola is at the top, followed by IBM, Microsoft, Google, and GE, which fundamentally make their money as B-to-B brands.

All of which brings me to business-to-business integrated marketing communications: a truly fascinating career with many opportunities for talented copywriters and art directors. In a business-to-business agency, you can do everything you do in a consumer agency, from branding to TV advertising to promotions to direct response to outdoor to social.

The difference is that you do all of those things for multiple audiences with multiple messages for products and services that cost multiple dollars (very often multiple millions) for multiple months and years. It took nanoseconds for you to decide to buy that Diet Coke and for your friend to choose Doritos—you trust the brands, you love the taste, and the cost was small. But the decision for the Coca-Cola Company to use aspartame as the sweetener had to have been much debated at every level of the organization, with the

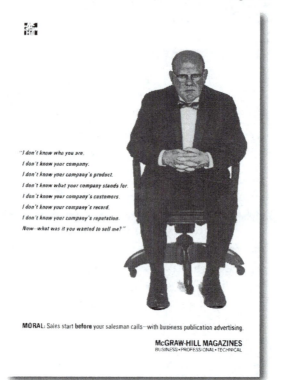

"I don't know who you are.
I don't know your company.
I don't know your company's product.
I don't know what your company stands for.
I don't know your company's customers.
I don't know your company's record.
I don't know your company's reputation.
Now—what was it you wanted to sell me?"

MORAL: Sales start before your salesman calls—with business publication advertising.

McGRAW-HILL MAGAZINES
BUSINESS • PROFESSIONAL • TECHNICAL

This is the classic ad that launched B-to-B marketing. It's McGraw-Hill's Man in the Chair ad. The statements this forbiddingly gruff man makes (he's actually the creative director who created the ad) are the ones that B-to-B agencies today still need to address for their clients.

final decision likely made by a committee based on information supplied over time. You can bet business-to-business marketing was deeply involved.

The opportunity in B-to-B is truly in integrated marketing communications, not just advertising. With all of those decision makers and influencers, you have to use programs that touch everyone in different ways and move them along a path to purchase and be an advocate. This means you get to take your big idea and then shape and expand it in so many different ways.

One more thing. B-to-B is not short for boring-to-boring. Some work can be dull and drab, just like lousy consumer work. But business decision makers are people, and appealing to their emotional interests will help the B-to-B marketer as much as the consumer marketer. Again, you just have to appeal to the emotional interests of many people to get a purchase decision made in your client's favor.

Seven Surprising Things You Can Do to Succeed in B-to-B

Be ridiculously curious. Read everything you can in our profession— and read everything in the *Wall Street Journal* and *New York Times*. We find that former journalists flock to B-to-B. They're used to digging deep and ferreting out the details that can make a difference. Cultivate your intense, geeky side when it comes to information. Be as much about art as you are about business, and explore all of your wildest interests, from bird watching to gluten-free cooking to Russian tattoos. The Renaissance man or woman is highly sought after.

Be a great creative. Yup. Talent wins here, too. Push yourself. Surround yourself with people who push themselves—and you. You can spot someone faking it in B-to-B almost immediately.

Put your ego on a shelf (up there with your awards). Our agency did research with clients and found that B-to-B marketers simply do not relate to the precious artiste archetype who uses jargon to make the work seem mysteriously important and meaningful. You have to be secure as a creative and confident about your vision and ideas in B-to-B, because the client is always, always going to know more about their product and service than you do. Your creative has to be powerful on its own because the coolly delivered presentation is not going to carry your day.

Blur the lines between you and the strategy folks. The creatives who truly understand the strategy and help shape it are the ones who go the furthest. Ask those questions. Do some research on your own. Hang out with your agency's research, planning, and account people. Join the Business Marketing Association (marketing.org). Your deeper knowledge also will inspire the client's confidence.

Be a consumer observer. Watch how you are marketed to. Learn how store shelves are arranged, Research the science behind décor and why the direct mail you get at home always has something for you to unstick or stick or put into a slot. Post reviews on Yelp and get a Twitter account. Use Facebook and watch how online display ads follow you all over the web. All of these things will come into play in B-to-B, and you may have better ideas for being inside them as a consumer.

Think globally. Keep up your second or third language from college. Travel—and travel some more. Put it on your resume and talk about it. Read news online from other countries. B-to-b is more global than ever. Show you can think broadly enough.

Have fun. Work at an agency where people laugh a lot. Start the jokes yourself. That's success.

Work Steps:

Here are six more surprising fun and easy things you can do to succeed in B-to-B (and beyond). You will see some of these work steps again in the essays that follow this one. They'll help you learn more about the specific area, so you can determine if you want to pursue it. Please note that we don't cover all of the specialty areas – for example, we don't cover agricultural advertising – but we recommend you research all of the areas listed in our essay "Finding Your Place: Part 1." After all, you may be pleasantly surprised at what you discover. In the meantime, try them right now, and you might be surprised to learn that B-to-B could be for you.

1. **Research:** What agencies in your area might be active in B-to-B advertising? (Please note that some might specialize in B-to-B while others might have a heavy proportion of B-to-B advertising clients – or assignments – at their agency.)

2. **More research:** After tracking down some of the key generators of creative work, who are some of the noteworthy talents? (Hint: the local AAF has ADDY Awards. These feature the best work by local clients, agencies, and design firms.)

3. **Find out even more:** Arrange an informational interview at one or more of these agencies. (You have a pretty good chance because B-to-B agencies tend not to get as many inquiries as the consumer agencies and design firms.)

4. **Verbalize:** What factors would keep you from accepting a creative position in a business-to-business agency? And what factors would make you interested in taking a creative position at a business-to-business agency? Be sure to be able to explain "why" for both.

5. **Keep notes:** Make a list for future reference. Some of these might not interest you yet – or you and your portfolio might not be ready for this type of agency. Why not then start a file of a folder for your notes?

6. **Create a campaign:** Try developing a campaign for a client that markets to other business. Even if you don't end up working at a B-to-B agency, there's a good chance you'll be called on to create advertising elements directed to other businesses.

7. **Follow:** Kelley ended her essay with seven key things that will lead to success in the B-to-B world. Many of them will also contribute to your success in other areas as well. So start doing them now.

━ ━ ━ ━ ━

Kelley Fead is a creative director and partner at Slack and Company (slackandcompany.com). Based in Chicago and with offices in Europe and Asia, Slack and Company has been a pure business-to-business agency since it opened its doors in 1988. The company uses traditional, new, and guerilla communications pathways to help clients build strong brands and generate profitable demand.

How I Became a Health Nut

Robin Shapiro
EVP, Chief Creative Officer, CAHG

Sometimes you know exactly where you're headed, and sometimes you have to figure it out.

Robin is now a top creative exec at a leading health care agency.

Here's the story of how she worked her way to a healthy career change. It starts with a childhood where she only knew about one kind of advertising. There's a lot to be learned.

The Onset

At precisely 6:35 p.m. every Monday, market research would officially commence. On any given night, topics up for debate and group dissemination could include my father's newest creative campaign (*What's your gut reaction?*), radio spot (*What's the main message this ad is communicating?*) or my personal favorite, a jingle (*Can you see yourself humming this even after the commercial ends?*). In between bites of the featured brand of the week (example: Kraft Macaroni and Cheese) my brother, my mother, and I were only too happy to serve as Norm's mini focus group. One night per week was reserved for portfolio review – including assessment of new print, radio, and TV for a range of copywriters and art directors trying to get a job in a big agency through Mom. My favorite candidate created the Fed Ex "fast talker" campaign at Doner, an Agency in Detroit. He was dying to break into the Chicago market. I recommended my Dad interview him. Why should we give him up to another agency? If you haven't already figured it out, life at 910 Michigan Avenue in Evanston, Illinois, was one great adventure.

My father, Norm Kantor, was a Group Creative Director. He worked for several top-notch consumer agencies over his 30+ year career in the industry – spanning from the 1970s through the early 2000s. During those same years, my mother, Donna Steele, was a leading creative recruiter in the industry. Advertising was their life, so it was our life. It was a family affair; a family career.

Weekends were reserved for insight mining, aimed at uncovering the mysterious motivations of a teenager. Dad smothered me with questions in order to uncover important insights into a normal 16-year-old mind, to whatever extent any 16-year-old mind could possibly be considered normal. What music do I love? What jeans are all the girls wearing? Who is my idol? What do I like to do with my free time? Free time? You mean there is actually something else to do besides work on the next campaign?

Sometimes the assignment actually included real client deliverables – naming projects and new ad campaigns. At first, my brother and I tried filing grievances with HR (Grandma) claiming we were being used as slave labor. But then I grew to love the pain, the addictive roller coaster of emotion that took hold when Dad would tell me one of my ideas was going to the client ... then to market research ... only to have it die. (Sigh) I always allowed myself one full day of mourning. Then I was on to the next assignment.

I was catching a bug, an advertising bug that would only be cured by a 20-year course of antibiotics, antidepressants, antipsychotics, and antivirals; a career known as healthcare advertising.

WARNING: Healthcare advertising is different from consumer advertising in several ways. All of the products promise to save, extend, or enhance lives. There is a lot more fine print. Yes, we have to tell the truth. If you have an interest in creating ideas for brands that make a difference in people's lives, please read on.

Cured

I didn't start out in healthcare. Like the rest of my job-seeking twenty something peers, I interviewed with the "Mad Men" of Michigan Avenue. I tried not to mention my parents for fear that people would hire me ... but for the wrong reasons. After a few offers to go to tropical places like St. Louis and Detroit, I accepted an offer at a mid-sized Chicago agency. It was a great job and a grunt job; every bit the Assistant Copywriter job I expected it to be. My days were filled with mundane writing assignments – tent cards for Bob Evans restaurants and brochures for Midways Airlines. Nights were more fun with friendly and not-so-friendly competitive shoot outs, endless hours spent on new campaigns and new business pitches. We worked our butts off, but we loved every minute of it. I created more than my fair share of TV spots, billboards, and print ads.

Then the tides started to turn. We were losing more pitches than we were winning. Politics set in, and Fridays became black ones. I was seeing my friends and mentors get laid off. Suddenly, it wasn't so fun anymore. At the ripe age of 23, I was developing a love/hate relationship with the consumer business.

I loved making ideas.

I hated the politics.

I loved the community of creativity.

I hated the egos.

I loved the wonder and possibility of every new campaign.

I hated selling products I didn't believe in or care about.

In the end, what really convinced me to leave was the ego of the consumer business. This was, after all, the early 1990s. The world was changing. Our agency was not. I felt like we were on the *Titanic* – too big to turn around; too broken to stay afloat. I saw the agency (and the industry) thumbing its nose to anything but 60-second commercials, turning a blind eye to direct mail and digital, and encouraging mean-spirited management.

So I left my job as a consumer copywriter only two years into it. My friends were amazed. Okay, they were horrified, especially when they found out that I was going into healthcare advertising. For me, healthcare advertising was just what the doctor ordered – a thriving industry, a business where the ideas were created *sans politics*. The campaigns contribute to the health or betterment of a human being.

Health History

For those of you who have never heard of healthcare advertising, you might be surprised to know that the industry has been around for over 50 years. In fact, the agency I work for, CAHG, is celebrating its 50th anniversary. In 1962, our agency opened its doors under the name of our founder, Frank J. Corbett. Corbett's first client was Westwood Pharmaceuticals, a client devoted to dermatologic products (creams, gels, and ointments for skin conditions). Fifty years and several mergers later, Westood-Squibb (now Bristol-Myers Squibb) is still a key client of the agency. Corbett was one of the first healthcare agencies, but it is surprising to know what a booming industry healthcare advertising has become. Currently a billion dollar, global, thriving industry, there are several hundred agencies devoted to the business of advertising good health.

You might think of healthcare advertising as being narrow or limited. Far from it! As a profession, healthcare advertising is as wide as it is deep. There are pharmaceutical brands, "nutraceuticals," devices, and hospitals. Target audiences range from professional (primarily physicians but also other healthcare providers) to consumers and from patients to pre-patients, those with biomarkers that make them vulnerable to a certain disease. It's a global business, with hundreds of agencies.

A Day in the Life

Like consumer, healthcare advertising is a business about ideas. Great ideas have the power to transform brands, mindsets, and even human lives. It is a business that works hard and plays hard. It's a business that seeks to understand what makes people tick and to capitalize on human emotion.

A day in the life of a healthcare advertising agency isn't really that different from any agency. At any given moment you are likely to find copywriters, art directors, and account people dreaming up the next great idea, account planners interviewing customers, project managers pulling their hair out in the midst of looming deadlines, and conference rooms full of teams, presenting their ideas to clients with the theatricality of a Cirque de Soleil performance.

We're lucky to work in an industry that is more good than evil and still fun.

A Word about Awards

Have no fear. Creativity is alive and well in this industry. Many of the large national and global award shows have healthcare categories or even healthcare versions of the same awards. The Clios sponsor Clio Healthcare, for example. The Global Awards is another fine show sponsored by the New York Festivals. The same rules apply when it comes to winning awards. Simple, surprising, visually driven, exquisitely executed ideas fare best.

The Outlook

There is much excitement in the healthcare industry. It's a time of great transformation. Physicians are leveraging new forms of media to educate themselves and their patients. Technology is changing the way diseases are diagnosed. The world is moving from treatment to prevention.

The business is more challenging than it has ever been before. Mergers and acquisitions are daily news. Managed care is a more pervasive and formidable force. Clients are under pressure to produce better results faster. Some companies are more risk averse. Others are inventing their way out with creativity and innovation. We prefer to attach to the latter.

The industry is in a state of evolution. So are the best agencies. New digital experts are being added. Roles like digital strategists, creative technologists, UX and UI designers, and digital producers are changing agency structure and process. Creative campaigns are being developed differently, as integrated multi-channel campaigns from the start. Agencies are executing for online and mobile media as much as print. Innovation and a spirit of entrepreneurialism are flourishing. As a senior leader in one of these agencies, I do everything in my power to keep it this way.

Is Healthcare Advertising for You?

Maybe. Maybe not. Not everyone can make it. This business takes a rare combination of passion, talent, patience and palpable inquisitiveness. In order to thrive in healthcare advertising, you have to appreciate delving in deep and discovering how things work. You can't easily hover on the surface.

Clients love and appreciate those who love and appreciate their brands. That means getting to know the brand's data (the promotable results from a brand's clinical trials) their customers, and their competition. Leveraging and showcasing that knowledge will lead to better work. I am 100% convinced of that.

30 Years Later

It's been a long time since the days of the Kantor-family focus groups. I have 3 teenagers and a loving husband, all of whom are working diligently on their hypochondria. How else is my 11-year-old supposed to help with an ad for macular degeneration?! But here's the best news. I still love making ideas, the community of creativity, and the wonder and possibility of every new campaign. Lucky for me, healthcare advertising was every bit the lasting cure I once hoped for.

Give it a try.

A career in healthcare advertising just might be the lasting cure for you as well.

Work Steps:

We all want a healthy career. So while these steps are the same ones as in previous essays, we recommend that you complete all of them. After all, you might be surprised to discover that healthcare advertising is for you.

1.   **Research:** What agencies in your area specialize in healthcare advertising? (Hint: there are several advertising awards competitions for the healthcare advertising arena. Look them up now as part of this work step. Then find the healthcare agencies in your area.) List them now.

2.   **More research:** After tracking down some of the key generators of creative work, who are some of the noteworthy talents? (Hint: Many of the awards mentioned in step one identify the people involved with creating the award-winning elements. You can also look on the agency websites to find the chief creative officer and other key creative personnel.)

3.   **Find out even more:** Arrange an informational interview at one or more of these agencies.

4.   **Verbalize:** What factors would keep you from accepting a creative position in a healthcare agency? And what factors would make you interested in taking a creative position at one? Be sure to be able to explain "why" for both.

5.   **Keep notes:** Make a list for future reference. Some of these might not interest you yet – or you and your portfolio might not be ready for this type of agency. Add your notes to your file.

6.   **Create a campaign:** Try developing an ad campaign directed toward the medical market. Remember, this campaign should include both digital and print as well as other elements.

－ － － － － －

Robin Shapiro oversees all creative efforts at CAHG, which is one of the largest integrated healthcare communications companies in the United States. She is responsible for building and upholding the agency's creative reputation.

Robin is fiercely dedicated to attracting, recruiting, and retaining top creative talent. Understanding that an agency is only as strong as its talent, Robin has created an environment of innovation in the area of talent development. Inventive training programs for conceptual thinking skills, strategic acumen, and leadership skills have become trademarks of the agency. Programs like these are the reason CAHG is ranked #1 among Omnicom companies for learning orientation.

Robin has created a culture of collaboration and cross-fertilization by artfully mixing talent from different backgrounds, skills, and areas of expertise. This approach has resulted in the creation of many globally recognized campaigns – campaigns that have helped catapult brands to market dominance and accrued multiple prestigious industry awards along the way.

Among her many creative achievements, she led the launch of ABILIFY, widely recognized as one of the most successful pharmaceutical launches in US history. CAHG remains Agency of Record for ABILIFY and the campaign Robin helped create is one of the most iconic and enduring ideas in the global pharmaceutical industry.

Robin began her career in 1987 as a consumer-advertising copywriter for Campbell Mithun Esty in Chicago. She attended Southern Illinois University and Columbia College Chicago.

Double Your Chances of Finding a Job: Start Your Promotion Portfolio Today (Offers Limited. While Supplies Last.)

Colleen Fahey
Principal, The Idea Haven

This classic piece, now slightly updated, explains Colleen Fahey's early field of expertise – sales promotion. It's a solid introduction to its basics of influencing action and creating measurable results. It was originally written to explain the field to people who only understood advertising. As the Executive Creative Director for sales promotion pioneer Frankel, and then Publicis, you grew up with Colleen's work – she supervised Happy Meals for McDonald's. Today, Colleen is at The Idea Haven where they're exploring the new frontier of Audio Branding. As we said, this piece is a classic, but it's still relevant. Today, there is lots of opportunity in sales promotion and the related fields of MarCom – so pay attention.

The Most Fun You Can Have and Still Be Working

I started out in an advertising agency; I liked it a lot. Then I moved to sales promotion. I loved it. I believe that promotional marketing is about the most fun you can have and still be working. It lets you be creative in truly unexpected ways.

In promotions, you get to use both your practical side and your wildly imaginative side, and, because it's so varied, you never get stale.

Promotion is the part of marketing that focuses on making a sale – or driving a behavior – within a predictable period of time. You tell the customer what you're offering, you say what you want in return, and you make it clear how long the offer will last.

This is usually done by offering some sort of limited-time incentive.

And you get to think up how you'll tell the customer. It can be anything from a hot air balloon to the great American T-shirt. Your work is often molded, die-cut, or backlit. You get to create premiums and prizes that have never existed before. You might come up with games, events, or unique experiences.

In other words, you get to think up the message (the offer) and the medium – or, more likely, the various media – to promote it. Not long afterwards, you'll find out whether your offer succeeded or failed.

In promotion, the most challenging task is to come up with a motivating offer. The most fun job is to find the twist that makes the offer fresh and motivating. And the most gratifying part is to watch the results come in.

How to Think Promotionally

Your first step is to translate the objective (e.g., build sales 3%) into something the customer can act on. Here are some of the actions you would typically be trying to encourage a customer to take:

- Try a new product
- Buy two packages at a time instead of one
- Come into a store or restaurant more times a month
- Buy several different products from the same manufacturer
- Buy a larger size

The Next Step Is to Get a Good Fix on Your Customer

This can be tricky. A product aimed at a child (who might think a whoopee cushion is the perfect promotional premium) might actually be purchased by his or her mother (who's likely to be more motivated by free school supplies).

A careful look at the audience will tell you where the offer will do the most good. Here are some broad groups clients often need to influence:

- Mothers of young families
- Business people who fly constantly
- Affluent, single working women

The next stop for your promotional train of thought is the traffic-driving tactic itself. Here's a partial list of tactics you can use:

- A premium is a gift that's offered free or at a lower-than-retail cost when the customer makes a purchase, takes a test drive, or visits a location. A perfect example of a successful premium promotion is the McDonald's Happy Meal. The offer is simple: The customer buys a child's meal combination, and, in return, the child gets a toy, which is available for a limited time. (That's why the toys change monthly.) There's even a premium that meets the needs of the parents: a container that keeps the child busy with puzzles, jokes, and games so that they can enjoy a relatively peaceful meal.

- A sweepstakes, game, or contest offers a big, eye-catching reward to a few people instead of a small one to everyone.
- A bonus offer gives the customer more of the product or service for the same price.
- A coupon, rebate, or special price reduces the cost of the product.
- A continuity program or frequency program is a long-term promotion that tries to keep people from switching brands. The airlines' frequent-flier plans are good examples of these promotions, so is My Starbucks Rewards, which enable participants to get a free drink after purchasing 15 drinks, among other benefits.

Where Does Creative Come In?

What makes the whole business exciting for creatives is the next step: figuring out how to combine tactics, embellish them, maybe add a bit of borrowed interest, or make them work especially hard to enhance the brand's image.

- That's how a Willy Wonka sweepstakes becomes "Wonkaaah!" and winners ride roller coasters from coast to coast. They win if they open their candy packets and hear it scream, "Wonkaaah!"
- An 80th Anniversary celebration for Nestlé Brazil becomes "80 Homes for You."
- A back-to-school promotion becomes "Afterschool Rocks" in which the audience earns playlists tailored to their individual after-school plans.

The possibilities go on and on.

To be good at this part of the promotion development process, you need to stay aware of what's going on in sports, entertainment, toys, and fads. Promotions that catch popular waves really create sales peaks.

Remember, if you choose a movie, sport, character, or event to add appeal to your promotion, do it with any eye to extending the image of your brand.

How to Start a Promotion Book

- You can use your best advertising ideas as jumping-off points for your promotion ideas.
- What would motivate a customer to purchase your brand? What will you give in return?
- For your book, it's important that you show an understanding of how you can create an immediate impact on sales without confusing the long-term image of the product. You don't have to follow the advertising slavishly, but you do have to be true to the brand's identity.
- Execute your work at the same level as your other advertising. While it needs to quickly communicate, it also needs to reflect – and build – your brand.

Here's What I'd Like to See in Your Book

1. Take one promotional assignment and try three concepts that address it. (This will show me how much creative flexibility you have within the constraints of a single set of rules.)
2. Pick your favorite one of these ideas and create the support pieces for it.
    - An ad or freestanding insert
    - A display
    - A TV commercial or radio spot
    - The premium itself, a PR idea, a trade sell-in piece or an especially original way of merchandising it. (This will help me understand your creative style and to see your ability to achieve continuity through different elements and to different audiences.)
3. Pick three products. Make sure one is in a different business category (i.e., if you used a product sold through grocery stores, make your next idea one for a retailer or for a service business). Do a concept board for each. If you see some natural extensions, you're welcome to include them. (This will let you show them off.)

What's a Concept Board?

A concept board simply conveys the core idea. It needs a theme, key visual, and some quick bullets describing any important mechanics.

Each concept should have a theme or "handle." These lines are shorter than headlines usually are. They announce the event and generally appear on all elements that carry the promotional message (e.g., floor displays, hang-tags, TV commercials, and window banners).

Writers, a concept board usually doesn't give you a chance to showcase your writing. So put longer pieces into your book, too. Even though we spend a lot of our time writing bullets and themes; there are always clients who need longer copy for websites, brochures, mailings, newsletters, and speeches.

- You've seen lots of blah themes; retailers recycle them continuously: "Fall Festival of Values," "4th of July Sell-abration," and "Strike it Rich sweepstakes."

Here are a couple of fresher approaches:

- Arm Yourself for the One You Love: A promotion designed to help Walgreens become the top retailer for flu shots.
- Game of Thrones – Maesters Challenge: An online game designed to support the launch of the *Game of Thrones* TV series for HBO.
- Huddle to Fight Hunger: A promotion from Kraft in September – Hunger Action Month – where Americans "donated meals" when they purchased various Kraft brands.

Art directors, note that a theme will often appear as a design element that repeats throughout the promotional materials. Here's a chance to show how you would approach a promotional "logo" design. (It helps to keep your roughs, too, perhaps as a separate PDF file on your tablet. We like to see how you made your choices.)

How to Prescreen Your Ideas

The creative director will be trying to understand how you think and can be even more important than how you execute a program. After all, we are all looking for someone to think up ideas that haven't been thought of yet. Here are some of the ways we evaluate promotions:

- Is it clear how it will help sell product?
- Does it extend the image of the brand?
- Is the idea or the execution fresh and inventive?
- Does it communicate quickly?
- Do I wish I'd thought of that?

If yours passes muster, put it in the book. Show your range. Big, flamboyant ideas are great. So are small practical ideas as long as they're a perfect fit. A fair number of ideas should show that you were having fun while you were working on them.

Believe me, if you do this, you'll have far more promotion in your book than almost any fresh-out-of-school applicant we've seen. And we'll be impressed with your commitment right off the bat.

If we're also impressed with your work, you could end up with one of the most fun creative jobs in marketing. And no matter how often you explain your new job to your mother, she'll still tell all her friends you're in advertising.

Work Steps:

Colleen has just given you a solid introduction to thinking promotionally. Let's see if we can add a promotional dimension to your portfolio. Whether or not you actually end up working in this area, you'll benefit from developing your promotional muscles.

So, let's look at your portfolio – pick any of the products you worked on, and we'll go through the steps. Ready?

1. **Make yourself more promotionally aware.** Now that we've got you starting to think promotionally, start to look at the world through promotional eyes. Go to any fast food franchise – see what they're doing. Now go to another. When you go to the convenience store, look to see what they are doing. If you're old enough to drink, go to a large liquor retailer and see all the displays and specials going on. Now go to a major supermarket and shop the specials. You don't have to buy anything – but you should start to see how these marketers are thinking promotionally.

2. **Identify the behavior.** What behavior do you want to encourage? You can start by looking at the list in Colleen's article. Basically, a promotional strategy is a behavior – buy a bigger size, try it for the first time, etc.

3. **Identify the audience.** Who do you want to do this? Let's think about the purchase situation. For example, it could be Mom or it could be kids. What's going on in their lives? Try to connect with new things that are happening. The same old Save Now – unless

these are HUGE savings – isn't going to get a big response. Try to put yourself in the customer's shoes.

4. **Determine the "bribe?"** Remember, sales promotion is a way of "rewarding" sales. That means you need an "incentive." What will it take to get it done?

5. **Make it effective.** Since your objective is to build a portfolio that grabs attention and provides the incentive to hire you, think about how good it has to be. Go for it!

▬ ▬ ▬ ▬ ▬ ▬

Colleen Fahey started her career in advertising in New York City. When she moved to Chicago, she decided to go into promotion for one year so she'd be a more well-rounded advertising person.

She never went back.

"What promotional creatives all have in common is an unwillingness to choose between being right-brained and being left-brained. They want to be in on everything. So do I."

If you'd like to read some more recent bright thinking, check out some of Colleen's writings at The Idea Haven – where she currently resides. http://theideahaven.com/?author=1

Building Brands
While Building Business

William Rosen
Partner, VSA Partners

We've already learned a little about sales promotions. But the practice has evolved to such a degree that its newer incarnations are better described as integrated marketing campaigns focused on driving sales in a branded way. You could think of it as a lot like the brand storytelling Robin Landa described in her essay, but with one clear mission: to drive behaviors that move people closer to transactions. This is the new world of brand marketing – or, as some still call it, consumer marketing services. Often overlooked by beginners, this is a highly creative and richly rewarding area of growing importance. Some even argue that this is the future of all marketing. Let's learn about it from one of its recognized leaders, William Rosen. Thanks, Bill!

In 1986, when Bud Frankel published his groundbreaking book, *Your Advertising's Great … How's Business?*, it was a revolutionary manifesto for a newly emerging marketing discipline aptly called "Sales Promotion."

While the world of marketing has evolved nearly beyond recognition since that time, the title of Bud's book and its underlying vision remains an apt answer to the question of why a new generation of creatives should and will enter the dynamic world of marketing services – the term used to describe the full suite of specialty disciplines that are focused as much on building sales as they are on building brands.

As Bud understood then, and the world's most sophisticated marketers demonstrate now, simply trumpeting a brand's positioning and benefits, no matter how engagingly, persuasively or entertainingly done, can only accomplish so much. One must find new ways to incent engagement, deliver value, navigate retail channels from Walmart to eCommerce, promote products, package offerings, leverage data, maintain loyalty, and create experiences that help marketers efficiently and effectively meet their very real business goals.

Those excited by that kind of no-holds-barred, creative problem solving are the ones who belong in marketing services.

Those next-generation marketing creatives are, in fact, going to lead the entire industry into the next evolution of marketing services.

The reason is simple: today's graduates are cross-discipline, cross-channel thinkers from birth. They grew up in a digitally enabled world where "online" and "off-line" lost meaning as quickly as they could scan an in-store price with a smart phone and share their purchase on Facebook.

This generation understands how the traditionally separated marketing disciplines interrelate and how, when they are connected, they can create real value for real people in the form of experiences, efficiency, utility, and personalization, just to name a few. When they realize and apply that insight on behalf of brands, they will hold the key to driving engagement and changing behavior – and continuing to unleash the power of marketing services to build business while building brands.

Over the last decade, there have been, depending on how you count them, four large categories of marketing services offerings: digital, direct/CRM, promotion, and shopper/retail marketing. In the next decade that is going to change.

Digital's ubiquity has moved it from a fringe discipline to the center of all marketing, so it will soon be as redundant and antiquated to say "digital marketing" as it is to say "electric light." That is convergence number one.

Digital technology is by definition data rich and highly personalizable, creating opportunities for one-to-one communications and relationships that bring it quickly into the world of direct/CRM/database marketing. That is convergence number two.

A personal, digitally enabled world gives people unprecedented power and capabilities, including the ability to block, opt-out, or otherwise disengage from relationships and messaging that they deem distracting, destructive, or of no value. As a result, creating real incentives and rewards for any form of participation will be increasingly critical. That skill-set and practice had traditionally been called "promotion." This is convergence number three.

Lastly, the newest marketing darling, "shopper marketing," is bringing, among other things, an unprecedented level of insight into how and why people actually buy what they buy, which of course is what all marketing is all about. This is convergence number four.

That is why the most efficient and effective creative marketing solutions will be informed by all four areas, and the next generation of marketers will think this way naturally. So with that leg up, how does this up-and-coming group of future marketing leaders ensure a successful entrance into and accelerated development of a marketing services career?

The first answer is to understand with sufficient depth the approaches, insights, ideas, and innovations going on in what are still distinct disciplines. There are key learnings and best practices in each discipline area that an up-and-coming creative needs to understand, if only to completely reinvent them. From creating an engaging and rewarding user experience on-line to effectively incenting trial of a product, there are proven practices that generate measurably superior results when appropriately applied. Knowing these techniques are the building blocks and "greens fees" of effective marketing. It is analogous to the tremendous number of classically trained jazz musicians. One must learn the fundamental techniques and theories if one is to have all of the tools available to them to improvise, invent, and innovate.

The second task is to understand the interrelationship between disciplines and channels in achieving marketing goals. This needs to be studied from two perspectives, which admittedly overlap. The first is by understanding what each of the disciplines is best suited for and does well in the marketing mix. The second is by utilizing your daily perspective as a consumer and shopper, by considering and noting how you use media on your way toward a purchase decision and ultimately a transaction in different product categories.

The third task is to apply the learnings from the first two to demonstrate your ability to utilize all of the marketing services disciplines in a strategic and creatively inspired way. This, of course, needs to go well beyond the "box checking" or "matching luggage" approach where an advertising idea is shown in-store ("check"), on-line ("check"), on the streets ("check"), and on a mobile social media platform ("check, check"), and it all looks exactly the same (luggage successfully matched).

The key to success is to demonstrate how the disciplines and media channels align in your idea(s) to engage real people, change their behaviors, and move them toward a transaction – all in a way uniquely ownable by the brand. To do this, you must show insight into how real people shop and buy the products and brands you are marketing and seize opportunities to engage them that demonstrates the brand versus simply talking about it. You must connect media and disciplines in unique ways that leverage the strengths of each into a seamless "conversation" between the brand and people that methodically moves them further down the path to purchase.

Lastly, demonstrate your understanding of the realities of what a marketer and/or retailer is likely to actually do and build-in ideas that overcome common barriers. The fact that you even thought about why Target would feature your client's brand or how you'd make sure the car dealer would manage the customer experience as you envisioned will score you huge points – and prepare you for the realities ahead.

The marketing world is being shifted by the promise of new technologies and marketers longing for partners who can deliver measurable results in the marketplace. As a result, there is no better place to be than marketing services, where one has endless opportunities to do both. Lay the groundwork in understanding and then creatively play with the best practices, and you will find yourself in the business that builds business.

Work Steps:

The following steps might sound familiar from others in this section – and some are new. But to truly find your area, it's highly suggested that you do all of them. After all, it's the best way to uncover the opportunity that's right for you.

1. **Research key approaches.** What are the key approaches, insights, ideas, innovations, and best practices of each discipline catalogued in the essay "Creative Careers for the 21st Century"?

2. **Identify delivery channels.** How are the different delivery channels affecting these key approaches, insights, ideas, innovations, and best practices for each discipline?

3. **Create a campaign.** Make sure that it goes across disciplines and media channels; be ready to explain how it engages the target, changes behavior, and moves people toward transaction.

4. **List the leading companies.** What firms in your area are active in brand marketing – i.e., that build brands while building sales? What is some of their noteworthy work?

5. **Find the Leaders.** Who are some of the key leaders of these agencies, and what is their noteworthy work?

6. **Arrange an interview.** Set up an informational interview at one or more of these agencies or departments. Make sure you keep detailed notes for future reference. And, of course, make sure you thank the individual.

▬ ▬ ▬ ▬ ▬ ▬

William Rosen is Partner at VSA Partners, where he is developing and overseeing their consumer marketing practice.

Prior to beginning his engagement with VSA, William was president and chief creative officer of North America for Arc Worldwide, the global marketing company and part of Leo Burnett Worldwide and the Publicis Group. He was responsible for the strategic and creative product across all disciplines – digital, direct/CRM, promotion, and shopper/retail marketing – for clients including McDonald's, Procter & Gamble, Coca-Cola, Nestlé Purina, Comcast, Walgreens, United Airlines, Whirlpool, and MillerCoors.

William took the top creative spot at Arc Worldwide in 2004, when Frankel, a leading marketing agency he headed as chief creative, merged into Arc Worldwide. There his team was recognized more than 300 times with major creative awards and rankings around the world including "Best New Media," "Best Multidiscipline Campaign," several "Best in Show" awards, and three Lions at the Cannes International Advertising Festival.

In 2011, William's work for MillerCoors, Symantec, and Walgreens received six Effie Awards, the industry's most prestigious prize for effectiveness. His work for Walgreens was honored with the Oracle World Retail Award's "Retail Advertising Campaign of the Year" as well as the MAA Worldwide Globes "Best of the Best in the World." In 2012, William's work for P&G and others was honored with seven more Effie Awards, placing it among the most awarded in North America.

William served as president of the jury at the Cannes Lions International Advertising Festival, as well as the Spikes Asia Advertising Festival, and has served on juries for the Clio Awards, the Effie Awards, the London International Advertising Awards, and numerous other leading industry award shows.

In addition to his advertising work, he is a produced playwright, whose 8 plays have received more than 12 productions in theatres around the country, including New York, Los Angeles, and Chicago.

Why Pursue a Career at a Digital Agency?

Ethan Smith
Creative Director, Gorilla

Every campaign is "digital" today, so why should someone consider working at a digital agency? We asked Ethan Smith, the creative director of award-winning digital agency Gorilla, to give us the answer. His answer might just inspire you to specialize in this important specialty.

At the beginning of every spring, I start searching for prospective interns. This year was no exception. The search process was long and arduous, and at one point I thought it might go unfilled. I spent a good amount of time talking to numerous candidates of varying skills levels with a lot of divergent career goals. In the end patience and diligence paid off, not only did we find an intern, we were able to find one that eventually got hired on a full-time basis.

What took so long, and why would I dedicate weeks of time to this process? I was insistent that our intern would want to focus his or her career on digital design. And a lot of good beginning designers are hesitant to specialize because they feel it might be too limiting. But here's what they need to understand about digital design:

It's Fun and You'll Meet New People

I've worked at all kinds of agencies and have done some consulting work for large companies; I can safely say the most fun I have had has been working in an agency that focuses on digital as its only practice. The type of people attracted to the digital environment on the whole are a pretty laid-back bunch, but the expectations remain very high. On top of that, you'll be exposed to a lot of different ways of thinking. If you want some really interesting feedback on your work, ask a developer to critique it.

Entrepreneurial Spirit

If there is any industry that is open to new ideas, it's ours. I can think of more than a few co-workers who have jumped ship to join a start-up, either someone else's or their own. If you've got the inkling to go out on your own someday, this a great stepping stone towards striking out on your own.

There's No Shortage of Work

Right now we're experiencing boom times, especially for those in the digital space. Competition for talent hasn't been this intense since the first dot com era. There are more jobs than people; if you're looking to break into something new, there are a number of different career paths you can pursue that embrace any number of personalities. The challenges of an interactive agency are intense, and the demands are high, but if you are willing to commit to learning the craft, the work will come.

Constantly Changing Demands

The new normal in the digital arena is a line that is constantly moving. You can't sit around or be complacent with your skills. This is a medium that demands you pay full attention and embrace change at all times. The constant state of industry flux leads me to believe while the jobs will change a lot over time, they aren't going anywhere soon. On top of that, you're focused on a profession that's constantly evolving; you'll never be bored because you'll always be learning new things.

Digital Is Becoming the Lead Voice

Companies are starting to recognize the digital channel as one that will be the centerpiece for all of their communications. Over the last three years we've seen a lot of companies invite digital agencies to take the lead in their overall strategy. This is a dramatic shift away from the standard "Agency of Record" practices of past years. While a lot of companies, especially the larger ones, still hold fast to that model, for a lot of the smaller, nimbler companies the associated overhead isn't economically feasible.

Built-In Performance

Agencies in other design areas are under constant pressure to prove return on investment to their clients. While that's no different in digital media, the ability to measure performance is inherently included. With digital almost everything is measurable; it's just a matter of how specific and contextual the numbers can get. It's a lot easier to tell just how many people came to you because of a site you launched as opposed to a billboard placed on the side of a highway.

You Won't Be Second Class

It's an unfair generalization, and I hate to say it, but for a lot of firms that started elsewhere, the digital staff is seen as second class. Even worse, their contributions can be viewed as a "value-add" and not a core service. I wish it wasn't the case, but it's something I've experienced firsthand and an unfortunate situation that exists at a lot of firms.

Forward Thinking Work

If you are lucky enough to work for a company that is forward thinking from a design and technology perspective, you will get some really forward thinking work in your portfolio. I see that as a major plus, and it's something I look for in all of the portfolios I look at. Is a candidate a good designer, and are they technically aware? Be mindful that in the long term this can hurt a little, as some technical fads don't stand the test of time.

Short Lifespan

This is both a benefit and a drawback depending on how you look at it. Working with technology means your work will have a shorter shelf-life than someone practicing industrial design or architecture might experience. That can be frustrating as I have several sites in my past that are long gone. The benefit here is that realizing an idea in digital format can usually be accomplished much quicker than other design disciplines. It's much easier to adopt a very iterative design practice when you can do multiple variations on an idea in a very short amount of time.

Global Reach

When you work in a digital agency, more people will experience your work than any other media besides television, and that's changing too. The potential to deliver a project that is experienced by a huge cross-section of the world is very real.

Cultural Significance

Working in digital these days most likely means ninety-five percent of the work you do will be in web design and development. While there is a tendency from some in the design community to shy away from web, I look at it as an opportunity to participate in the most culturally significant artifact of our time. Living a network enabled life has dramatically shifted us in directions that are both good and bad. Whether or not you agree with the cultural shift attached to becoming a fully networked culture, it's effect on our lives is without question. I would rather be an active participant in shaping this part of the human experience than sitting on the sidelines watching it happen.

Work Steps:

Let's get working. The following steps might sound familiar from the end of Kelley's section – and some are new. But to truly find if digital is right for you, we highly recommend that you complete all of the steps. Let's start right now.

1. **Research:** What agencies in your area specialize in digital? List them now.
2. **More research:** After tracking down some of the key generators of creative work, who are some of the noteworthy talents? (Hint: the local AAF has ADDY Awards. These feature the best work by local clients, agencies, and design firms.)
3. **Find out even more:** Arrange an informational interview at one or more of these agencies. (As we noted, you also have a pretty good chance here of arranging one because they don't get as many inquiries as large general agencies and design firms.)
4. **Verbalize:** What factors would keep you from accepting a creative position in a business-to-business agency? And what factors would make you interested in taking a creative position at a business-to-business agency? Be sure to be able to explain "why" for both.
5. **Keep notes:** Make a list for future reference. Some of these might not interest you yet – or you and your portfolio might not be ready for this type of agency. Add your notes to your file.
6. **Create a digital campaign:** Try developing a campaign where digital leads or is the primary component. It could be a website, an app, or messaging that resides elsewhere. You might even want to include

all of these touch points. After all, there's a really good chance you'll be asked to create digital elements even if you don't end up working at a digital agency.

- - - - - -

*For over a decade **Ethan Smith** has been practicing interactive design and user experience. Over the course of his career he has fulfilled the roles of visual designer, front-end developer, information architect, strategist, art/creative director, consultant, and project manager for a collection of agencies and clients (both big and small) in California, New York, and Chicago.*

In addition to his freelance and agency track record, Ethan has served as a digital design faculty member for colleges in both the public and for-profit sectors. His topics covered include 2D fundamentals, web design fundamentals, advanced digital design and digital imaging techniques.

His body of work includes clients such as 3M, The American Library Association, Canyon Ranch, Chick-Fil-A, Custo Barcelona, Discovery Communications, Fox Searchlight Studios, The Joffrey Ballet, Lowe's, MasterCard, Quintiles Transnational, Ronald McDonald House Charities, Sub Zero/Wolf, TurboChef Technologies, Weber Grills, Wells Fargo, and Xerox Corporation.

His work has appeared in the Communication Arts Interactive Annual, Webby Awards, IMAs, and WebAwards from the Web Marketing Association.

Ethan holds an MA in multimedia from California State University as well as bachelors degrees in both visual arts and music from Illinois State University.

His current post is Creative Director at Gorilla, an E-commerce agency in Chicago.

Welcome to the Experience That Is Experiential Marketing
(Please Keep Your Hands and Feet inside the Ride at All Times)

Credit: Rebecca Peplinski

Erik McKinney
VP – Strategy & Creative,
Legacy Marketing Partners

What do you know about experiential market-ing? Not much. Don't feel bad because all that is about to change. We asked Erik McKinney, VP of Strategy and Creative at Legacy, to give you a brief introduction. In one chapter of reading, you may go from not knowing what experiential marketing is to altering the focus of your creative career path. We guarantee you will profit from the experi-ence – his.

Welcome. If I can offer you one piece of advice that you remember above and beyond anything else I share with you, it is this: pursue your passion. The creative career path you choose should have you excited to wake up every morning to conceive the unexpected, unthinkable, and unforgettable. That is why I do what I do at Legacy.

My career path probably differs slightly from most of the other authors of this book. I started my career on the "dark side," also known as account management.

However, in the world of experiential marketing at that time, the idea of a creative department was just in its fledgling stages. In account management, not only did we have to handle the day-to-day client responsibilities and ex-ecution logistics, but we also did most of the ideation for any assignment we were working on. You can probably guess where my passion was focused.

In 2006, I helped to develop and launch the first ever creative depart-ment for my agency at the time, Relay Worldwide, the Publicis network's U.S. based experiential marketing agency. And I never looked back.

Since that time, I wake up every morning excited to take on the day's challenges and strive to find new and innovative ways to create meaningful connections between brands and consumers.

That passion is crucial because it is the crux of experiential marketing.

When it comes to engaging consumers, I'm sure you are familiar with the standard marketing terms: awareness, trial, consideration, and adoption.

At Legacy, we follow a different model. We aim to intrigue, engage, inspire passion, and amplify it. Our mission is not just creating new consumers, but new brand advocates.

What Is Experiential Marketing?

Since experiential marketing as an industry may be new to you, let me start by asking you about your best friend.

What makes your best friend just that?

Is it because they talk about all the things that make them great?

Is it because you're friends on Facebook or you follow them on Twitter?

Is it because they offer you special deals?

Or, is it because of the experiences that you have shared together and relive time and time again?

I'm going to venture a guess that it's the latter. If not, my analogy may be shot, but you have a much bigger problem in how you selected a best friend.

At its core, experiential marketing is about creating shared experiences between a brand and a consumer.

Great experiential marketing is the ability to create those experiences in a way that consumers can't wait to talk about with friends and can't avoid talking about the brand in the process. At Legacy, we use the term Brand Love, which is the intersection where rational product benefit intersects with an emotional brand connection.

Recently I've heard experiential referred to as a "popular trend." It has actually been around for decades. Heard of the Oscar Meyer Weiner mobile? That was a branded mobile tour created in 1936, which coincidentally falls under experiential marketing.

You've probably come across more than one pop-up store. That originated in experiential marketing as well.

Have you been engaged at a branded experience at a sporting event or music concert? Once again, that too is experiential marketing.

Finally, have you ever been engaged with branded sampling or education in a store or a bar or even on the street? If so, you've experienced experiential marketing at its most basic level.

Whether it's at retail on the road or in a brand-owned space, we are constantly trying to find new and innovative ways to engage, educate, entertain, surprise, and delight consumers.

Regardless of the final product, that process begins with a creative idea.

Experiential Marketing Creative Careers

There are a number of different creative careers within experiential marketing. However, one quality that everyone we hire at Legacy Marketing Partners must possess is being an idea machine. Before we get into specific needs for designing or writing, we need the big idea from which everything else is born.

The key to being a big idea generator is, shockingly, not about just being creative. You can have the most imaginative ideas in the world, but if they're not grounded in the brand strategy or consumer insights, they are just clever thoughts, not big ideas.

Remember this when you put your book together. It's not just about showing your most creative work, but also being able to explain the thinking behind it and why it makes sense for the brand and the consumer you're trying to reach.

To communicate an experiential idea for your portfolio you need a concept drawing and a brief explanation of the idea. Here is a concept drawing for an experiential event produced by Legacy…

I employ a simple filter to evaluate ideas. I ask four questions.

Is the idea relevant? To check the box in this area, the idea must be on brand strategy, make sense within the target audience's world, and work within whatever environment it will be brought to life.

Is the idea memorable? The idea must provide an experience that stays with the consumer and delivers the desired mix of education and entertainment.

Is the brand part of the story? When they remember the experience, we must ensure they also include the brand in the story.

This leads me to the final question. **Is it "shareable"?** A unique part of experiential marketing is that normally we are not engaging millions of people at a time. We are working against much smaller, targeted audiences. As such, it is essential that every idea we create generates word of mouth and includes digital and social media components that allow consumers to easily share the experience.

Once we settle on the big idea, then the specific creative disciplines go into action to bring the idea to life. Experiential marketing is unique in the sense that creative is not just confined to design and writing. Our goal is to create a truly sensorial experience that will be brought to life three-dimensionally and interact with the consumer in a live environment, not separated by a TV screen.

With all of that in mind, here is an overview of the two primary creative

… and here is a picture from the actual event.

career paths within experiential marketing. While I am focusing on the general description, there are clearly defined career paths within each that provide an entry-level opportunity as well as the ability to grow.

Career Path #1: The Idea Writer

The Idea Writer is experiential marketing's version of a copywriter. Their role begins by creating the verbal identity of the idea with a concept name and, potentially, a tagline.

However, writing is only part of the job description. The Idea Writer's primary role after the big idea has been created is to create a framework for the entire experience. They truly need to view the experience through the eyes of the consumer from the moment they enter until they leave.

Basically, they are creating the ideas within the big idea that round out the consumer experience. Whereas a TV spot only needs to educate and/or entertain consumers for thirty seconds, our branded experiences may engage a captive audience up to several hours. This is done through interactive elements, performances, and any other means that creates or deepens the connection with the brand.

Once the entire experience has been constructed, Idea Writers take on the role of scriptwriters. Within any live experience, we have onsite brand ambassadors who will engage consumers and facilitating a two-way dialog.

The Idea Writer is responsible for developing the scripts that guide these conversations. Because we are talking with consumers and not at them, we must take an open-ended approach that provides the staff with options and flexibility. This requires thinking through every potential conversational direction, overcoming objectives, and providing the brand ambassadors with the tools to customize the dialog based on the consumer's interests.

Finally, once the experience has been defined, our Idea Writer reverts back to a more traditional copywriting role. While the branded experience is paramount, it will never be successful if no one experiences or hears about it. The Idea Writer is involved in developing the copy for any pre-promotional materials such as ads or invitations.

On the back end, they ensure the experience is amplified by lending their writing skills to any social media or digital sharing initiatives. Ultimately, they provide a consistent "voice" throughout the consumer's journey with the brand.

If this is a career path that sparks your interest, here is what we would be looking for if you were to interview at Legacy:

- A passion for marketing, big ideas, and our agency's culture
- A showcase of your most creative ideas. They need to be as strategic as they are innovative
- A variety of examples that display your writing skills
- An unquenchable curiosity and understanding of popular culture and consumer behavior
- Any previous work experience such as an internship or work with a local or non-for profit company

Career Path #2: The Designer

From an entry level Graphic Designer to a Creative Director, these are the people that make the experience a visual one. It starts by creating the visual identity through an overarching look and feel for the idea, generally including an iconic logo, which is pulled through every element of the experience.

Designers in experiential marketing must have the ability to think in both two and three dimensions. Their look and feel will come to life in a variety of creative elements that exist before, during, and after the experience itself. This includes amortizing the creative across promotional materials, on-site branding, and throughout any digital or social media extensions. Their mission is to create consistency, continuity, and impact at every consumer touch point.

Transitioning to the three-dimensional world, our designers have become master collaborators working with a variety of outside vendors to bring their vision to life.

For a mobile tour, they will work with fabricators to develop and design a mobile vehicle. For a pop-up experience, they may partner with an interior designer or architect to develop the branded environment.

Beyond that, our designers are consistently partnering with pencil sketch artists and CAD renderers to develop three-dimensional visuals to bring all aspects of the idea to life.

Finally, our designers may also partner with multimedia designers in the development of video content for use before, during, and after the experience.

If you have a passion for design, here is what we would be looking for, if you were to interview at Legacy:

- A passion for marketing, big ideas, and our agency's culture
- A portfolio of your work available online as well as a PDF version you can e-mail and print out
- An ability to work within a team environment
- A consistency in how you brand yourself from your resumé to your work through your interview

Collaboration: The Final Piece of the Puzzle

No matter how big an idea is, it is not worth anything if it does not come to life in the right way. Ensuring success requires an experiential marketing creative to value collaboration above all else.

Firstly, our Idea Writers and Designers must be in lockstep throughout the entire development. They need to challenge each other to push the overall creative vision but then be able to collectively ensure a completely seamless final product.

However, collaboration does not end in the Creative department, especially in experiential marketing. It is a misconception that the people working in the Creative department are solely responsible for the big ideas.

You must be engaged with your Planning department to ensure you are on brand strategy and that your ideas are grounded in real consumer insights.

You must partner with Account Service to ensure your ideas are in line with (but, ideally, exceeding) client expectations.

Finally, you must trust in your Operations team because they are the group that will take your ideas and bring the vision to life. They are crucial in ensuring that anything we propose is actually feasible.

If you are a skilled collaborator and the type of person that thrives in a team environment, becoming a Creative in experiential marketing could be the right kind of job experience for you.

A Few Final Thoughts

Regardless of what creative discipline you pursue, I'd like to share a few helpful hints that have served others and myself over the years.

Showcase your passion and energy.

While your creative skills may check the box on everything in the job description, when I make a decision on a new hire, it always comes down to that person fitting within our agency's culture. I want someone with drive and ambition who is a sponge for knowledge and is willing to put in the time to grow as a creative.

Always look for a way to stand out.

You are an aspiring creative, so act like one. Don't take the easy way out and use the same approach for your cover letter, resumé, and portfolio for every single job opportunity. Think of each agency you apply to as its own separate target audience. Take the time to learn about their values, work, and approach. Then, customize your approach to speak to them. This extends beyond getting the interview to how you follow up and thank them for their time. I find that it is always the little things and attention to detail that help a candidate stand out.

As a Creative, just like pretty much every other job in the world, part of your role will be salesperson. It will be one of the most crucial growth areas as your career unfolds. Having great ideas is the start. Being able to clearly explain, strategically defend, and sell those ideas internally to your agency and externally to your clients is how they become a reality.

Try to be yourself.

It's human nature, when you get into interview mode, that you try to play the role of the character who you think an agency wants to hire. However, for the sake of your long-term happiness and success at a place of employment, make sure the true you shines through, and it's you they hire. Not some made up character. That way, you actually get to be yourself at work and don't have to continue portraying someone else.

Never be satisfied.

The beauty of creativity is there is no end game or finish line. You always have the ability to raise the bar just a little higher, and you should always strive to do so. This goes beyond your day-to-day work. Always stay on top of trends and popular culture. Make time to gain new perspective through reading magazines, books, or relevant online articles. Look for opportunities, workshops, and seminars to learn new and different skills or ways to enhance your thinking. If you are constantly curious, then your creativity will always continue to grow and evolve.

"Knowledge speaks, but wisdom listens."

That is a quote from Jimi Hendrix, who was pretty creative in his own right. This is advice that will not only serve you as you embark on a career as a Creative, but it will also serve you throughout your journey. Always be a sponge. Always be open to constructive criticism. Always understand that you can learn more and evolve your work further. Always seek out mentors and input from others. Your best creative work will always reflect the wisdom you have obtained by listening.

Finally, always have fun.

Before I went to college, my dad had me spend a summer working at a factory that manufactured wheels and rims for tractor-trailers. I spent that summer working on an assembly line, welding, and grinding out welds. Ten hours a day in a dark, dismal factory doing the same monotonous tasks over and over again. The goal of his social experiment was to show me why I was going to college.

While that work was definitely an honorable pursuit, and I respect those who do it, it was not the future I foresaw for myself. If you're reading this book, I'm assuming you have similar aspirations. No matter how stressful or challenging my job gets, I always think back to that summer.

As a Creative, in any discipline, we have an amazing job. We are paid to dream the undreamt and imagine the unimagined. Every day presents a new challenge. Every problem is our newest opportunity. It is a rewarding journey, and I wish you nothing but the best as your journey begins.

Work Steps:

Yes, many of the steps are the same as from the previous essays. But there are a few new ones here. And all of them are important. Let's complete them now.

1. **Research:** What agencies in your area specialize in experiential advertising?
2. **More research:** After tracking down some of the key generators of creative work, who are some of the noteworthy talents?
3. **Find out even more:** Arrange an informational interview at one or more of these agencies.

4. **Verbalize:** What factors would keep you from accepting a creative position in an experiential agency? And what factors would make you interested in taking a creative position at one? Be sure to be able to explain "why" for both.

5. **Keep notes:** Make a list for future reference. Some of these might not interest you yet – or you and your portfolio might not be ready for this type of agency. Add your notes to your file.

6. **Convert your creative:** Erik Hauser, founder of the experiential marketing forum, likes to point out that "experiential is an approach to advertising rather than a tactic." As a result, any form of advertising can be "experiential" – even print. Therefore, review your current portfolio and see if you can make any of your pieces more experiential.

7. **Read up on Gossage:** Need help converting your work to an experiential format? Or want inspiration? Look up Howard Gossage (or read, no, study, *The Book of Gossage*); in many ways, he formed the foundation for experiential advertising, and many of his print ads were highly "experiential." Way ahead of his time and influential in the work of such agencies as Goodby Silverstein and CP+ B, his approaches are as relevant today as they were back when he created them in the 1960s.

8. **Create a new campaign:** Try developing an experientially focused campaign. What are the elements you should include? Why?

— — — — —

Erik McKinney graduated from Susquehanna University in the year 2000 with the 20th Century thought that something in radio broadcasting might be fun. However, it was already the 21st Century, so he pursued a career in marketing instead, joining Bates Worldwide as an Assistant Account Executive. After a brief stint in advertising, he discovered his passion for experiential marketing and transitioned over to sister agency, 141 Worldwide where his career began to take off. Four years and two companies later, Erik was already the youngest Account Director at Relay Worldwide, the experiential and sponsorship division of the Publicis Groupe in the United States.

Though he had a bright future ahead of him, his desire to pursue a more creative existence could no longer be contained. This led to a slot as Senior Director of Creative Services at Relay Worldwide where he developed the agency's first creative department from the ground up. He led the agency's ideation to develop experiential programs for clients such as Coca Cola, Beam Global Spirits & Wine, and Sharp Electronics.

From there, Erik's entrepreneurial spirit kicked. He helped to launch Situ8, a sustainability marketing agency, where he served as VP of Strategy and Ideation

In 2011, Erik joined Legacy Marketing Partners, one of the top Experiential Marketing agencies in the country, specializing in developing consumer engagement campaigns that connect with consumers through events, promotions, digital, and social media efforts. As the VP of Strategy and Creative, he works across the agency's impressive roster of clients including ABSOLUT, Malibu, Jameson, Navistar, Corona, GE, WWE, Cabela's, and many more.

LEGACY
MARKETING PARTNERS

Opportunity Awaits In-House

Thomas McManus
Group CD, Prudential Advertising
Part-time Faculty, Parsons School of Design

In-house agencies and corporate advertising and creative services departments are a large, but largely hidden, segment of our industry.

Most of the agencies you read about are AOR (agencies of record) for a number of clients. In-house agencies have only one client.

Much of the work is quite good. And many of the work situations are just as positive.

Here, Thomas McManus, who also teaches at one of the world's finest design schools, gives you a look inside an in-house agency.

The Inside Story on In-House Agencies

In-house agencies are supposed to suck: lousy pay, terrible offices and incompetent creative.

I found that the pay and the offices really do suck.

But the work?

Well, that is another story.

When I switched from a regular agency to an in-house agency, I quickly realized I could get away with murder.

It was weird. Clients listen to us. They bought work, and then we actually produced it the next week! Without testing.

I was in heaven. I started with a creative staff of five. Only one was a digital person. Within five years, we had over 45 creatives – most of them were digital.

Working in-house has lots of benefits. And some drawbacks, too.

On the following spread, I compare the two – In-house vs. AOR (Agency of Record) I hope that it helps you decide that in-house is a viable option to pursue.

Bureaucracy
AOR have more layers than an artichoke. With In-House you are the client.

AOR knows how to have fun. In-House is kinda uptight.

IN-HOUSE

Work/Life Balance
AOR has much longer hours. Especially when you are pitching. But you can get long vacations for the holidays and summer Fridays. In-House is more accepting of people who have kids.

Creative perception
AOR creatives are kings. They help create the product that agencies sell. In-House is often considered to be a cost center.

Job Security
There isn't any in this business. Don't kid yourself, we are all freelancers. If the account fires the In-House agency, the whole place goes down.

AOR salary much higher.
The money here is really good. To attract creative talent to crappy accounts they throw lots of coin at you.

In-House money lower.
Pay is substantially lower. But the bonuses and the benefits aren't that bad – and could be even better than an agency.

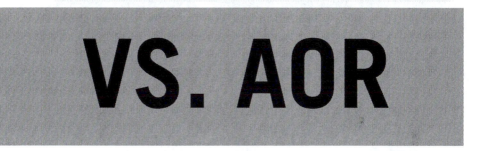

VS. AOR

TPS reports
You think "Office Space" had it bad? There's an incredible amount of paperwork at in-house agencies for performance reviews. But the good news is they don't require time sheets.

Your portfolio
At an agency you can work on different accounts so your portfolio can be diversified. In-House clients are more trusting. If you play it right, you can sell great work.

Interior Decoration
Agencies work really hard at making their spaces look like a Rem Koolhaas landmark. In-House agencies work really hard making their spaces look like a bank.

After all, you can only build a great career with great work. And in-house is one place you can do great work!

A Quick Closing Story

When I first started to work at Cheil, Samsung's In-House agency, I was afraid that I couldn't turn it around.

But Samsung's clients really wanted great work. The only thing stopping this in-house agency from getting it was themselves: they didn't know better.

Unlike a lot of clients, Samsung actually produced work. Lots of work. With the best photographers and directors. Like Annie Leibovitz, Steven Klein, Michael Schnabel and David LaChapelle.

And it's not just print but digital, too.

Once we outsourced a digital project to Barbarian. They liked the work so much they wanted to take credit for it. We told them they couldn't (later Cheil ended up buying them). That project was named a Cannes Finalist.

We could also freelance any creative. Really smart people from the best agencies. Some were even still in those agencies and freelanced on the side. And we could easily guide them because we knew the business so well.

The outside agencies, on the other hand, would always have to spend months trying to get up to speed with the business.

And then the creatives would leave and they'd have to start over.

So my experience with in-house agencies has been great. I just wish they would have better interior decorators.

Work Steps:

Thomas McManus helped us compare in-house agencies to more traditional agencies of record. Before you continue shopping the creative marketplace, let's learn a little bit more about in-house agencies. Try these work steps to help clarify your thoughts on this possible career option.

1. **Research local businesses.** What companies in your area have in-house agencies or "creative services" departments? (Hint: Companies that produce lots of work tend to have in-house agencies. These include most large retailers, financial services firms (that includes insurance companies), high-tech firms like Apple and

Microsoft, companies that publish catalogs, and fast food restaurant chains – to name a few.

2. **Identify the key leaders of these agencies.** What is some of their noteworthy work? Let's not forget fashion companies and fashion retailers. Companies like The Gap, Target, and Calvin Klein often do work in-house. Clever posters or funny signs in a franchise restaurant – someone did those. Who?

3. **Arrange an informational interview.** OK, you found one. Now let's visit one. (You've got a pretty good chance – they don't get as many inquiries as AOR agencies.) What did you see? How does it compare to the other agencies you've visited? If you visit more than one in-house agency, which one do you prefer? Why?

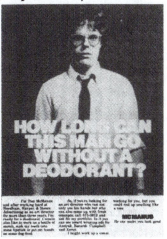

4. **Know yourself.** What factors would make you consider accepting a creative position in an in-house agency? What factors would keep you from accepting a creative position in an in-house agency?

5. **Promote yourself.** Here's an ad Tom created to help himself get a job many years ago. What can you do today to help with your own job search?

Thomas McManus is a Creative Director who has worked at TBWA/ Chiat Day, Y&R, and Samsung. He currently is Group CD at Prudential Advertising. He also runs the Integrated Advertising Lab at Parsons School of Design in NY. Tom and his imaginative work have been featured in articles by the New York Times, the Washington Post, USA Today and the Wall Street Journal. From his Absolut Vodka work being one of the most celebrated in the industry to the user generated content for Samsung's HDTV being short listed at Cannes, his work has consistently won every top advertising-industry honor. He has twice received the $100,000 Grand Prize with the Stephen Kelly Award.

Go Green and Black, Yellow, Brown, Red, and White

Mike G. Williams
VP, Creative Director Commonground

Creative messages can be extra powerful when they are more specifically directed at us as individuals. Sometimes that has to do with things we're interested in, and sometimes it has to do with our cultural context, and, most of the time, it's both.

Here, Mike Williams, CD at one of the top multicultural agencies provides some interesting perspectives on an exciting and growing part of the communications industry.

By now we all know the statistics. That America's ethnic makeup is changing, and pretty soon the minority will become the majority. That now more than ever agencies are being forced to rethink their structure, how they talk to people, and how they craft and deliver their messages. We also know the abysmal percentage that represents the number of non whites in our industry, non males in creative, and those that have similar values, beliefs, cultures, and mindsets of the very people that we, as advertisers and marketers, depend on to buy what we're selling.

There is no need for me to expound on this as it has been well documented and is routinely spewed in every new business pitch across the nation by both General Market and Multicultural agencies alike. Yes, we all know the facts, the marketplace has changed.

Instead, if you will, forget the above for a second, and think about what this exciting industry is "you" are getting into, what is it that "you" have to offer, and what is it "you" are trying to accomplish.

For me it went a little something like this. I wanted to play my part in depicting a real and positive portrayal of people of color in the media. The vehicle was advertising. It was a national stage. If the communication was authentic, the brands would gain loyalty, people of color could get hired, and the message delivered would help balance out some of the negative images that existed. It would be a Win Win for all. So after working at a large GM agency by anyone's account, I caught wind of an assignment for a local museum that wanted to promote their latest exhibit on Hip Hop Culture. The exhibit would give a chronological in depth overview of Hip Hop Culture from its inception in the Bronx to the early 2000s when this assignment was given. It would include interactive stations, the original equipment from early pioneers, videos, installations, history lessons – the whole gamut. The assignment initially was only given to one very accomplished creative team who undoubtedly would've done a good job. However, I wanted it. I needed it. I felt compelled to work on it. I was fairly new and didn't want to step on any toes and decided to write my ECD at the time an impassioned email while on the plane headed to a shoot. To his credit the ECD plainly told me he didn't put me on the assignment as he thought it would be stereotypical to give the one African American the task. It made sense because when first hired I made it known that I wasn't going to be the "black guy" who only worked on "black assignments". My multicultural perspective was much, much broader than that.

I appreciated his thoughtfulness but pressed the issue and was granted the opportunity to work on it as well. For me it was simple. Hip Hop was undergoing a major metamorphosis. Images of Hip Hop were all about the bling and the booty. Hip Hop purists were angry. Newbies were intrigued and fascinated. And the country at large was disillusioned with Hip Hop's far-reaching impact and soon to be global presence. The exhibit would display the facts and let people educate themselves without any opinion. Now sure, I could've done some clever headlines or some sort of visual metaphor that the industry lauds, but I wanted people to feel it. Feel what I was saying whether they identified or not. Think about what I was saying whether they agreed or not. But most importantly be intrigued enough to go the museum with an open mind and experience a culture that I was fortunate enough to be living. The idea literally was to strip down Hip Hop culture to the point where you were forced to decide if it was still Hip Hop. I only used a few inanimate objects and a dog that by themselves were just that but when put in the context of a rap video could take on a whole new meaning or not. And the headline that accompanied each visual: "Hip Hop?"

That's it.

The remaining copy invited people to come to the exhibit and decide for themselves based on what they already knew and soon would learn. The images used consisted of everything from a diamond earring to a Rottweiler to a spray paint can. Then the strategy was to promote the exhibit like a Hip Hop album release. Street teams would pass out Go Cards/flyers and tack the posters up side by side all over the city. Although the campaign was the museum's most successful to the date and was awarded by the ad community, the point is a voice was heard from a multicultural perspective.

Now could someone not familiar with the Hip Hop culture have come up with the same campaign? We'll never know. But my experience, my perspective, my life afforded me the insight to naturally offer a unique lens into a world that at that time was not popular culture. I was able to link the brand to the people because I had an idea that was authentic. It's why General Market agencies clamor to acquire or create multicultural agencies within and why multicultural agencies clamor to prove that they are diverse beyond what they've been pigeonholed. Everyone is searching and seeking authenticity as a means to connect people to brands. In other words, if you want to be on the forefront of where things are growing, you need to be a diverse thinker, have a multitude of authentic experiences from which to draw, and embrace a multicultural perspective.

Work Steps:

Knowing yourself is key to becoming a success in the industry. So, based on Mike William's essay, we have two very simple questions for you. Let's see if you can answer them now.

1. **Find your point of difference.** Everyone is truly different and can bring a unique perspective to solving the marketing or advertising problem – a perspective that goes beyond stereotypes and contributes true insights. Your challenge now is to identify that perspective.
2. **Set your goals.** What do you want to accomplish? A really good answer should go beyond a goal of making creative director or earning a certain salary. Rather, we believe it should have meaning beyond the monetary. Then, once you have your answer, be sure to answer why (even if it is obvious). And then be sure to answer why the first why is important to you.

— — — — — —

*Prior to joining commonground, **Mike Williams** created work at Leo Burnett for such global and national brands as Nintendo, Kellogg's, Proctor and Gamble, Altoids, Disney, and Quaker. His professional range is due to more than a decade of experience across categories ranging from the U.S. Army to feminine products (yes, he has a sensitive side too). He has a knack for uncovering life's little nuances and transforming them into big ideas that resonate with consumers. By leveraging his insights and expertise in diverse consumer segments, Mike was able to successfully broaden Leo Burnett's ability to deliver on strategic creative that went beyond the traditionally defined general market consumer base. The effort proved to be valuable to brands such as the U.S. Army and Proctor and Gamble's Always. Mike has extensive work experience in both general and multicultural agencies and has been heralded for his creativity along the way. He has gained recognition and has been honored with an array of awards, including Gold Lions at Cannes, a Gold Addy, and the Best in Show award from the Chicago Creative Club.*

I'm a Project Director

Mary Ryan Djurovic
Freelance Project Director

We realized that there is another category of creative career that is generally not covered. It's not quite like writing and design, but it's critical for creative success, and it's a job where you are a vital part of the creative team – it's project manager, or project director.

Instead of creating individual ads, you coordinate the creation of events and programs. You may be involved in major creative productions, photo shoots, or video or audio production – with important responsibilities.

If you have an organized mind and always seem to be the one who gets things done, this creative career might be a good fit. Since it's not formally taught (at present), your career path may wander a bit. Let's have Mary tell you about how she got there.

I am a Project Director. It's what I've become over the years. I started my career quest at Columbia College Chicago, where I first chose to learn the advertising trade.

It began with two semesters majoring in marketing communications, heavy on the advertising/media classes.

Then I transferred to Southern Illinois University – SIU. I continued as a communications major with a specialization in advertising. I chose sociology as my minor. I had no idea how significant this would be.

In SIU's AAF ad club, I experienced what agency life might be like. I was one of the best writers at our little student agency. That success led me to believe I should think about pursuing copywriting.

Pursue it I did.

Thanks to a successful internship, I landed a job at The Copy Workshop. They publish advertising and marketing books, including this one.

It's owned by a partnership of award-winning copywriter Bruce Bendinger and his wife Lorelei (more on her in a bit).

If you want to be a copywriter, a better mentor could not be found! Unless … unless you come to realize that copywriting is not the career for you – which I discovered.

But I also discovered something more important – I have a real talent for producing – supporting, nurturing, assisting, and enticing excellence. It's a different kind of creative contribution, but it's critical.

The person who helped me realize this was The Copy Workshop's Publisher (and producer), Lorelei Davis Bendinger. Before starting The Copy Workshop, Bruce and Lorelei were creating advertising together. One year, the two of them produced 104 TV commercials! That's right, just the two of them. I'd found the perfect team to teach me the trade! And they did.

Fast forward 10 years. My resumé now includes stints as production assistant, craft service provider, casting agent, media planner, account coordinator, director of marketing services, account director, promoter, production manager, publicist, and spectacle performer. All different. All the same.

I learned a lovely lesson – my heart lies in production.

Better yet, I'm good at it!

My preferred title on any assignment is that of Producer or Project Manager (or for the big gigs: Project Director) because it is in this role that you can support, nurture, assist, and entice excellence from all your team members.

A key role on any team will be the client. They may be close to the job or off in the distance. Often, they're looked at as "The Client," but they are the expert on their business. Projects originate with them, and it's imperative to keep their interests and approval as top priority throughout the process.

Remember how I said that sociology thing would be significant? OK, time for me to call up my combination of communication major and sociology minor. Where are my old textbooks? Ah, here they are. If you look at the following definitions of sociology, I think you can see where my connection of communication and sociology with real work experience resulted in production and project management being the best fit for me. Some quotes …

"Sociology is the scientific study of society." Auguste Comte

"It is a social science which uses various methods of empirical investigation and critical analysis to develop a body of knowledge about human social activity."
— Ashley Orenstein

"Sociology is the science whose object is to interpret the meaning of social action and thereby give a causal explanation of the way in which the action proceeds and the effects which it produces." —Max Weber

See what's going on here?

I realized that I was putting my sociology minor into action. OK – enough philosophy – you might still be asking…

What does a Project Director actually do?

In general, the answer is "whatever it takes." That's why it really is a creative job. Specifically, here are some examples of projects where successful teams made it happen and where I was an important part of that team:

Interpublic Women's Leadership Network Live Webcast Event

Producer of The Interpublic (IPG) Women's Leadership Network (WLN) webcast. WLN is an IPG-wide organization that promotes the advancement, retention, and recruitment of women. The event was simulcast to 1000+ members in 12 markets in the US and London. Attendees represented a diverse array of IPG companies including Draftfcb, Gotham, Hill Holliday, Initiative, Jack Morton Worldwide, McCann, Mullen, Universal McCann, Weber Shandwick, and many others.

HP Neoview FSI Animation

Delivered a four-minute Flash animation for the HP Business Intelligence's Neoview program. I managed the development of storyboard and animation, script, programming, animation rendering, art direction and design, audio, and overall project management. Neoview's focus is financial services.

SAP on HP Integrity Animation

Delivered a six-minute Flash animation for HP Solutions Group.

Accenture: International Women's Day

Producer of 60-minute video focusing on one of the company's top diversity initiatives: International Women's Day. The video featured an audience address by Accenture CEO, William D. Green; Managing Director of Human Capital and Diversity, Armelle Carminati; and keynote speaker Gail Evans, author of the best-seller *Play Like a Man, Win Like a Woman*. The video was presented as the opening piece of a whole day celebration of women in the workplace. The video was viewed at 23 Accenture events around the globe that included more than 6,000 onsite participants and thousands more that dialed in via computer.

Allstate Financial: Help Produce a Merger!

This was a project and a half! I represented the Integrated Marketing Communications team for a company merger. This involved working with individuals from Legal, Product, State Filing, Compliance, Tax, Distribution, External Design Agency/Internal Design Agency, Internal Production/ External Production, Fulfillment, Technology, and Systems. Both the Assistant Vice President of Allstate Financial and the Project Manager for the merger recognized my importance in the merger and my success in accomplishing the objectives.

Redmoon Theater

This is Chicago's spectacle performance group, and this project was really something. They hired me to configure volunteer positions for Redmoon's 6th Annual *All Hallows' Eve Ritual Celebration*, a one-night outdoor performance and installation that attracts more than 10,000 spectators. The objective was to gain first-time support for the artists and performers by providing safety, crowd-control, traffic patterns, information distribution, donation gathering, and a participant warming shelter.

In this new position, I developed a system to enlist, train, manage, and direct 100 volunteers for the *All Hallows'* event. Next, I was hired by the theater's marketing department. My responsibilities initially included researching and targeting untapped revenue resources to secure both earned income opportunities for the theater and group sales to Redmoon's season performances. I was then promoted to the position of Publicist. Sometimes getting it done has different titles attached to it.

And So It Goes...

I want to stress I've never done any of this alone – project management and the creative process are a team sport, but if you're consistently on a winning team, people notice.

It seems to me that the reasons project management is a good fit is due to a relentless attention to detail, an "in-the-moment" presence, and – to get a little philosophical – a quest to seek answers to life's unknowns. After all, creative project management means you're creating something.

As it turned out, my education in communication and sociology helped a lot. Combine that with 20+ years of real work experience and you tend to get recommendations and jobs.

OK, time to wrap it up. I like this explanation of project manager by J. Davidson Frame.

"Project managers bear ultimate responsibility for making things happen. Traditionally, they have carried out this role as mere implementers. To do their jobs they needed to have basic administrative and technical competencies.

Today they play a far broader role.

In addition to the traditional skills, they need to have business skills, customer relations skills, and political skills.

Psychologically, they must be results-oriented self-starters with a high tolerance for ambiguity, because little is clear-cut in today's tumultuous business environment. Shortcomings in any of these areas can lead to project failure."

That's a pretty good definition, but I'd like to add that "failure is not an option."

For a by-the-book definition of project management, you might want to look at *An Introduction to Project Management* by Duncan Haughey, PMP (PMP sounds impressive, doesn't it? It indicates certified Project Management Professional). Duncan observes that a project goes through six phases:

- **Project Definition:** Defining the goals, objectives, and critical success factors for the project.
- **Project Initiation:** Everything that is needed to set up the project before work can start.
- **Project Planning:** Detailed plans of how the work will be carried out including time, cost, and resource estimates.
- **Project Execution:** Doing the work to deliver the product, service, or desired outcome.
- **Project Monitoring & Control:** Ensuring that a project stays on track and taking corrective action to ensure it does.
- **Project Closure:** Formal acceptance of the deliverables and disbanding of all the elements that were required to run the project.

He's right, but I have to tell you that when you're in the middle of it, those six stages are kind of a blur. Duncan Haughey, PMP continues ...

"The role of the project manager is one of great responsibility. It is the project manager's job to direct, supervise and control the project from

beginning to end. Project managers should not carry out project work, managing the project is enough.

Well, yeah. But sometimes it's "grab the nearest shovel."

Here's more from Duncan; he talks about the range of activities that often end up on your plate:

"The project manager must define the project, reduce it to a set of manageable tasks, obtain appropriate resources and build a team to perform the work.

The project manager must set the final goal for the project and motivate his/her team to complete the project on time.

The project manager must inform all stakeholders of progress on a regular basis.

The project manager must assess and monitor risks to the project and mitigate them.

No project ever goes exactly as planned, so project managers must learn to adapt to and manage change." (Amen to that.)

You're kind of a tool box and a Swiss Army knife and a roll of duct tape all at once. Duncan lists the following range of skills required of a project manager:

- Leadership
- People management (customers, suppliers, functional managers and project team)
- Effective communication (verbal and written)
- Influencing
- Negotiation
- Conflict management
- Planning
- Contract management
- Estimating
- Problem solving
- Creative thinking
- Time management

"Project management is about creating an environment and conditions in which a defined goal or objective can be achieved in a controlled manner by a team of people."

Creating an environment where defined goals can be achieved is often challenging.

Many projects are awarded by clients before everything is worked out. The client and agency teams have not defined the project components. Sometimes, as Bruce would say, "you're hangin' ten on the cosmic surfboard." Well, I'm glad to say that I'm pretty good at that! I'm able to determine tangible deliverables from lofty concepts. We make it real.

Did I mention budgets? I've learned how to develop accurate budgets for producing those tangible deliverables as the project is already up and running.

One final resource you need is people. You'll have to develop a network. Don't worry; you will. You know the people you want to work with again. Over time you'll also need to get good at staffing – because you need exceptional talent to create those tangible deliverables.

When you've helped create those tangible deliverables that delight clients on time and within budget, you've done your job. Time to party! You celebrate with your team, and that's one more thing that makes for a satisfying career.

Do I like being a Project Manager?

What do you think?

Work Steps:

If you're interested in this field, you might want to learn more.

1. **Read a book.** Here are some books you might find interesting…

    a. *Creative Project Management: Innovative Project Options to Solve Problems On Time and Under Budget* by Michael Dobson (©2010)

    b. For designers, here's a link to… *The Art of Business: Project Design for Creative Professionals.* By Eric Adams. http://www. creativepro.com/node/60994

    c. and, of course, *An Introduction to Project Management* by Duncan Haughey, PMP.

2. **Find out what they call Project Managers in the field that interests you.** For example, sometimes it's Marketing Communications Manager or Account Manager. In some fields, that's an uncreative staff job, but in other companies, that's what they call the project

manager. (Hint: just about everyone in marketing communication uses project managers, but they may use different titles.) Find a company that interests you and find out what they call them.

3. **Find a project. Manage it.** It could be an event (like a gig for a band – complete with pre-concert publicity, poster production, and T-shirt design and distribution). It could be a project for a non-profit – a benefit, a fund-raising drive, or a bit of "cause marketing." And it could be something for your school. See if you're any good at it. See if you like it. If so, this is a skill that the job market is interested in.

By the way, there are also business school courses in project management. You may or may not find them to be what you're looking for. Many are designed more for engineers, software developers, and IT people. These kinds of projects tend to be more analytical and long-term (like designing and managing an IT system or a supply chain) as opposed to creative and short-term – like producing a video for an event.

■ ▬ ▬ ▬ ▬ ■

Mary Ryan Djurovic. After my first job out of school with The Copy Workshop, I went on to several key positions in the marketing communications field – including Account Director and Director of Marketing. In addition to creating and executing integrated branding campaigns, I also have extensive experience in promoting arts, music, photography, and theater. My heart is in production, and at this stage of my career, I'm familiar with all facets – from bidding through post for film, video, print, music, live meeting, learning/training, digital, and multi-media formats. The clients on my resumé range from Accenture, Allstate, HP, and Kraft to Redmoon Theater and Rockin' Billy & The Wild Coyotes. Currently, I fill the role of Producer or Project Director on a contract basis for several Chicago companies. However, my major production responsibilities are shown here – very satisfying, though not without their own unique production challenges. Specialties: Project Leader, Production, Strategy Development, Communication Writing, Management, Budgeting, and, of course, storytelling and nap management.

Wexley's Words of Wisdom

Cal McAllister
Founder, Wexley School for Girls

Tucked away in Seattle, they may be the future of communication.

At the same time, there is some evidence that this is but a momentary energy particle bouncing its happy way through an all-too-orderly universe currently clogged to the brim with an abundance of all-too-orderly and all-too-ignorable blather.

It's Wexley School for Girls – a unique communications agency with an extra dimension of modern media consciousness – no extra charge.

The founder of Wexley shares some of their thoughts and practices in this semi-coherent narrative. As you look for new opportunities, perhaps you should follow Wexley's lead and invent them.

What is Wexley, exactly? Are we a nontraditional marketing company? Definitely. An alternative ad agency? Sometimes. To use the industry's buzzy categorization, we are a "media agnostic" outfit – the idea being that we don't worship at the shrine of paid media, particularly television.

We believe everything is advertising: traditional media, design, packaging, PR-generating ideas, video games, branded entertainment, short films, guerrilla tactics, and events. Even squirrel races, done properly, can be advertising.

And we reach the consumer through websites, publicity stunts, viral videos. Whatever you call it, we represent an important, relatively new approach in the advertising and marketing world – small, creative operations born in the digital era and nurtured by the rise of the Internet, which provided a new and vast market for media buying that was not only cheap (or free) but also offered access to very specific groups of consumers. Our playing field combines social media, experiential marketing, old-fashioned publicity, and the brand new opportunities created from the interaction of the Internet and increasingly techno-savvy consumers tired of the same old same-o.

Do You Believe?

Jonah Bloom, the editor of *Advertising Age*, says it's impossible to pinpoint the originator of the media-agnostic idea, but he credits the rise of the movement to "a bunch of independent agencies in the U.K., like Michaelides & Bednash and Naked Communications. What those guys realized was that some other agencies were tending to solve every business problem with the same answer: 'Let's do a flight of TV commercials.'"

"It's less about the mass conversation as opposed to a whole lot more individual conversations," notes Rae Ann Fera, editor of the trade magazine *Boards*. "The buzzword now is engagement."

Welcome to Kick Ass

OK, what does that mean exactly? For new business, here's a favorite Wexley technique – build a one-page website known as "Welcome to Kick Ass." Target the site to a specific person, and write an original song on his or her behalf.

Micro-site. Micro-targeting. Hmmm.

Among other things, it's a cutting edge new business technique – sometimes it works. And, to look at the Wexley client list – Microsoft, Virgin, Starbucks, Nike – it seems to work very well, indeed.

Fan Factory

In one sense, we are a fan factory. We take your money and turn it into thousands, tens of thousands, millions of thousands of crazy people. We can create them. We can reinvigorate them. We will deliver them. Fans that stay for a lifetime of loyalty, with the spending and championing that comes with it.

Our biggest value as an advertising agency is not just getting fans in the door, but earning and sustaining their fanship over the long haul by entertaining them time and time again. As they hold you in their hearts and minds and on the tips of their tongues, we engage them in ways you can imagine and others you cannot. It's pretty simple, really.

What's Our Secret?

Actually, we have five.

Secret Number 1. Look beyond the Obvious.

People are spending more time getting branding messages than ever before. To reach them, think entirely differently. For instance, just because you're a fast food joint doesn't mean every message has to be burgers and fries. For Virgin Mobile, we designed a Miss Virgin Mobile Beauty Pageant using photos taken on mobile phones. Oh yeah, and we owned the trademark – we participated as an equity partner. Crazy? Like a fox.

Secret Number 2. Customize Your Message.

That one-size-fits-all communication approach won't do much to grab attention. In today's world, a small core audience may be more valuable than a lot of people who don't care. This thought process aiming for a smaller, deeper connection can generate surprisingly unique and effective brand experiences.

Microsoft hired us for college recruiting, and we launched a campaign called *Hey, Genius!* It targeted top students across America. We sent the students e-mails with links to websites that – literally – sang their praises.

We also drew up sandwich boards with students' names on them ("Hey, Sean Lynch!" for example). We had actors stand outside classrooms wearing them. We built the first ever *Jobcuzzi,* a hot tub parked in student unions and occupied by a sycophant in a suit who barked congratulatory greetings at prospective hirees.

The campaign hit more than 60 colleges and had 72 distinct creative pieces. It cost Microsoft less than $1.5 million and made a huge impact on a critical target. Microsoft hit their ambitious hiring goals four months early.

Previously, they spent their budget on traditional advertising and stress balls, with less than optimal results.

Secret Number 3. Take It to the Streets.

Getting in front of your customers live can pack a powerful punch. Copper Mountain Ski Resort wanted to push its marketing beyond print ads with pretty scenery. In a campaign called National Snow Day, the agency brought snow to Austin, TX – literally. They sprayed it onto the streets and made sure it covered the lawn of Austin's #1 morning DJ.

Look up there! What is that wrapped around the top of the Tully's Coffee headquarters? Why, it's a giant scarf for the Seattle Sounders soccer team.

How about that.

Secret Number 4. Preserve a Bit of Mystery.

Sure, plastering your BIG LOGO everywhere will get you a certain sort of awareness, but the magic of personal discovery has its own power. To promote Microsoft's Live Search Maps, we placed giant push pins on buildings throughout Seattle. The only clue was a Web address on the pin and nearby signage. Street theater. Art. Communication magic.

Secret Number 5. Always Remember to Have Fun.

With all the messaging cluttering our lives, we try to make a connection through the contemporary funny bone. We look for something smart but a little ridiculous.

It also sends a signal to clients. When they have a meeting with the Wexley School for Girls, they'll know the fun people are coming.

OK, What Does This Mean If You Don't Happen to Be in Seattle?

First – see if you can't target your job-hunting in a slightly more intrusive and outrageous way. Don't be stupid – but don't be shy. You're supposed to make a connection and make an impact – remember?

Second – understand social media, involvement, and theatrical impact. To us, it's all advertising, and the whole wide world is a media opportunity. This is where much of the business is headed. The young men and women here at Wexley School for Girls are leading the way, singing a song of their own creation. Class dismissed.

Work Steps:

The Wexley Way isn't for everyone, but let's look at your approach through the Wexley lens. Dial up the five secrets …

1. **Look beyond the obvious.** What/how are you being surprising? Take that insight and see if you can take it to the next level. OK, so

maybe it seems a bit ridiculous. Your brain needs the exercise.

2. **Customize your message.** Target audiences can be individuals. What would happen if you focused down into a single laser-like message aimed at ...

3. **Take it to the streets.** Sure, you're going to be inside an office – but that office is surrounded by a larger world. That larger world, according to Wexley, is a media opportunity, a stage, and an unending sequence of events worth celebrating – particularly if they have just been freshly created.

4. **Preserve a bit of mystery.** Since these wonderful thoughts came from the mind of wonderful you, perhaps the magic of discovery should be part of it. Who did this? I don't know, but he left this portfolio ...

5. **Always remember to have fun.** Think about your target audience – someone who is hiring. What if that event – meeting you and seeing your book – becomes an entertaining and memorable experience. Think. What would Wexley do?

Don't just stand there – go visit Wexley School for Girls (wexley.com).

▬ ▬ ▬ ▬ ▬ ▬

Cal McAllister is a proud Detroit native who cut teeth as a beat writer for the Chicago Tribune. *After getting in a lot of trouble for making things up, he switched to advertising.*

Before co-founding Wexley School for Girls in 2003, he worked on regional, national, and international business at small shops like WONGDOODY and global agencies like Foote, Cone and Belding and Publicis Worldwide.

Cal has worked in every major consumer and trade category on brands like Nike, ESPN, Microsoft, Xbox, T-Mobile, MADD, Coca Cola, The Red Cross, the Seattle Seahawks and Sounders, RealNetworks, Amstel Light and NASCAR, to name a few.

His work has been recognized by most every international advertising award show, including Cannes, the Clios, Communication Arts, New York Art Director's Club, and the One Show. He also judged the Lotus Awards in Vancouver, regional and national ADDYs, and the OneScreen Film Festival, among others. As a screenwriter, his films were selected and screened at the Seattle International Film Festival, Slamdance, the Chicago Short Film Festival, Atom Films, and the RESFest International Film Festival, among others.

Cal sits on the Board of Directors as an officer for WorldChanging, a non-profit media organization focused on covering the world's most innovative solutions to the plant's problems. He also sits on the Board of Directors for The Creative Circus, an advertising portfolio school in Atlanta. He recently completed two terms on the Board as an officer for People for Puget Sound, an environmental non-profit organization working to protect and restore the health of Puget Sound and the Northwest Straits through education and action. In 2007, he was named one of the Northwest's Top 40 Under 40, a list of promising young business leaders by the Puget Sound Business Journal. *In 2008, Seattle Magazine named Cal one of Seattle's 25 most influential people. He spoke at TEDx Seattle and is a frequent contributor to regional and national media outlets, including* Inc. Magazine, *the* Seattle Times, NPR *and* KING 5TV, *Seattle's NBC affiliate, discussing branding and advertising.*

Time for Transmedia

Andrea Phillips
Writer, Game Designer, and Author

Robin Landa introduced the idea of transmedia storytelling in her essay. But it's so important right now, that we thought you deserved more information about it. And who better to give it you than Andrea Philips, the author of A Creator's Guide to Transmedia Storytelling *and award-winning game designer for such clients as HBO, Sony Pictures, and Thomas Dolby.*

Transmedia is *so hot* right now. It's so hot, in fact, that you might have just rolled your eyes and turned the page – as with virtual reality, Second Life, and Friendster, at first glance, transmedia might seem poised to flame bright and fizzle out.

I'm here to tell you that's not so. To really dig into the reasons why, though, we need to look at what transmedia is and why it's such a powerful tool.

The academic definition is this: transmedia is the art of telling one story across multiple platforms, such that each platform is making a unique contribution to the whole. That definition comes from media thinker and USC professor Henry Jenkins, author of *Convergence Culture*.

The classic example is *Star Wars*, with its films, books, animated series, and so on. Star Wars isn't transmedia because it's got action figures; that's just licensing. It's transmedia because you need to watch the films to see Han Solo and Princess Leia fall in love, but you need to read the books to see them get married and have twin babies. No one medium is giving you the full story. Consuming both gives you a fuller picture, and each adds insight to the events in the other.

The full power of transmedia isn't just in linking together static pieces of content, however. Many of the platforms available today are interactive and social. They are participatory. This opens up new realms of engagement and art. The character you read about suddenly becomes the friend you get emails from. The events of the story don't unfold before your watching eyes; instead, you actively unroll them with your own hands.

Consider *Why So Serious*, the award-winning marketing campaign for *The Dark Knight*; *Pandemic*, Lance Weiler's indie film; the Old Spice Guy, Levi's *Go Forth*, Thomas Dolby's *Floating City*, the extended interactive presences of shows from *Heroes* to *How I Met Your Mother* to *Psych* and beyond. Transmedia storytelling has been used for film, TV, music, but also consumer goods, branding for companies like GE, training for companies like Cisco. Documentarians are using transmedia; theaters are; publishing is.

Marketing, entertainment, media, culture itself is changing, and transmedia is the natural result of changes already underway. This has broad implications for how we approach content creation. Suddenly we're no longer in the business of merely telling stories. Now, we are instead creating experiences.

One of the key benefits of transmedia storytelling is that you create a deeper, richer flavor of engagement. An audience begins to feel like they have a personal stake in the story you're telling. Characters become friends – and even abstractions can become characters. Even the tiniest piece of interaction can evoke an emotional response. The Mars rover Spirit had a simple Twitter stream on NASA, talking about movements and measurements. But this simple tweet stream humanized the robot to such an extent that Twitter wept when the little robot finally shut down.

Ultimately, you can make an audience feel, not just happy or sad about the story, but emotions not often evoked by flat media. Choices made by the audience can have lasting results – in inadvertently giving away a character's location so the bad guys can murder her or persuading a security guard over the phone to rescue a kidnapped boy. This dynamic can make an audience feel a broader palette of emotions incorporating frustration, guilt, or pride, because they feel like they have some weight of responsibility for the events in the story.

But the tools that make transmedia storytelling so powerful aren't limited to the kinds of storytelling that involve a plot or games with challenges to solve. Look no further than the success of the Old Spice Guy. The commercial was a brilliant concept, brilliantly executed. But then came a live event where users could ask the Old Spice Guy questions on Twitter, and he uploaded videos all day answering them. That dynamic pushed an already successful campaign over the top. What began as marketing turned into entertainment – content sought out for its value to the audience.

We live in an era of convergence. Everything is turning into everything else. It's no longer possible to rely on old models; the media buy in ten markets for your 15-second spot isn't long for this world, because it's increasingly easy for the audience to simply avoid messages they aren't interested in. Your only answer is to be more compelling, more dramatic, funnier, more engaging than the next guy.

That's why the transmedia toolbox is increasingly being used for marketing, for documentaries, for commercial experiences. Unlike buzzwords of the past, transmedia is about layering wonder on top of your existing life, not about disconnecting you from it. It's about adapting to changes to how people consume media that are already happening, not pressing for changes that you hope will happen.

And yet, and yet – let's say transmedia does flame out in another year or three. Will that mean that your years tapping into transmedia will be wasted?

Absolutely not. Couldn't happen. No freaking way, buster. That's because the skills that make you great at transmedia storytelling are future-proof. Designing and executing a transmedia story will teach you to pay attention to the big picture and the details at the same time; to adapt to new technologies and platforms as they emerge; to connect with an audience in a warm, human way across electronic media. These skills will always be relevant.

So how do you actually get a transmedia job, then? There are two paths. One is to try to add transmedia elements to work you're already doing at the job you already have. This is the path to take if you already work at an agency or marketing firm, an entertainment studio, a brand. Ask yourself, "What can I do to make an amazing experience for my audience or customers?" and go from there.

Not everyone is in that position, though. If you don't have the luxury of bringing transmedia to your day job, then you need to foster the entrepreneurial flame and do it on your own time. Build experimental weekend projects. Make work out of pocket lint and elbow grease, using free resources like Tumblr, Twitter, and Gmail. Hone your craft, expand your skillset. Make stuff and see how it goes.

You'll eventually discover that you have a portfolio to sell yourself to a company. But you may also find you have your own audience and your own brand – and it's worth more to you to keep creating under your own banner.

You'll never know if you don't take that first step. Don't wait for your employer or a funder or for someone else to give you permission. Roll your sleeves up now and see what you're made of.

The media landscape is undergoing tectonic upheaval right now. With the future of everything from newspapers to network TV to the Internet itself in question, the only way to prepare yourself is to be ready for anything. And the way to be ready is to start right now.

Work Steps:

Let's put the transmedia toolbox to work for you. So try these activities right now. With the ongoing upheaval in the media landscape, they just might position you for greater success.

1. **Learn how to become a transmedia storyteller:** To start, read Andrea Phillips book, *A Creators Guide to Transmedia Storytelling*. It's the best book on the subject.

2. **Research campaigns:** Look at an awards annual and identify the marketers who are using the transmedia toolbox to create their overall campaigns. What do you take away from them, and how can you apply this approach to your work? Remember: Be specific in your answers.

3. **Revise your spec campaigns (again):** Look over the work in your portfolio and seek to find "deeper, richer flavors of engagement" with each one. What parts can you extend? And, what should you eliminate?

4. **Expand your skillset:** Like others you're meeting in this book, Andrea suggests you create projects for yourself and use it to work in new areas, try out new techniques, and prefect your craft. It just may lead directly to paying work. And you could have some fun in the process.

— — — — —

Andrea Phillips is an award-winning transmedia writer, game designer, and author. Her work includes a variety of educational and commercial projects, including The Maester's Path for HBO's Game of Thrones with Campfire Media, America 2049 with human rights nonprofit Breakthrough, and the independent commercial ARG Perplex City. Her indie work includes the Kickstarted collaboration Balance of Powers, the Twitter horoscopes of Madame Zee, and the forthcoming serial transmedia project Felicity.

Andrea is a co-moderator for the first community of ARG players, the Cloudmakers, and a Fellow of the Futures of Entertainment. She has spoken at SXSW, MIT Storytelling 3.0, the Power to the Pixel/IFP Cross-Media Forum, ARGfest, DIY Days, and FITC Storytelling X.1, among others.

Andrea cheats at solitaire (a victimless crime) and Words with Friends (which is less forgivable). Consider yourself warned.

Section III:
Going to Market

"Know your work and how it fits into the marketplace,"
Alison Sullivan, Photo Researcher and Photographer's Agent

It's all about your "book."

In this section we've collected some of the top professionals and professors to give you the best advice we can find on making it happen for you and your career.

- Frank Blossom of The Polishing Center kicks it off with some words to the wise on "Understanding your Market, Targeting Your Market, and Marketing to Your Target."

- Next, the history of the portfolio from the person who made history – by inventing the portfolio school. It's Ron Seichrist – of the Miami Ad School – now a worldwide creative development program. This article isn't just about how it all happens – it's also about how a creative career can develop in exciting and unexpected ways.

- Then, we'll hit you with "The Portfolio of the Future," from Ignacio Oreamuno, who has made some creative impact in his own career. Founder of ihaveanidea.com, he is now running the Art Directors Club in New York. (Hopefully, your work will show up in his award books some day soon.)

- Stan Richards, head of The Richards Group, the largest independent agency in the country, provides some insight on how a professional looks at who they'll hire and what they look for.

- So, how does your portfolio look to someone who sees them every day? Kara Taylor, who does it for the Leo Burnett agency in Chicago offers some useful advice in "Please Don't Bore Me with Your Advertising."

- You say your portfolio still needs improving? What a surprise. You're in luck. Frank Blossom at The Polishing Center provides you with some "Portfolio Prowess."
- Jeff Epstein, of the Chicago Portfolio School, has a memo to share and a message to remember, "Student Work Shouldn't Look like School Work."
- Wait a minute. Looks like you still need a bit more advice. Now we'll bring on Suzanne Pope with "The Top Ten Mistakes in Portfolio Development." Let's see how many you made.
- Did you know that some agencies have a "pre-screen interview"? That's the interview before you get the interview. Lena Woo at Commonground will help you get ready for it with "How You Can Approach a Pre-Screen Interview with an Advertising Agency."
- Now another bit of good advice from Dan Balser of the Creative Circus in Atlanta – "Create Yourself." Sounds like fun.
- Finally, Rich Binell, former copy chief at Apple, lets you in on some "Nasty Secrets." By the way, at Apple, even the little brochures were as perfect as they could make them. Makes you think.

Ready? Let's roll!

Understanding Your Market, Targeting Your Market, and Marketing to Your Target

Frank Blossom
Affiliate Professor Grand Valley State University & Coach, The Polishing Center

Deciding where you want to work and preparing for it is a daunting task. How do you start? Do what the big guys do – segment – target – position. This chapter will take you through the steps and show you how to position yourself (brand) to get the first great job.

Now that you have a better handle on where you want to live, this chapter focuses on getting a lot smarter about where you want to work and whom you want to work for.

But why is this a good move for your job quest?

Ad agencies, design studios, and marketing communication departments want to hire smart ad people. Your challenge is to demonstrate your smarts. But don't depend on your grade point. This may be a blessing for some of you.

Ironically, as hard as you've worked to get a good GPA, the people who can hire you don't care about it. They care that you've graduated, but you'll probably never be asked what your GPA is. That number is not a good indicator of future performance. What they want to know is how smart you are about the ad business and how well you can solve problems. So how do you demonstrate them?

Follow, Wise-up on Good Work

Keep current on what good work is and who is doing it. Follow *Communication Arts* and *CMYK* magazines to see great ads, designs, photography, illustration, and interactive work on both the professional and student levels (subscription information at the back of this book). These publications are considered solid sources of the best work and good places to work. They take the guesswork out of trying to figure what's good for you.

In fact if you ask most ad and design people where they'd most like to see their work, it would be *Communication Arts*. And for students it would be *CMYK*.

But don't stop there. Also follow *Advertising Age*, Seth Godin's blog and Marty Neumier's blog. Stay up to date on new campaigns, the strategy steering them, and the people behind them. Discover your own list of smart ad people and get smarter about them.

Then, when you're asked in an interview, "What work do you like? What communication people do you follow?" you can demonstrate your smarts. You can talk like someone already in the business, not a clueless student hoping to get in. You can show your resourcefulness and initiative. This research will give you an edge and also a lot more confidence going into those interviews. Remember it's a job to get a job, so work it.

Target Segmentation

Second, follow the companies and people you want to work for. Target the market by segmenting it.

Segmentation is smart tactic in advertising. It's also smart in job hunting. It gives you a better chance of getting the right message to the right audience at the right time.

But too many students take a mass media marketing approach and send out hundreds of resumés figuring that at least a couple will stick. They seldom do.

You can't be everything to everybody. And you don't want to be. Focus on your top shops. As you research them you'll probably discover more reasons why you want to work there or why to drop them from your list. Either way you're better off.

Segment your job search. Research the market. Who are the top agencies, design firms, and corporate ad departments that you want to work with? Who are the people you want to work for? Put together your dream list. And go after them hard.

Dig deep; find out everything about your dream agencies. Put together a profile on each. Discover their philosophy, culture and approach to the business along with their clients, awards, and recent news. Cyber stalk the key people at each shop, especially any that might interview you.

> **Student Tip:** "I applied to internships across the country, over 100 in all, to no avail. In hindsight, this was a huge mistake. I should have selected the 10 or 15 places I'd kill to work for and then created a plan to stand out in their eyes. Companies want to hire people who want to work for them, not just people who want to be in advertising."

Then assess, "How do I match up with those profiles and people? What do I have in common?" Find the connections and apply them to your communications and interactions with them.

Why? Companies like to hire people like the people they already have in most cases. They want people who are a good fit for their culture. Birds of a feather flock together.

So know more about your dream agencies than any other candidate. Do your research. In many cases your research will tell you what they are looking for and how to approach them.

If there is a job description, great, because now you have a game plan. Think of the job description as a recipe. Study it; break it apart. Assess your qualities, skills, and experiences against the job criteria. How do you match up? What are the buzzwords or phrases? Work them into your cover letter and resumé. Customize your materials and communications to the target. Make it obvious that you know the job description really well and that you are great fit for it.

Google and Cyber Stalking

Ad people and ad agencies tend to have strong egos and a touch of personal or corporate vanity. They are not shy about putting their opinions and thoughts and accomplishments out for all to see. So it's pretty easy to get smarter about them. Follow them on their Facebook, LinkedIn, and Twitter sites. Search them out through blogs, online publications, award shows, and local news services. Google them. Google yourself, too, to see what's out there about you.

After you've followed them for a while, engage them. Comment on their posts. Add your voice to the conversation. Find out what you have in common. What do you like that they like? What experiences have you both been part of? You might get them to start following you.

It's human nature that you become more interesting to someone who can hire you when it becomes apparent that you are interested in him or her.

> **Consider this scenario:** Two people want to get a date with you. Each makes their pitch. One tells you all about themselves. How smart they are, how cool they are. The other talks about you, and not in a creepy way. Things you've done, accomplished, common friends. Who is more interesting to you?

Also, the top ad, design, and marketing people you really want to work for are often too busy to post job openings and read a ton of resumés. They don't have time to follow you. So follow them. And when you are following and interacting with someone, again in a professional way, they will notice. They might even begin to follow this smart college student who's engaging them in conversation. Get noticed by noticing them.

Share the Passion.

Ad, design, and marketing people are passionate about the business and their companies. They want to hire people who share that passion. They really want to hire junior versions of themselves. So by digging, researching, developing an understanding of them and their companies, and getting smarter about the business, you are showing your passion and your commitment to the business. You are going beyond the typical, the average, and the ordinary. That's what they did to get where they are.

Work Steps:

1. **Segment.** This will help you understand your target more clearly. Segment your list of potential employers in your dream cities. Once you understand what makes those target companies desirable, you'll be on the road to finding more of them.
2. **Get smarter.** Identify the smart work and who's doing it.
3. **Make a "Hit List."** Who does that smart work? Start putting down contact information.

4. **Do some research.** Those top people? Wouldn't it be smart to find out more about them?

5. **Add a profile to your "Hit List."** You're getting smarter, now let's get a bit more organized.

6. **Follow-up and contact.** Time to make contact. Not quite ready? How about an "informational interview," or an "I'm working on my portfolio, and I'd like some advice" interview?

7. **Develop your personal marketing plan.** It's not just personal for you – it's personal for your target. The more you know about them – and want to know about them – the better you'll know how to make a more effective connection.

8. **"Craft" the communication.** Make it match up with what's important to each company on your list. Prove how much you want to work there through how well you have prepared and how smart you are about them.

9. **Make a "roll-out" schedule.** Time for a timeline. Don't just sit there. Let's set some objectives and start making organized contacts and follow-up.

10. **Keep at it.** Do we have to explain this? Didn't think so.

I've Seen Things

Ron Seichrist
Founder, Miami Ad School.

This entire book is about creative careers. This particular piece is about a unique creative career.

It started in one place, and along the way, turned into something else entirely. Or, perhaps, it was just the logical consequence.

The author began as an art director and creative director, and, along the way, created the first real portfolio school and then grew that into an international force in advertising.

Please settle back and enjoy Ron's journey. Then, think about what your journey might be. Each and every creative career can have some of this same adventure. It begins in one place, and then, as we create our own career path, it can become something unique and special.

Also, reflect on the changes Ron has seen – and created – and use them as a way to get prepared and anticipate the changes that you'll face and, we hope, create.

After all, if you don't create the changes, you'll be controlled by them.

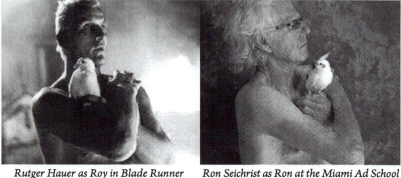

Rutger Hauer as Roy in Blade Runner   Ron Seichrist as Ron at the Miami Ad School

"I've seen things you people wouldn't believe. Attack ships on fire off the shoulder of Orion. I watched c-beams glitter in the dark near the Tannhauser Gate. All those moments will be lost in time, like tears in rain. [pause] Time to die."

Movie buffs recognize this scene in Blade Runner, when Roy (played by Rutger Hauer) is at the end of his short life cycle. After a horrendous fight with Decker (Harrison Ford), Roy saves Decker's life. Roy's last words tell of the extraordinary things he has witnessed in his short life.

I love this movie. Like Roy, I am closing in on the end of my life cycle – at 76 – and I also have seen many, many wondrous things. I watched a man walk on the moon. I've seen a black man in the Oval Office.

I've watched the world change from analog to digital and television turn from black and white into color. Now telephones are mobile and tell you jokes. My car talks to me and gives me turn-by-turn directions. E-mail. Facebook. Twitter. Google. Apple. Microsoft. Last year I had stem cells implanted into my badly damaged heart so I can still play soccer. At my age.

My wife and I adopted two young children from Ukraine (from the Chernobyl region), and now they are driving cars, texting, tweeting, and facebooking. OMG! LOL.

Since I was asked to write this piece for a book about creative careers, I should now shift to the changes I've witnessed in training young people for a job in this business. I can do that. I've been in advertising a long, long time. And I've also been in advertising education for a long, long time.*

Let's go back to the days when a young person came fresh out of a four-year college, with a black cardboard portfolio – with little black strings at the sides and top. He (few young women in those days) knocked on the door of an ad agency, somehow got to see someone, and spent ten minutes trying to untie the little black strings – then pulled out sketches, life drawings, and a hodgepodge of this and that.

In those days most college professors in most colleges had never worked in an agency – although they gave it a good college try. In most cases, the result was pretty bad. It was a sad state of affairs. Back then, I was an agency creative director, and I couldn't help these poorly trained graduates. Some had talent, but we had no time or resources to train them. I had no school to recommend that could train them properly. There should be a place, I thought, a school that mirrors what the agencies really need.

Teaching in the Time of Flower Children
My Fate stepped in. Abruptly. I had a perforated ulcer. Recovering from a

---

* Editor's Note: Ron is too modest – he helped invent it – as you will see.

seriously debilitating operation, I took a year off – with a bit coming in from some clients who liked my work. (That meant a lot of money coming in each month.) With my new smaller stomach, I wasn't going to starve.

Fate, apparently, had my phone number. I got a call from the president of the Minneapolis College of Art, asking if I would consider coming as a visiting professor for a year. This was interesting. Sure, I'll give it a shot.

Well, I went there and fell in love with teaching. Everybody smoked pot and was happy all the time, so the students laughed at whatever I said though I've never been all that funny. These students were the hippiest of the hippy. Hip hooray.

The Seed of My First Portfolio School

The school turned out to be a giant challenge but an even bigger opportunity. Fate stepped in again – now in charge of promotions. I was made temporary chairman of the Design Division. I accepted on the condition that I could change a few things. I hired many part-timers who were working in local ad agencies and design studios.

Lady Fate continued her kindness. I just happened to have a group of smart, talented, hungry students who thrived on the changes. Some of our early graduates: Nancy Rice, Pat Burnham, Dean Hanson, Mark Johnson – you can see their names in award books – they were the creative nucleus under Tom McElligott to form Fallon McElligott and Rice, the Minneapolis agency that signaled a new era in advertising.

I made a few more changes and had a few more thoughts that stayed with me years later. Together they formed the spine of all my portfolio schools in the future.**

I began teaming my design students with writers on projects. It was only common sense, but it wasn't being done at the time.

I started getting real projects for the students to work on – like the new Minneapolis skyway system.

I began bringing in teachers from all over the world to teach for six months to a year. I could invite any speaker – such as Tom Wolfe and Milton Glaser. I had local creative directors mentoring the students on portfolios.

I learned to tell the students that they themselves were part of their portfolio – they must include pieces that revealed the kind of person they were.

** *Editor's Note: and pretty much all the other portfolio schools.*

For all this, I got a "D," a good thing. The Minneapolis College of Art changed its name to Minneapolis College of Art and Design – now known as MCAD.

Around this time, I designed the school's catalog. Oversize. Almost totally visual. The cover had students dressed as characters in the Wizard of Oz, standing on a retouched yellow brick road leading to the Minneapolis College of Art and Design in the distance. Today, that seems kind of old-fashioned and quaint. Back then, it was revolutionary. Actually, that might be an understatement.

It caused a tsunami, an earthquake, and A-bomb explosion! Some of the fine arts faculty actually made a blazing bonfire of my Yellow Brick road publication in one of the school buildings. A fine arts Fahrenheit 451 – wow!

The effect? Applications skyrocketed. And we were attracting the right people.

Portfolios Back Then - Made by Hand

Yes, literally by hand. There were no computers, no printers, no copy machines. When an art director did a "comp," he could make a photographic print – a "stat" or Photostat. The AD would trace the letter from a typeface. It was all a very time consuming process.

But the process did have its merits. Tracing letters got you very good at remembering the typographic form. Since you were placing the type character by character, line by line, you also got very good at character, word, and line spacing. This could lead to a love of typography – as well as a love for shorter headlines and copy.

We had a revolution in layout execution techniques about the same time – changing from colored pencil and chalks to markers.

But even with markers, putting a portfolio together still took endless hours. That meant your "book" was almost priceless. You couldn't have two of them. Only one. You protected it with your life.

Atlanta, 1978 and Portfolio Center

After a few years overseas (long story – had a great time), a network of schools offered me a job in Atlanta with two opportunities: First – raise the level of their big school in Atlanta and do much of what I'd done in Minneapolis. Second – travel the USA and find schools for them to add to their network.

They offered me the job, but that was not my fate. I realized that my eventual goal was to have my own school, and it was time to get started. In addition, I didn't want to do anything remotely like they were doing.

I found a building in Atlanta on West Peachtree Street. It seemed ideal. I started Portfolio Center. Fate did not make it easy.

After two months, the street in front of our leased building was torn up for the new Atlanta subway. It was nearly impossible to get into the school. Once inside, the noise from explosions and monster digging machines did little to enhance the creative environment. But, somehow, some brave souls slogged through the mud, climbed the stairs, and signed up. Somehow a couple of agencies wanted to know what we were up to. In particular, Leo Burnett's Flinn Dallis – she offered us our first scholarship. A Florida agency owner, Chuck Porter, offered another small scholarship.

The subway noise moved on, and pedestrians began to stroll past our school. More people climbed the stairs. And we had our first graduation. Every graduate got a job and spread the word about this new kind of school.

In a couple of years, we'd outgrown our location and moved to a warehouse just off Peachtree Street. Agencies were now solidly behind the school, anxious to teach and anxious to hire our graduates. We were over 250 students.

Portfolios Could Now Be Mass-produced

About the time I started Portfolio Center there were some dramatic changes in technology. They changed the requirements for portfolios.

The first breakthrough was rub off letters (Letraset). Next came copy machines. Then photo lettering. Now you could produce – and reproduce – your entire portfolio with relative easy. Never again would you have to trace or paint a letterform.

The option of multiple color copies also allowed students to produce agency "leave-behinds" as well as professionally printed business cards and resumés.

With these new technological innovations, students still carried their work in a black portfolio case, but now they could easily have several identical portfolios. This meant they could *leave* a portfolio at an agency for the agency to show around. This changed hiring dynamics drastically – for both the graduate and the agency. As books piled up, having a staffer to manage the flow throughout the agency became very important. Now portfolio school graduates could have portfolios in many agencies. In fact, portfolios could now be in many cities at the same time.

Ads in the real world were beginning to be almost purely visual. The same thing was happening in students' portfolios. Headlines got shorter. And the difference between an art director's book and a writer's book became more difficult to see.

During this time the use of stock photographs became a common practice – in both portfolio schools and the agency world as well. This news was good and bad. Fallon McElligott & Rice did much extraordinary work with a clever headline and a stock photograph. The combination of stock photo and very funny headline was often powerful. But a lazy practice. A lot of the work began to look and feel alike.

I sensed the advertising world was changing, though there were no black storm clouds on the horizon. Yet.

It seemed that New York and London were no longer the only games in town. You could feel it in the international advertising awards competitions. Brazilian work began to pop up. And the Germans were beginning to make small waves, too.

Things were going too well. I sensed Fate was getting ready to deal me a new hand. Something was up.

Goodbye Portfolio Center. Hello Miami Ad School.

The Portfolio Center was doing a lot better than breaking even. Graduates were being hired left and right. We'd graduated a number of super stars. The concept of a portfolio school had been accepted by the advertising business, and to many of the better university programs we were now "grad school."

But, as John Lennon noted, *"Life is what happens to you while you're making other plans."* Fate decided to give me a fresh start. And, to make it wonderful, she introduced me to the perfect partner to do it with. Advertising is a team sport. So is life. Pippa Seichrist became my partner in the international adventure you may know as The Miami Ad School.

It was time to change. I'd left Portfolio Center but didn't want to start another school in Atlanta. I had another kind of school in mind in another location.

As we worked on our plans, Pippa and I started our own little ad agency specializing in German and Dutch clients doing business in the USA.

We had a great time. We put our agency on a farm a few miles out of Atlanta in horse country. Life was very pleasant. (Incidentally, we work very hard in our business. You should also work hard at having an enjoyable life.)

We bought another horse farm in the North Georgia/North Carolina mountains and spent our weekends there restoring an old house, making furniture, doing pottery, hiking, taking photographs in the morning and evening mists. And more. Clients brought their families to visit long weekends because they were reminded of their childhood in Bavaria. Life was indeed very pleasant.

But I missed teaching. I missed watching the young people become brilliant. I missed contributing to that. One evening, watching the horses graze in the dusk, I put down my glass of wine and blurted out to Pippa that I was ready to start another school.

So the process of starting a school from scratch began again. We were fairly certain we should start in South Florida. I found my way to South Beach and sat in an outdoor cafe. The ocean breezes wafted over me. Yes, this is the place for our new school.

That same night I called Flinn Dallis at Leo Burnett and asked if she could join me in Miami because I needed her advice. Without hesitation Flinn hopped a plane. The next day we sat at the very same café, and before I could finish talking she was already convinced of the idea.

Flinn was as enthusiastic as I was; she promised her agency's support and asked to be the first member of our board of directors.

We found the perfect building. And, as it turned out, Miami turned out to be the perfect choice for the new school concept we had in mind. The location attracted an international student as well as being a magnet for Latin America. There was a good base of ad agencies who wanted us in their city and were prepared to support the school. No problem finding teachers. Chuck Porter was on our board and encouraged his creative staff to teach at our school – that included his rising star Alex Bogusky, who taught in the beginning and became an important advisor to us on curriculum, promotions, and whatever we needed advice on.

It was now 1993. Even with just a handful of students in the school, we began to win important awards. Not just local Addys, but national awards, then very quickly our first international awards.

Miami Ad School Becomes a Global School

The first group of graduates got jobs right away. The second group did just as well. Agencies were now offering scholarships and internships: Leo Burnett was our biggest supporter in the early years. But our market – like our student body – was global.

Think back. The '90s were early on in the advent of the computer revolution; few recognized this at first. We, like everyone else, put computers in a "computer room." Like everyone else, we struggled to keep them running; computer tech guys (IT) were not easy to find. Before we knew what was truly happening, the term "computer graphics" exploded on the scene, and the frenzy started. (FYI it hasn't stopped yet.)

With this dramatic change came a dramatic opportunity. We could now implement the next stage of my idea for portfolio development – that our kind of creative education needs to include a *global* perspective.

Before MAS (Miami Ad School), students would go to one school and stay there. But this new thing called the Internet gave students the confidence to go anywhere.

My idea was for a school with programs all over the world – and it was now viable thanks to this new world-changing, life-changing invention.

More importantly, the big ad agencies are global corporations. Their executives moved from country to country, city to city. The whole world is now one giant network. Even small shops can have offices in different continents.

Within the space of a couple of years we added full-time schools in San Francisco, Minneapolis, and Hamburg. A year later we added Madrid. Then São Paulo. While this was going on, we added many quarter long (three months) programs in London, Paris, Amsterdam, Stockholm, Boulder, Chicago, Moscow, Mumbai, Dubai, Buenos Aires, Brussels, Sydney, Berlin, Manila, Beijing, and many others.

Most of these programs included internships in the leading agencies in those cities. Some evolved into more full-time schools: Berlin, Sydney, Mumbai, Buenos Aires. It seems like every month I have a request from a party wanting to start another full-time Miami Ad School in their city.

New York was a more recent addition. Yes, New York should have been one of our first, but real estate there was out of our financial reach. We waited. Finally, many of the digital agencies moved to Brooklyn. That was affordable.

Of course we won't add cities everywhere; the people who participate must have their heart in the right place for education instead of a quick ROI. If money is their reason for starting the school, I advise them to start an ad agency or open a restaurant.

Now we have this extraordinary global network where students go to one full-time school for one year and then go to four (they choose) of the leading advertising capitals all over the world. They are exposed to so many cultures and languages, and they have incredible experiences that are truly life-changing.

Pippa and I agree, this is the kind of school we wished we had gone to.

Face2Face = Telepresence

With this kind of network, we realized we can take further advantage of our world-wide resources with technology. We added telepresence systems in all the full-time schools. We call our system "Face2Face."

With Face2Face we can teach classes where, for example, the art direction students are in Hamburg, the copywriting students might be in San Francisco, and the instructor might be in Moscow. We try to have every student in every location take one Face2Face class each quarter. We know this is the future of education and of business as well. In fact, CP+B uses their telepresence system not only from Boulder to Miami but from the first floor to the second floor as well.

This telepresence system greatly expanded international exposure for our students as did our long-standing program that brings important speakers from all over the globe every week to our school to speak/teach for varying amounts of time. So the Miami Ad School graduate has worked in agencies in at least four remarkable cities, had personal contact every week with important creatives from wherever, and telepresenced with other creatives from every place – except perhaps the moon or Mars. We're working on that.

The Innovation Lab: The Next Stage of Creative Evolution

Today, as you know, it's about more than advertising. But it's still about *ideas*. With that in mind, we developed an Innovation Lab. We are pleased to say that it is rocking with results

Our involvement with the real world is not limited to advertising agencies but has evolved into working directly in various ways with clients in producing ideas for their products and services. (Frequently, however, this is in partnership with their ad agency.)

Since the first of **Miami Ad School's** Boot Camps for Account Planners was held in 1998, the climax of that Boot Camp has been the presentation of strategies and creative work to a live client. From the very beginning, these presentations – the culmination of 10 weeks of concerted effort by up to 10 teams of **students** – featured eye-opening, unconventional thinking that challenged the status-quo. As a global school we could offer so many cultural points of view and so many creative minds to focus on their issues.

Gradually, with this success over the years, word has spread, and so has demand. This led to the development of the **Innovation Lab**. The Lab allows clients to access the bleeding-edge creativity of our students, the Pop Culture Engineers. The students, in turn, gain invaluable, rubber-meets-the-road experience in dealing and addressing real-world communications issues and their attendant complexities.

Innovation Lab clients have included: American Express, Apple, Dairy Queen, Dunkin' Donuts, FedEx, Ford, Go Daddy, Hormel, Mini, the *New York Times*, Nike, Office Max, Saturn, Wendy's, and Yahoo!

The latest addition to this client roster is **Starbucks**. Back in January, marketing staff from Starbucks, PepsiCo and their joint venture, the North American Coffee Partnership – along with their lifestyle-marketing agency, Freedom Zone – came to Miami to brief an assembled gaggle of 40 Pop

Culture Engineers – art directors, copywriters, and account planners – divided into 10 mini-agencies.

The mission: create a campaign promoting the DoubleShot Espresso energy drink that would extend a project Starbucks had participated in with HBO Films. *"We knew we had [in the HBO Films project] the nugget of an idea,"* Richard Burjaw, General Manager of the North American Coffee Partnership recalled, *"but we needed more creativity, and we needed it from our target –which is people in their late teens and early 20s. This opportunity was a neat way for us to get some different thinking and engage our target market."*

The client returned to Miami Ad School for the team presentations, and they were not disappointed. *"Today was amazing,"* enthused Jim Milligan, President of Freedom Zone. *"We got to sit down and go through the work of 10 different groups, and there is no better way to figure out what a peer group wants than to get input from their peers."* He continued, *"It's for the Millennials, by the Millennials. It's pure thinking; that's the stuff we were hoping for, and that's what we got."*

Google Partners with Miami Ad School for a Year-Long Training Program

Google just recently designated Miami Ad School as the school to learn all the Google applications and spread the training globally.

The partnership between Google and Miami Ad School is a unique concept. And it could not come at a better time – when employers need people who are skilled in *analytics and online marketing*.

Over the next year, the Google team will go to the Miami location of the Miami Ad School network to teach how to use various Google products and tools in a creative way. Something as simple and everyday as starting a search can lead to great insight into a brand or company. Armed with this knowledge and expertise, Miami Ad School students will graduate with a special skill set that prepares them for the real world and makes them an asset to the agencies that hire them.

And it is not just the students in the Miami location that are getting this edge. All of the lectures, classes, and feedback are recorded and edited to push out to the eleven other schools within the network, making this initiative truly global. Miami Ad School is honored to be the school chosen by Google and is excited for our students to learn and develop more creative, strategic, and engaging brand ideas.

UNICEF: A Heart-tugging Opportunity

We work to expand our students' hearts as well as our heads. UNICEF's social marketing group, which at the time was only a month old, asked if Miami Ad School would work on an initiative with them. They needed a creative partner that had scale and could move fast.

They wanted to work with the school's Innovation Lab because, with our locations all over the world, our students have a global perspective and know how to leverage social media in a savvy way.

UNICEF needed help raising awareness of the severe malnutrition crisis in Africa's Sahel region which claims the lives of 1 in 5 young children. UNICEF desired a fast-moving creative partner with scale experienced in the digital-social domain. Because our students master social media and of their global experience, a great partnership soon formed.

This project for UNICEF was really special. It was about saving lives.

UNICEF wanted to leverage their existing social network of nearly 2 million Facebook fans and Twitter followers.

The process began when key UNICEF staff from their New York and Africa offices briefed the students. Within a week we mobilized over 70 students around the world to develop creative campaigns. Once the students had developed their preliminary strategies, they shared them with Unicef to make sure they were on the right track.

After integrating UNICEF's feedback, the students developed final case study videos of their ideas. Six weeks after the initial briefing the Innovation Lab delivered 30 unique social media campaigns to UNICEF.

UNICEF selected their five favorites, and the winner was announced at a special press conference at UNICEF headquarters in New York.

The winning team, Su and Rafa, truly had an international perspective. She is from Singapore. He is from Brazil. Between them they have studied in Miami Ad School locations all over the world and teamed for this project during their last quarter in New York. B Reel, which *Creativity* named Production Company of the Year, is on board to launch the campaign on Facebook this Spring.

Hosting McCann World Group/Latin America - Innovation for MasterCard

This was a two-day event conceived and organized by McCann World

Group Latin America for MasterCard, that brought together all the marketing executives of Latin America – on both the agency and client side – to identify and discuss key innovation triggers.

The school housed a multifaceted melting pot of creatives congregating to find new ways to push forward the MasterCard brand. An added twist came in the form of ten handpicked Miami Ad School students that took part in the activities.

The relaxed environment of the School – as opposed to a more conventional venue such as a hotel conference room – proved to be a potent inspirational catalyst.

Carlos Ernesto Gutierrez, VP Regional Account Director, McCann World Group Latin America, had this to say. *"When we started designing the Innovation Summit, it became apparent almost immediately that not only the content had to be innovative but also the agenda, the speakers, the dynamics and, of course, the venue. Miami Ad School was the perfect partner, and we engaged them at several levels: They provided the physical space for the summit, and we gave a couple of presentation slots to their brightest students, who were absolutely fantastic."*

The summit proved to be a success. Everything from the school, to the speakers, and the students proved to be, in a word, priceless. Edgardo Tettamanti, SVP and Marketing Group Head of MasterCard Latin America & Caribbean, agreed that our school added to the process. *"Having the MasterCard Innovation Summit at the Miami Ad School was a priceless experience, not only because of the venue itself, but because we had the great privilege of working in close collaboration with some of its top students."* Why? *"They provided truly innovative ideas and fresh insights,"* Edgardo added, *"which made our discussions that much richer and bolder."*

MAS for Pros

The success of our graduates and the unsurpassed record of international awards our students have won has brought us attention from nearly every country large enough to have an ad agency and with that attention––a request to start a Miami Ad School there.

The list of requests for a Miami Ad School is growing longer and becoming ever more interesting: Azerbaijan, Portugal, Greece, Russia, Ukraine, Egypt, Aruba, Saudi Arabia, Iran, Shanghai, Beijing, Malta, Brussels, Peru, Ecuador, Colombia, Chile, Holland, United Arab Republic, Qatar, Poland,

Nigeria, South Africa, Denmark, and dozens of others.

Many of these requests were from countries that were too small to support a full time school. But their need for training is real. And we worked hard to find a new format to help them out. The result? We've added a program called MAS for Pros. We teach live on-classes in specialized courses to the professionals in an agency, both on-site and online. For the past year, we've been teaching the complete creative department of DDB in Lagos, Nigeria with online classes. That was so successful, DDB asked to offer classes to their senior executives as well.

We have a big challenge in front of us to expand this new format to all the agencies and companies who want a partnership with Miami Ad School to improve the skills of their staff. This is truly the future of our kind of specialized education.

You Are Now Leaving the Neanderthal Era

For my entire life in education, the typical classroom was identical to how Neanderthals went to school. The oldest adult with the whitest hair stood on a boulder and sketched on the wall of the cave as little Neanderthals sat cross-legged scratching notes in the sand – most likely ignoring the old man pontificating.

Lately, the youngsters have simply looked at their lap tops – ignoring the teacher and wasting what they are spending good money for. I wasn't happy about this. So, some months ago, I tried an experiment in a wordsmithing class I was teaching.

I told the class to open up their lap tops and get on Google Docs. Using two screens, I had a student post his or her writing project on one screen. Then the rest of the classes would post their comments on the Twitter-like feed – they all were asked to go on to the document posted and make comments/changes/suggestions which are visible in real time and even show the photo of the person making the comment.

This was remarkably successful. The entire class was engaged. There would be a dozen or more running comments on each piece of work; I would be lucky to have one or two in the past. Shy students who rarely made vocal comments made many comments in writing. My comments were no more important than anyone else's. This is truly the best format for learning – peer to peer education.

The experiment was so successful that we began looking at ways to expand this approach. We looked and tried other applications – many were equally successful.

This use of technology may also be the best way to listen to any speaker, any lecturer. I found that by seeing the running comments of the students I could adapt what I was saying to what they were commenting about – all in real time.

I am on a crusade now to have this technology used by every teacher, every speaker in every Miami Ad School location. That won't be easy; a year of convincing my staff of the merits of telepresence was nothing compared to the dramatic change of open-computer/open-cell-phone classrooms.

Pippa tells a funny story of attending a session at an SXSW conference where the speaker was using a running Twitter feed on a giant projection screen behind him. At some point in his speech the entire audience was laughing and another panel member told the speaker to turn around and read the latest tweet. The tweet was from a young woman to the other women present, *"He's hot. Is he married ?"*

The Most Awarded School in the World

We have been remarkably successful in international competitions. In addition to the awards list below of past years, at the writing of this chapter, we were just selected at Cannes as Future Lions School of the year; Best of Show in the National Addy's, 10 gold pencils at D&AD, 4 pencils at the One Show, and Gold at El Sol.

One rewarding aspect of all the awards is that they are spread between all our locations and not just centered in one campus or country. Keep in mind that, since all our students in all locations are a tossed salad of cultures, an award won in Brazil may be from one student from Hamburg with another from Madrid or any of a hundred other country combinations. Our students consistently win an award in Spain where the prize is a new automobile. And, since our student winners are from all over, they have to end up selling the car and splitting the award money.

Also at this writing one of our students, Bennett Austin, from the San Francisco school is winning the top award in just about every national and international competition. Bennett is following the footsteps of one of our Dutch graduates, Menno Klunin, who was the most awarded student in the world when he was at Miami Ad School. We predict Bennet will do the same as an agency creative.

I'm Writing a History, Is It Fair for Me to Talk about the Future?

Well, I'm going to anyway. Human beings that we are, we will misuse every new technological invention. Then, being what and who we are, we will develop new technology to solve the misuse. And on and on.

For example, texting: texting in movies, in the car, in the classroom, in the restaurant, texting everywhere. We will develop new technology to solve the misuse.

Rudimentary technology available today would use voice recognition to transmit your texts to earphones; night vision would allow you to text without a light that interferes with the others in the movie. Present technology would allow your wife to see texts on her eyeglass from her mother, her lover, or her kids while she has a pleasant dinner with her husband and his boss. Present technology would allow your automobile to go in autopilot while you send and receive texts while driving.

In the classroom of the future, all computers will be open, and the instructor will be able to view all their screens at once. Instructors and students will communicate with each other by texting even though they are in the same room, just as my wife does with her kids at the dinner table now. Everyone will know what everyone is thinking before we think it because an iPhone app will anticipate our thoughts because the phone knows us so well.

Every form of advertising will be personalized since data on all of us will be recorded – every thing each of us desires, likes, dislikes, as well as what will motivate us to buy every single item in the universe.

Amazon, or some future version of it, will write books exclusively for me with all my friends as characters in my favorite genre. Billy Collins will write poems exclusively for me. A resuscitated Mozart will write sonatas for me.

All for Me. Me. And the world will be completely boring, and everyone will long for that special time after *Mad Men* and before WebWorld.

Oh, I forgot. I won't be here when this all happens. Fate again.

I lived in the best of times and the worst of times, didn't I?

But, as I said in the beginning, I have seen things you people would never believe. And I have given back on the gifts I was given. Think it's time for a true story.

What Got Me Started in Education Anyway?

Fortunately, that's an easy question to answer. In high school I told my parents what college I wanted to go to. They thought I was joking.

We were poor. We lived in a poor town of blue collar workers. Nearly all available men worked in the Navy Yard or Naval base of this military town. That was your future.

My father was an immigrant from Germany. He'd joined the American Navy to get his citizenship and then stayed when his gig was over – it was just before the outbreak of World War II. He knew what side he was on.

I was expected to work in the Navy Yard when I finished high school. I was devastated. I always planned on going to college. Or maybe dreamed would be a better word.

I went to school the next day, morose and bitter. I've always been a fairly happy person, and every teacher asked me what was wrong. After another day or so of gloom, one of my favorite teachers took me aside, and I confided in her. She told me not to worry. Later that week she said for me to meet her at 6am the next morning. Our meeting place was in front of a local supermarket.

That morning she led me into the supermarket, and we went to the back of the store and up a small staircase. I was introduced to a remarkable man – one who changed my life profoundly.

He offered me a full scholarship to college, all expenses paid, to any college. There was only one caveat; at some time in my life I would have to send someone else's child to college.

I found out later that he had sent twenty-seven other young people to college with the same condition. He did this anonymously; I only knew the name of one other person.

Many years later I decided to take Pippa to meet this man. We drove from Atlanta to Norfolk, Virginia and we went to his small, modest house. We arrived as he was coming out the door, helped by his son. He must have been in his nineties by then. But he was still dapper wearing a bright bow tie, walking without difficulty. He glanced at me and at Pippa, then stopped and stared at me.

I said, "Hello, Mr. Overton. I'm Ron Seichrist. Do you remember me?"

"Of course I remember you." He said, answering me in the same raspy voice I heard years ago when I would visit him between semesters at college.

Then he said, *"Did you ever make anything of yourself?"*

It's a wonderful world. Pass it on.

Work Steps:

As we begin our careers, we don't usually think much about history.

After all, when you're starting out, it's about the future … not the past.

That said, the piece you've just read covered a lot of ground, and the changes in the technology of portfolio production had a profound effect on how people went looking for a job. Let's think about this and ask a few questions.

1. **Stay current.** What techniques and production technology are you currently using to produce your portfolio?

2. **Show your craft.** Older portfolios demonstrated "craft skills," such as writing and drawing ability. Does your more modern portfolio show off any of these traditional skills?

3. **Look ahead.** What techniques, production technology, and new communication formats (for example, new types of social media) are you thinking about adding to your portfolio? In what formats will you be delivering your portfolio?

– – – – – –

Ron Seichrist is the father/ founder of the modern portfolio school.

We thank Ron (and Pippa) not only for this piece but for their tremendous contributions to our industry – developing the teaching models that help young talent prepare careers in creativity.

The Portfolio of the Future

Ignacio Oreamuno
Executive Director, The Art Directors
Club & Founder, ihaveanidea.org

*Now that you've learned about the history of port-
folio schools and their role in making portfolios
more competitive, let's look to the future. And no
one is better equipped to talk about the future than
Ignacio, the founder of ihaveanidea.org – one of
the oldest-running online publications dedicated
to shaping the future of the advertising industry through an intellectual
archive that provokes creative professionals (and students) to think or act.
In fact, an earlier version of this piece originally appeared on that website.*

I know it makes me sound old, but eleven years ago I was hunting for my first
art director job. Since I'd decided to study web design and art direction at
the same time, I had a combination of interactive and print campaigns in my
book. The advice I got from creative directors was always the same: "If you
want to be a web developer, make a web portfolio. If you want to be an art
director, make another one – but don't mix them up. We don't care if you do
web." That was then.

Fast-forward five years. Suddenly traditional print portfolios began getting more interactive, as gutsy juniors added banners to their print campaigns.

Fast-forward two more years, when I got an angry email from a promi-
nent CD who had attended Portfolio Night, complaining that a junior
brought his portfolio on his laptop and that it wasn't the "correct way" of
showing it.

"How wrong he was," I thought last year, as I looked at the juniors attending Portfolio Night 9 in Amsterdam, armed with all sorts of tablets, mobile
applications, and laptops. Campaigns included interactive elements, films,
games, and more that they had coded themselves.

This is the first time since the days of the *Mad Men* that portfolios have
truly transformed, and it puts a lot more pressure on creatives trying to get

that dream job. Not only do the ideas have to be great, but the media they live within has to be a perfect fit.

Here are the most important trends I see leading up to the next Portfolio Night.

- **Tablets will dominate.** Last year saw a massive increase in tablets vs. laptops. I expect 90% of portfolios to go on tablets this year. Yes, a laptop can do everything a tablet does, but for some reason it's just a cleaner, better way to show it. Also, battery life is better so you don't have to worry about running out of juice or having too much clutter on your desktop.

- **More complex mobile/interactive campaigns.** Two years ago, most portfolios began to include at least one campaign with a mobile element. In most cases they were weak, since juniors often just took the idea of a TV or print campaign and dumped it on a very crude or too complex iPhone app, assuming that made it okay. Early on, that may have been ahead of the game, but now that everyone has the same iPad/iPhone app comps in their books, they must be developed further. Remember, the purpose of your portfolio is to demonstrate that you have the thinking the agency needs, so you should have fun and push the limits of your thinking.

- **Play with the technology.** I've met a lot of creatives who have learned to code apps and interactive games. While this skill set was not a requirement four years ago for, say, a copywriter, times have changed. If the people competing for your job have that skill set, it means you have to embrace it. You don't need to become an expert, but if you can work with a creative technologist to build out some of the ideas you've developed in your book, it's going to score you big points. Remember, if you get that dream job you're after, this is exactly what will be required of you.

- **Surprise me.** Leading agencies around the world are diversifying further. Look at the last shortlist of the Tomorrow Awards and you will find that some of the most innovative advertising work around the world is not just ads. Some agencies are building apps for themselves and putting them to market, others are creating social movements to build buzz for the agency and brand, while others are launching into new arenas like architecture. The portfolio of the future should have between 15-20% of non-ads in its arsenal.

- **The level of polish has changed.** If you wanted to show off your TV skills in the past, you could get away with writing a TV script in your book. Years later, juniors began shooting their own videos and composing grunge-looking versions of ads. Nowadays the bar has been raised by technology. Everyone has access to HD cameras and to advanced-but-cheap movie editors. If consumers are able to create video content that is watched by millions of people, so should you. This applies to copywriters as much as art directors. In the past you could get away with it looking amateurish, but that's no longer the case. What do you mean you can't compose your own music for your video using GarageBand?

Work Steps:

Want the portfolio of the future? Here are a few key work steps from Ignacios's advice to get you going.

1. **Checkout ihaveanidea.org:** The content on that website can really help you understand the business and give your strategies that enhance your career prospects as a creative professional.

2. **Push your thinking:** As Ignacio said, simply translating a television spot or print ad into an app isn't enough. You need to make sure it's appropriate and completely thought through.

3. **Learn about the technology:** Remember: You may never get called on to program an app, but as Ignacio indicated, being conversant in technology can help you get hired – and can help you get your vision produced.

4. **Polish your work:** First make sure your ideas are strong. Then, make sure you've presented them in the right media.

5. **Bring your work to life:** If you want to show a television idea in your portfolio, go and find some aspiring filmmakers and shoot it. Have a radio idea? Produce it. Same for your apps. The more you do, the more it will enhance your chances.

— — — — — —

Ignacio Oreamuno, *Executive Director of The Art Directors Club and Founder of IHAVEANIDEA, never believed he needed anyone's permission to change the industry he loves so much. That fearlessness inspired him to found IHAVEANIDEA in 2001, with the intention of creating a community-based publication that shared quality know-how by creatives for creatives. Soon thereafter, Ignacio launched Portfolio Night, the world's first-ever international simultaneous portfolio review. Both initiatives grew at lightning speed, which solidified his path toward inspiring creatives around the world.*

In the following years, Ignacio was named one of Marketing *magazine's "Ones to Watch Under 30," and he launched two new initiatives; the Tomorrow Awards, the first international awards show without categories, focused on teaching and learning, and Giant Hydra, a first-of-its-kind mass collaboration unit for agencies and brands.*

Ignacio's recent move to the leadership position of the ADC marks the integration of two of the most esteemed industry advocate organizations in the world -- furthering his goal to "dramatically change, for the better, the industry I love so much."

Having lived in ten countries throughout his life, across Latin America, Europe, and North America, Ignacio is no stranger to travel and new cultures. He is known for living his life in an airplane, for his taste for fine foods and wine, and for never stopping in his tireless quest to improve the global creative industries.

I Think People Who Go into Advertising Should Do So Because They Absolutely Love It

Stan Richards
Principal, The Richards Group

In general, we've emphasized all of the new opportunities opening up and all the new technologies that are making today's portfolios – at their best – digital dynamite.

But we felt that we also needed to remind you of some of the classic craft-driven values that are still a part of our industry.

And we can't think of a better person to tell you about it than Stan Richards, founder of The Richards Group, America's largest independent agency.

Here, he offers excellent advice on portfolio building – advice that was true 20 years ago and is still true today.

This interview is from How to Succeed in Advertising When All You Have is Talent *– used with permission.*

"These people watch television at night, paying little attention to the show, but perk up when a commercial comes on. They're so vitally interested in the way people communicate that they see it as a life's work," observes Stan Richards, founder and leader of The Richards Group in Dallas, Texas.

Richards is someone who truly made a life's work out of studying communications—from his days as an art student, to founding a leading Dallas design studio (some call him the dean of Texas design), to turning that studio into one of the largest privately held full-service agencies in America—one that is consistently considered among the best in the world.

His organization creates work that is consistently recognized as among the best in the country—by *Adweek*, the *New York Times*, and New York Art Directors Club— working for such clients as Chick-fil-A, Corona Beer, Fruit of the Loom, Motel 6, Hyundai, and The Home Depot, among many others. He has also served a number of nonprofit organizations on a volunteer basis, including Junior Achievement, United Way, and the Salvation Army.

Richards is the author of *The Peaceable Kingdom*, which describes how he structured The Richards Group, built its culture, and maintains it today.

Richards' early years were spent in Philadelphia and Atlantic City. He settled in Dallas after graduating from Pratt in the mid-1950s. Today, he balances his business and personal responsibilities by setting aside evening hours for his family.

He leaves the office every night by six o'clock. If he has four hours of extra work, he returns at four o'clock the next morning. Richards has been married for 49 years and has two sons. One is a partner in his own ad agency in San Francisco, and the other is a Ph.D. in clinical psychology. He also has two grandchildren. An avid jogger, he's logged over 43,000 miles.

Drawn to Design

What makes someone successful in one creative area and not in another? Nature or nurture? Whatever instills talent, Richards firmly believes environment is what leads an individual to manifest one or another. "A designer is a designer in any medium," he says. "I'm convinced that if a great designer were taught the tools of musical composition instead, he or she could write a pretty nifty piece of music. The judgments are essentially the same. Designers just don't have the facility to use the particular tools that a composer uses. I believe the same talents apply to playwriting, sculpture, all the arts."

In this section, we're going to explore this concept—as well as see how this idea developed. Richards started his arts exploration very young. Even at ten years old, he was one of those children who could draw better than anyone else in the class. (In fact, his mother was convinced that not only could he draw better than any kid in the class, he could draw better than every kid in America.) "That led me to believe that I was going to do something in art," says Richards.

Then, in high school, he learned from a teacher that he could actually make a living as a commercial artist. On a recommendation from this teacher, he went on to Pratt in New York. He chose that design school because it was the only one with a basketball team, an important consideration for him at the time.

The school consistently turned out students with great potential in advertising and design. Richards credits Herschel Levit, one of his teachers at Pratt, with greatly influencing him, as well as a group of two- or three-dozen other art students.

Along with Richards, these people went on to have outstanding careers in advertising or design.

Levit helped Richards understand what graphic design was all about.

"In the very first session," says Richards, "he marched us all down to the school auditorium, sat at the piano and explained, in great detail, Arnold Schoenberg's 12-tone row system for composition. He explained how Schoenberg built his compositions and the wonderful symmetry involved without explaining its relevance to the class. At the end of this class session, we were dismissed, and it was never mentioned again."

This taught Richards his greatest lesson. Here was a group of people who planned to work their entire lives without having to ever write a piece of music. As he reflected on it over the course of his studies, he realized that Levit was saying that to be a great designer, everything you know is relevant.

"Every time I went to class, I never knew where the discussion was going to go. We could critique our work and then the conversation would move off into very interesting discussions of architecture or dance," recalls Richards. "All of us gained tremendously from those discussions."

Heading West

Richards graduated from Pratt in 1953 and got some job offers in New York. But he noticed that some talented designers who worked in New York improved when they moved on to Los Angeles. "So I thought Los Angeles was the place for me," he says.

He headed out for Los Angeles, but took a detour to Dallas because he had seen terrific work being done by Neiman Marcus. The exclusive Dallas retailer's advertising design was ahead of the industry and very well regarded. "It was brilliant," he says. "It was always great fun and had a nice light touch." He applied there, but, although he received encouragement, he did not get a job.

This frustrated him. "I was this 20-year-old kid out of one of the best art schools in America," Richards says. "Maybe I wasn't the very best kid in my graduating class, but there were a few of us who dominated the class. I was coming to a city that was not much more than a frontier town. It had a very sedentary, quiet, unexciting advertising industry."

Richards' portfolio consisted of a dozen highly experimental pieces from school. "I sat down and talked with a creative director who headed the biggest agency in Dallas at the time. He looked at my work and got very excited. He offered what turned out to be extraordinary counsel."

He told Richards that nobody in Dallas would hire him because his work was too advanced. But Dallas was going to grow and flourish. "He said if I could stick it out through the lean years, I'd be in a position to dominate the market. Because I'd be responsible for all the good stuff."

The creative director's prediction made Richards' detour well worthwhile. He took this advice and started a freelance design and advertising practice. He won local advertising awards over the next couple of years. Then, in 1955, the head of the Bloom Agency, the second biggest agency in Dallas, called and asked if he'd be interested in working as a creative director there.

A Career Blooms

"I took the job thinking I'd enjoy heading up the creative efforts for a big agency," says Richards. "But I hated it. It was all the classic things you hear about advertising agencies. It was bureaucratic, hierarchical—a stultifying environment. It was one in which the account managers said, 'No, that's not what my client is looking for and so I won't show it.' Then we battled over it. I left a year to the day after starting and reestablished my freelance practice."

Richards had to struggle very hard to reestablish himself. He had virtually no income for several months, but soon his business began to flourish. Business from Dallas-area companies and agencies came first, then from around Texas, and soon from the rest of the country. Eventually he built up a 20-person staff.

His organization developed relationships with advertising agencies based on print work. Sometimes a television assignment would come up, and the studio would be asked to work on it. Richards would conceive it, write it, and storyboard it—and on some occasions produce it. "I always felt that it was the most natural thing in the world to do both advertising and design," he says. "I might sit down in the morning and work on a logo and in the afternoon work on an advertising campaign." Over the next 20 years, his organization grew into an important creative resource for advertising agencies.

An Ad Agency Is Born

Then, in 1976, when his design firm was firmly established, the CEO of a major Dallas bank asked him if he'd be interested in handling their account as a full-service agency. "It was an interesting moment," recalls Richards, "because if we became an advertising agency, we'd say good-bye to all of our clients. So I thought long and hard about that one and decided it was time to make the transition."

When The Richards Group became a full-service ad agency, his design group was kept intact and moved a few blocks from the agency. Eventually, the business grew to also include groups that specialize in direct marketing, interactive communications, public relations, sales promotion, and employee brand training.

Different by Design

As an advertising agency, several factors set The Richards Group apart from other organizations. He was one of the first to eliminate seating departmental groups together. Even early on, art directors are just as likely to be next to account executives or researchers as another creative at The Richards Group. "That way, they'll see that the others care just as much about their side of the business. That's enormously helpful in avoiding confrontations," observes Richards. "I don't tolerate barriers that make it difficult to do great advertising. I want to remove those barriers and have all the decisions based on the merits of the work."

Another Important Difference

Richards doesn't pattern his organization after current trends or the traditional practices of other agencies. He maintained his agency's independence in a period of buyouts and consolidation.

"If you're part of a holding company agency, your mission from the moment you walk into the office in the morning to the time you walk out in the evening is to enhance the wealth of the shareholders," says Richards. "Here, we don't have to do that. We also don't borrow money," he adds. "So we don't have to concern ourselves with bankers. It means that all of us, all day, every day, can focus on the only thing that counts, and that is the work. At the very top of our priority list is, how good is the work and how good can we make it? If that is fundamental, it changes the way you look at your job."

This independence also enabled him to avoid deep cuts in his staff during the severe industry downturn. So while his competitors were laying off 100, 200, 300 people, and the agency business as a whole lost nearly 19,000 jobs—a high number for such a small industry—The Richards Group maintained its staff (except for a few they lost through attrition and a handful of others).

"It was a choice that I made," says Richards. "It meant accepting a dramatically reduced level of profitability. But I'm in a position to do that because of our lack of shareholders, partners, and investors. I didn't have to concern myself with anyone else's welfare, except for the welfare of the people who are part of the company."

"The business is cyclical. It always has been, and it always will be. And I felt that it was much more important to maintain our strength during a down period than to maintain profitability."

As part of his unique culture, Richards prefers that his employees spend time with their families and avoid late hours. "It's a business that requires considerably more than nine hours a day on a fairly regular basis," he says. "So I learned early in my career to set aside my evening hours for my family. If I have extra work to do, I just come in early. Nobody at my house cared whether I was gone at 4:00 a.m., but they cared a lot if I wasn't home at 7:00 in the evening."

In addition, Richards expects all his creative staffers to present their own work. "We don't shield any of them from our clients," he notes. However, this does not demand exceptional presentation skills. Richard believes, "Good work speaks for itself. You can be absolutely silent and put five ads on the table, and a person sitting on the other side is going to find it pretty easy to pick the best one."

But individual work styles are respected, too. Richards prefers to work alone but recognizes that others may need a partner to be productive. So most of his creative teams work in partnership, while others choose to work by themselves.

His unique take on the business also extends to what he looks for in a client. "Avoid working for clients in multi-layered organizations where the work travels through an endless series of approvals," he suggests. "At each level of approval, reviews make the work weaker and weaker. That's frustrating for a creative."

Four Client Questions

In deciding whether to take on a new client, he asks four questions:

"The first question to ask is can we do great work?" says Richards. "Is the client open to great creative? Do they trust fresh ideas? And are they willing to provide enough input to get it?"

The second question focuses on getting results. "Can we measure how the advertising works or are we going to have to be satisfied that the client's spouse thinks it's nice?" he asks. "It's important to measure results. Being able to look at sales and determine whether the advertising did the job is important to effective campaigns in the future."

Remuneration is the third question. "Can we make a profit?" asks Richards. "The client has to understand that we both assume the responsibility of helping each other profit in the relationship."

And the final question looks at the personal relationship with a potential client. "Can we have fun?" he asks. "That's the human side. Do we like the people? Do they like us? When we show up for a meeting are we going to be treated with respect? Will we enjoy the experience?"

He asks these questions because he believes the client is one of the greatest determining factors in producing great work, which reflects on his view of the industry overall.

A Look Back

Looking back on his more than 50 years in communications, he says, "There is no business that is as emotionally rewarding as the one I'm in—with the exception of being a performer. And the only reason is that with a performance, you get to hear the applause. We don't. We have to assume that there is applause. You legitimately want to please.

"In dealing with clients, you want very much for them to sit across the table from you, listen to your presentation, and when you're finished say, 'That's wonderful.' That's the applause I'm talking about."

And clearly, Richards has gotten lots of applause over the years.

"I'd do this whether anybody paid me or not," he says.

"I work with very, very bright people who care about their craft. We spend our days trying to figure out how to create something wonderful. What more could anyone ask for? Every morning I get up, and I'm excited about coming to the office. And I'm overpaid for doing it!"

Today, Richards feels that his biggest challenge is maintaining the kind of electricity and vitality at his agency that it had when it was a much smaller firm.

"We've managed to do that," he says, because of its culture, philosophy, and business structure. "It is still the same place today as it was ten years ago, 20 years ago. And we now have 662 people."

How to Endear Yourself to a Potential Employer

Richards has an unusually honest approach in making his hiring decisions. "I hire people I like. That may sound stupid," says Richards, "but personality counts. Integrity counts. It's an intuitive process. I get a feeling for the beginner, not just for the work in the portfolio."

When he interviews, Richards wants to find out what the beginner is like. "I try to draw that person out—beginning with high school years," says Richards. "I want to find out if he or she played sports, was involved in politics, or what his or her folks do. I try to understand what kind of person he or she is. I want to be satisfied that, when I expose this person to my client, he or she will represent both himself or herself and our organization very well. And if I hire people I like, there's a pretty good chance they'll like each other, too."

In the portfolio, Richards looks for two or three pieces that are so brilliant he could expect to see them in the annuals. Says Richards, "If a beginner is capable of doing that, I'd hire him or her." Here is some advice that can help you get to that level.

Review the annuals: Richards believes this helps you develop your instincts and abilities to make sound judgments. "Spend time reviewing *CA*, the *One Show* annuals, *New York Art Director's Annual*, and *Graphis*," says Richards. "Those books help you to recognize what is possible in advertising. While it's important to look at current ones, it's also useful to look at older editions to understand where advertising came from, why things are done the way they are done—and how we got here. If you only read this week's *Time*, whose ads are 90 percent garbage, you won't ever develop a sense for really terrific work. Emulate the best work that's being done in the field."

Stir up your creative juices: To come up with ideas, Richards tells us that anything can trigger a stream of consciousness. "I can pick up a magazine, the annuals, or the Yellow Pages and make some sort of word association that starts a thought process. Something might trigger a whole string of thoughts and lead me to a place I wouldn't come to otherwise," he says. "Also, I'm a runner, and when I'm running alone, I find that helps me to solve advertising problems."

Understand the customer's position: Advertising's primary mission is to sell a product or service. That's simple. But to do that means identifying the potential customer's point of view. Ideally, research will tell us that. "We need to understand what information will change a potential customer's point of view," says Richards, "and what information will motivate them to do business with the client."

Use familiar products for a spec book...: Your portfolio should have ads for products anybody can understand. Says Richards, "If somebody comes in with an ad for some highly sophisticated software program, an ad that only he and an engineer understand, it's very difficult to evaluate the work. The simpler the product, the better it is. Also avoid fictional products. Presenting real products, with real marketing considerations, has more impact."

... With obvious marketing considerations: "Suppose a beginner chooses WD-40. You don't have to be a genius to figure out that most households in America have a can of WD-40 sitting on a shelf. And it could last a lifetime. Therefore, the marketing strategy should be to motivate people to use it up. That's simple."

Include radio in a copy portfolio: Richards sees very little radio work in spec portfolios. However, he feels this is an important component of advertising. So he is always encouraged when a beginner presents some terrific radio. Richards recognizes that beginners should also include TV because some employers want to see it, but he believes TV is difficult to evaluate. "It's a collaborative medium. It involves many people. In a television spot, there can be ten people who played a major part in the process," he says.

Be prepared to talk about anything: Richards wants to work with people who will be able to work with his clients. "I ask applicants to talk about subjects they are unprepared to talk about," he says. "I prefer to hear about their parents, brothers and sisters, and what they like to do for fun, rather than the details of their last position."

Don't worry about the packaging of your portfolio: "I never even reflect on the outside packaging of a portfolio," says Richards. "All I care about is what they've tried. I want to sit across the table from them and get a sense of what they're like as people, but the packaging of the portfolio is inconsequential."

Evaluate the agency: In the same way that a beginner needs to look at the walls of the agency to evaluate the work during a job interview, you need to evaluate the culture. "If it is not a place that exudes energy and electricity, then it may be the wrong place for you," says Richards. "It's important that the people around you have as much fire in their bellies as you do. If you're surrounded by a bunch of functionaries, then sooner or later you'll become functionary."

Be a grown-up: Richards particularly wants to avoid hiring people who seem arrogant. "I don't believe in artistic temperaments. I think that's often an excuse for infantile behavior. In my own organization, I simply will not accept that. I won't accept arrogance, and I won't accept temper tantrums," he says. "We want to present the work. We want the client to respond. And we want to be able to respond to the client's comments and then make the changes that satisfy all of the concerns. That's hard to do with people who are arrogant or cocky."

Always question your work: When you finish an ad, Richards suggests asking yourself questions about its effectiveness. "Does the ad make a point? And does it make that point clearly? Does it make the point without the body copy? If it's an outdoor board, can it be read at 70 mph? All of those questions are important," says Richards.

Include only about a dozen pieces: "You can have a few more," says Richards. "But not many. Secondly, they ought to be the very best you've ever done."

Attend an art school: "I hire a lot of kids out of art schools," says Richards. "They do a marvelous job of preparing people to enter the business. They're, for the most part, highly competitive. Those who distinguish themselves in an exceedingly demanding environment are going to be successful in business. So it's about as predictable as anything can be."

Invite client participation (once on the job): "We go into every client/agency relationship understanding that we'll never know our client's business as well as he knows it," says Richards. "But we'll know his customer better than he ever can. And we'll know advertising better than he ever can. But we will never know his business as well as he does because he has ways of casually picking up information that will never come to us. We want to take full advantage of that. So we want our client to be a participant in the process. Consequently, if he or she has reservations about an ad, we want to understand why. That insight will help us reach the best answer."

A Branding Process for Building Your Book

Throughout this book, we hear a lot about brands. Here's The Richards Group take on brands and the branding process, which they call Spherical* Branding. While you can't use it on the same level as The Richards Group because you don't have the same level of resources to put against it, you can apply the thinking behind their process to help you put together your portfolio.

"I have a very simple definition for a brand," says Richards. "A brand is a promise. That brand needs to deliver on its promise at every point of contact over an extended period of time. That's how a brand is built. That's why some brands are strong and some are weak.

"Our branding process is to provide, at the end of it, the consistency that every brand needs over every point of contact.

"Our system demands that there be conviction behind that brand promise, and that it has to be held at the highest levels of management in the company. If we can develop the conviction about the brand promise, if we can then assure consistency at every point of contact, then we can build a strong brand.

"The process itself begins with qualitative and quantitative research to understand the characteristics of the brand. We go through that very diligently. It also involves an extensive series of management interviews to talk with the people who have the responsibility of managing the brand and understand their point of view. How they feel about the way that brand presents itself to the consumer.

"After that, we hold a workshop for one or two days (occasionally it's even three days), where our key people are in a room with their key management people—there could be as many as 15 people—and we begin to define the characteristics of the brand that are going to dictate where we head for the next several years.

"We begin with the development of a brand vision statement, which is the highest calling of the brand. This is not a mission statement. As an example—this is not one of ours—the Disney company in defining its brand vision could talk about animated films, cruise ships, resorts, but instead their brand vision is 'keeping the magic of childhood alive.' We try to find a brand vision statement that is as lofty as that.

"Then we go through a positioning exercise. This is not terribly different from conventional wisdom: we define the target audience (not demographically, but as a mind set), the category in which we compete, and identify the brand's most compelling benefit.

"So, we wind up writing a sentence that says, for example: 'To frugal travelers, Motel 6 is the comfortable place to stay that's always the lowest price of any national chain.' That's pretty close to our positioning statement for Motel 6.

"Once we've defined a positioning statement—that's really the intellectual positioning—we need to look at the emotional side of why the brand is selected. So we do a personality statement, which is usually not more than five or six words to describe the personality of the brand. And then we do something that few other people do, and that is an affiliation statement.

"That is, what club do I join when I buy into this brand? Let's say it's a retail store like The Home Depot. Somebody sees me opening the trunk of my car and taking out a Home Depot bag. I've just shopped at Home Depot, what do they think of me? What club am I a member of?

"Those are important issues we're dealing with today in our new Hyundai relationship, because the Hyundai is a remarkably good car at a remarkably good price, but it doesn't enjoy, at this point, the benefits of having a strong affiliation. And certainly they should not be proceeding as a car that's purchased because one doesn't have the means to buy a better car. Rather, it's a car that you purchase if you have your head on straight, and you recognize what's important in life. You don't want to spend a ton of money for a badge on a car. What you want is a really good car that'll do everything you want it to do. So the affiliation statement for Hyundai is people who are winners at life."

Work Steps:

Let's review some of Stan's advice for building your book.

1. **Read CA, CMYK and the annuals.** This will be important throughout your career, but it will be even more important at the beginning.

You will find some companies and individuals you admire. You will start developing some standards to shoot for.

2. **Show that you "understand the customer's position."** This is good advice. As we work on our projects, we are more and more involved in our own thinking. How can we get good at seeing the world from the customer's point of view?

3. **Create for radio.** Stan's agency has had great success with radio campaigns – like the one for Motel 6. This is not necessarily great advice right now, with radio listenership shrinking and most players not up to the possibilities of the new technology. But that's about to change! Soon, you will be able to respond to radio on your computer or mobile device. You'll be able to respond to advertisers and order music and products by touching the screen. New platforms will make it easy, and – like so many other things – what was old will be new again! Radio! Stay tuned!

4. **Be prepared to talk about anything.** How are your conversational skills? Stan makes a good point about the social skills needed to be successful in this business.

5. **Review the branding process that Stan recommends.** His comments on developing a brand vision and then a positioning statement is still rock solid. You should do that for every client in your portfolio – and you should think about making it a part of your creative development process.

Thanks again, Stan.
—The Editors

Please Don't Bore Me with Your Advertising

Kara Taylor
Director of Creative Recruiting, CP+B

Now that you have the start of a good portfolio, your next step is to get though the agency's creative recruiter.

What is a creative recruiter, you ask? It's someone whose job it is to find all of the best possible candidates for any open positions – creative professionals who are a match for the agency and for the needs of the particular clients.

Therefore, it is creative recruiter's job to know about all of the potential candidates and then remember about the good ones, so he or she is prepared when a position becomes available. And it is your job to get to know as many of them as possible.

But what is it that a recruiter is seeking, at least initially? Let's find out from a veteran, Kara Taylor. Her advice just might change the way you approach your job search.

If I had five bucks for every time someone asked me what I look for in an entry-level candidate and in an entry-level portfolio, I could probably retire. Maybe. Actually, probably not, but you get the idea.

I can say truthfully, however, that in the 10 plus years that I've been asked this question, so much of the business has changed, but the things that I look for in a book and in a candidate are still pretty much exactly the same.

The Portfolio

Let's get right to it. In a book, I want to see smart **concepts**. I want to see smart **content,** and I want to see lots of love for the **craft**. While I've divided these three points up, you'll notice they overlap quite a bit.

Concepts

Your portfolio needs to demonstrate that you understand how to solve marketing problems. Your concepts need to prove that you are smart, that you are inventive, and quite simply, they need to make me be intrigued by how your brain works.

Onward.

Content

Content is really important, and it means more than one thing. Content is not only the amount of work you share, but the kind of work you include in your book, as well.

Let's first start with the kind of work to include in your book, because I actually think that is more important than the number of campaigns you end up with. I think that the types of products you have in your book are an indication of how well you understand what your day-to-day life will be like at an agency.

There are millions of products out there. Millions of brands that need advertising, but think back to point number one up there, and remember that you will score big points for solving real marketing problems.

So include campaigns for brands that are in a tough spot, like for product that may be launching in an over-saturated market, or a brand that may be near bankruptcy, or a service that has been challenged by a new, smarter version of itself.

Pick up a publication like the *Wall Street Journal*, read about all the companies that have plummeting stock prices, and really think about why they are in that position. What happened to Blockbuster? What happened to Borders? Will anyone want to spend $200 on a Blackberry one year from now? Could a great marketing campaign have helped save those companies and/or products? Hell, yes!

So when you are creating your book, try to think of some real world brands that are in real world trouble and could use some serious creative problem solving. It's really impressive to see someone take that on in an entry-level portfolio.

In fact, even if the solution isn't perfect, as long as it's not way off base, you will score a lot more points for getting close than you will for nailing an easier assignment.

I can't tell you how many books come through full of ads for easy products like Post-It notes, White-Out, White Strips, Q-tips, name your favorite beer, Ugh! I can't stand it! They all lend themselves to the same type of solution and very rarely make me want to learn anything at all about how your brain works.

But, if you really, really love a campaign you did for an "easy" product and feel like you just might die if you don't put it in your portfolio, then my advice to you is to make sure it is nothing short of awesome. Otherwise you're not going to look smart. In fact, you'll look stupid. Stupid is bad.

Also, when determining your book pieces, think about what categories you see the most advertising for on a daily basis. You probably see a lot of ads for cars, banks, food, toiletries, travel services, insurance, gas, cell phones, and fashion.

If you need more help thinking of categories, go online and look at an award show entry form, like for the One Show or for Cannes, and you'll see the various categories products and services fall into.

Also, as you start to think about brands within these categories to make campaigns for, think about the brands that need advertising the most.

Try not to make campaigns for specialty or high-end brands. Instead, take a stab at the "common folk brands" that are really quite identical to their competitor, otherwise known as parity (not parody) products.

Make those great, and you'll look smart. Smart is good!

Let's talk about the number of pieces to have in your book. I would say that less is more, but I would try not to put any fewer than 4 campaigns in your book. 5 is probably ideal. Any more than that, and I get overwhelmed.

I have to look at portfolios all day long, every day. Keep this in mind. You should also know that no one really likes to look at books. Not even *your* book.

So do a favor and make my job easier, and make it fun, by making your book **smart** and **quick**. It will be hard for you to choose what ends up in your book. It will be hard to eliminate campaigns that you poured your heart and soul into, but self-editing is a very important skill, and your book is the perfect place to start practicing it. That being said, this is probably a good time to mention that most of the ideas that you will have in your advertising lifetime will die. And it will be painful in the moment, but the sooner you accept that, the better off you're going to be. So cull your book down already! Only include work that demonstrates your very best thinking and your very best craftsmanship. Period.

Speaking of **craftsmanship**, something you will quickly learn after you do get your first job is that you've entered an industry full of control freaks. You should also know that most of these control freaks say that your generation can't write or art direct and that there's no more love for the craft. So you've got to prove lots of folks wrong right out of the gate. Something I heard once that really rings true for anyone starting out in any career, but feels especially appropriate when we're talking about craftsmanship, is that it is your number one priority to make your boss's job easier. Always and forever, no matter what. So, if he or she, who is already predisposed to be a control freak about all things creative and crafty, needs to constantly rewrite your copy, or re-do your lay outs, you're not making anyone's job easier. You're doing the opposite of that. Even worse, you're further perpetuating the bashing of your entire generation's craftsmanship skills. Don't do that! That's bad!

Write copy that isn't boring. Write copy that makes folks actually feel something. Besides bored. Life is too damn short to be bored by advertising.

Art direct with style, with attention to detail, and let it show that you are a hands-on, visually inspired person who truly loves to make stuff.

Honestly, if you have the gift to write or to art direct, then you need to love it, treasure it, and nurture it. Whatever you write or design, make it perfect. Then make it more perfect. Then make it even more perfect after that. If this sounds like too much work, do something else. Seriously. There is all this talk about the changing media landscape, that the TV commercial is dead, blah, blah, blah, but even if that nonsense proves true, we'll always need talented craftsmen and women in this business. So love it up, people.

Love it up!

The Person

The most important lesson I've learned over the years of hiring folks is that the best portfolio means nothing if the individual who made it is a jerk. Or can't take feedback. Or complains. Or is lazy. I've heard more than one Chief Creative Officer say that there is a "no asshole policy" when it comes to hiring in their creative department. But on occasion, those a-holes slip through the screening process, and when they do, they make life hell for everyone. Don't be that person. EVER! This is an intense business, but it's also a really fun business. And if you're nice to people, most often times they will be nice back to you. So be appreciative. Be willing to learn. Be willing to change. Be competitive. Be humble. Be hardworking. Be likable. Be lovable! Be a winner. Be thankful that you are in an exciting, ever-changing, fascinating industry, and if you ever get to a place where you can't be, go drive a garbage truck!

Work Steps:

1. **Review your portfolio (yet again).** Get rid of the easy solutions. Then look at the remaining executions. Do they show you know how to solve real marketing problems? If not, broom them, too. Finally, replace your eliminated concepts with smart executions for brands that really need advertising.
2. **Proofread and edit mercilessly.** Make sure the details are all in place, that you only have your best ideas in your portfolio, and that it's easy to get through your work. In other words, edit.
3. **Show you're human.** Your co-workers will be around you for long hours at a time. If you're not likable now, they'll imagine that you're really not likable on the job. The best way to do that: relax, but show you're a hard worker.

━ ━ ━ ━ ━

Kara Taylor graduated from Iowa State University in 1995 with a degree in Journalism and a really bad portfolio. From there, she headed to the big city of Chicago with hopes of becoming an art director at a major advertising firm.

27 bad interviews and no job offers later, Kara gave up on art direction and went to work at JWT as the Executive Assistant to the Chief Creative Officer. One year later, she found herself across town at Leo Burnett eating apples that were never thrown down the elevator shaft and in charge of the agency's award show submissions.

Soon after that, Kara parlayed her newly developed eye for award-winning advertising into the entry-level creative recruiter position. For seven years she traveled across the country critiquing student books that were light years better than hers ever was and hiring the best in class entry-level talent to work for Uncle Leo in Chi-town.

In 2004 Kara left Burnett to be the Director of the Miami Ad School in Minneapolis. Here she recruited students, recruited teachers, taught classes, took out the trash, and on one occasion she even talked the city cops out of issuing a noise ordinance at the school's first Karaoke party.

Kara found herself back in Chicago and at Leo Burnett one year later. This time around she was in charge of hiring all levels of creative talent for the agency. She stayed with Burnett for four more years until CP+B in Boulder, Colorado came calling for a Director of Creative Recruiting.

Kara has been with CP+B since October of 2009. She hires all levels of creative talent for the agency's offices in Boulder, Miami, Los Angeles, Toronto, and London.

Kara lives outside of Boulder with her husband, two young daughters, and two naughty dogs. She is undeniably addicted to Starbuck's Skinny Vanilla Lattes and is obsessed with beating her husband at Words with Friends.

Portfolio Prowess

Frank Blossom
Affiliate Professor Grand Valley State University & Coach, The Polishing Center

This chapter is not a portfolio 101 on how to make a portfolio. You've probably poured through a bunch of other books, articles, and posts on that. This section is how to make your portfolio smarter – key concepts and perspectives to make your portfolio stand out to Creative Directors, your target audience.

First let's take a look at the purpose and perspective of your portfolio or as it's sometimes called your book.

The objective of your book is to move you on to the next level in your job journey – hey, that's the goal of everything in this book, hence the title. You want your portfolio to be smart and engaging, demonstrate your thinking, your skills to get you a face-to-face interview or more likely phone-to-phone.

In most cases, your portfolio alone won't land you the job offer. But it can move you to the next step in your job journey.

What's the perspective of an ad agency?

Agencies look at portfolios to learn about you. They want to know:

- How you think and solve problems through communication
- How you demonstrate your writing or art direction/design skills

How CDs Look at Portfolios

First, they'll look at it online through your website, PDF, or digital mini book. If they like what they see, they'll call you in for an interview.

In the actual interview they look at portfolios the same way they look at magazines or award show books. They flip through the pages to see what catches their attention and what stands out. They don't linger on a page and pour through the ad, studying the copy and design if it doesn't grab them in the first place.

They are very good at discerning smart ideas quickly. That's why they are creative directors. And like all of us, they are time crunched, especially when they have dozens of portfolios to go through, plus their client work and management stuff.

So what does that tell you?

Your concepts must communicate quickly. Develop your ads based on simple ideas – single benefit focused, compelling concepts executed in a smart, unexpected way over a variety of media interaction points. A coordinated campaign delivering one consistent message through a combination of touch points with the target audience.

Each campaign in your book should be built around one core idea. For example: Jimmy John's is fast. Lexus is luxury. Heinz ketchup is slow. Levi's are authentic. Coke is happiness.

> **What's your personal core idea?** It's simple. You are a great copywriter or art director or digital designer or digital media strategist. Your book, like a campaign, should demonstrate it, prove it, and clearly position you as it.

Keep your copy to the point, make each ad easy to read no matter if it's a print ad, banner ad, video, mobile message, outdoor, or guerrilla execution. The power of your ideas is directly proportional to the speed at which they communicate. And best of all, if your ideas are simple, clear, and concise, they'll work well across multiple media platforms. Remember, it has to work well on screen in order to make the cut. K.I.S.S.

How Much to Show?

Just enough to show that you are a smart ad person. Only show strong work. CDs can tell in a few campaigns if they like your work and if it's smart work. That's usually four to six campaigns. Remember, they are time crunched.

Start your portfolio off with your best campaign. Create a positive first impression. First impressions last. Set the expectations high for the rest of your work. Finish with your next best campaign and try not to screw it up in between. This advice, by the way, is Steven Spielberg's strategy for making movies.

Do not show mediocre work just to fill out your book, even if that means you only have a few campaigns. You'll be judged by the weakest work. You do not want to show that you do and are satisfied with mediocre work. If you only show great work, even if it's only a couple of campaigns, what's the perception of you?

Portfolio Mix

Demonstrate your smart thinking and versatility across several categories of products, services, and organizations. Build your book around a mix of consumer products and services, business-to-business products and non-profit organizations.

Show Creative Directors that you can motivate and persuade individuals, organizations, and businesses. Demonstrate that you can create rational and emotional messages. Confirm that you can communicate in different tones of voice based on different target audiences. Prove that you can talk to bankers, boaters, bakers, and snowboarders.

You are positioning yourself as more versatile and giving yourself more opportunities to fit in at an agency. For example, in your portfolio you could have campaigns for a ketchup, bank, forklift, and clean drinking water. You pick the mix; just make sure it's a mix.

Campaign Scope

For each campaign, work across multiple media platforms: print, video, digital. Show your ideas on billboards, TV, packaging, You Tube, magazines, Facebook and other social media, games, radio – you get the idea. Show you can take your simple, core ideas and make them work across a variety of media and touch points.

Common/Uncommon

Most products and services are common, everyday things – blue jeans, shampoo, checking accounts, coffee, bananas, and headlights. They are not glamorous, exciting, one-of-a-kind, uniquely different products and services. They're great for portfolios because you can demonstrate how you can take something common and present it in an uncommon way. You can get the creative director to say, "Wow, I never though of toilet bowl brushes that way."

Avoid doing campaigns for hot sauce, condoms, tattoos, lingerie, hot motorcycles – products that are inherently provocative, interesting, and sexy on their own. Avoid products that have a history of great advertising like Jack Daniels, Absolut, Nike, Apple – products whose ads have become coffee table books, products whose ads regularly show up in award books, because you don't want your work always compared to the best work. Why set yourself up for a comparison you'll probably lose?

Instead focus on common, everyday products and services and present them in uncommon ways. Show what you can do with dish soap, condiments, cereal, plumbing fixtures, kitchen tools, hi-los, lamps, beds, mattresses – you get the idea.

Look in your cleaning closet, under the kitchen sink, laundry room, medicine chest, fresh product department, or office supply store. Find products not known for courageous creative like cleaning products, tractors, insurance, tooth care and get the CD to think, "That's a cool idea for dental floss."

Emotional Consequences

Explore the feelings and emotions that ordinary products can provide or the consequences of not using the products or running out of the product. Got Milk, anyone? Or Tide to Go Instant Stain Remover?

Why do this? It's easier and more fun to do ads for condoms than condensed soup. Exactly, it's easier.

First, most agencies have me-too products and services for clients. Show the agency that you can make them remarkable. Second, as the creative newcomer on the team, you're probably not going to be working on the high-profile products. More likely, you'll be assigned to the common and boring products and services that the senior creatives don't want to work on. Prove them wrong. Show your uncommon stuff.

Spec or Published? Paper or Plastic?

The better question is which is strongest? I repeat, only show your strongest work, regardless of whether they are speculative work (non-published) or produced. Creative Directors know that your job over the last few years has been as a student not a working creative with access to photographers, illustrators, music houses, and production studios. They don't expect you to have finished, produced work.

What they do expect is smart work. Spec or published is not important; smart is the key. One Creative Director said that she's tired of pretty looking ads, what she wants are smart ads.

If you do have published work, and it's smart, focused, well written and art directed, great, show it. But if your published/produced work is mediocre, keep it in the back pocket. Show it only if asked. Acknowledge that it's not great creative; show it as an example that you have worked in that medium or category and know how to put a file together that will print. If it's weak creative, do not put it in your book. Pitch it, or you may get pitched. Remember, you'll be judged by the best work and weakest work in your book. If you don't think it's smart, strong work, it probably isn't; keep working.

Oh Crap! I've Seen It Before.

Research the category of the products or service that your campaign is about. Know your advertising history. If you think that you've seen or heard one of your concepts or headlines before, you probably have. And the CD reviewing your portfolio probably has, too.

So kill, trash, or convert any idea you think may be perceived as a duplicate. You want to position yourself as an original thinker, not a hacker copycat. It's a lot better for you to catch the duplication of thinking than the CD.

Shout Out for Outdoor

Outdoor is a great platform for your portfolio. It forces you to be clear, concise, and strongly visual. But it also communicates like a rocket and makes it easy for creative directors to see your concept. Consider a billboard or poster as the first piece in your campaign to set up the concept and clarify the direction. You'll get the CD on board with your idea before she moves on to the rest of the campaign. And if your idea works in outdoor, it'll work in everything. If it doesn't work in outdoor, figure out why.

Outdoor makes it easy for CDs to understand your concept. And there is so much bad outdoor currently out there, that the bar for you to beat is pretty low.

Type Power

All type campaigns can be all powerful. Good typography is becoming a lost art in advertising. So consider an all type campaign to show either your writing or your understanding of fonts, letter spacing, kerning, etc. Show your design skills without the pizzazz of photos and illustrations. Prove the power of your words. Make the type stand out, and you'll stand out.

Great, thought-provoking copy set in a dramatic way makes for distinctive campaigns. And they're cheap to produce. Take a look at the *Economist* ads. All type and winning all awards. If your concept communicates and engages people in all type, it's a big idea.

Student Tip: "I was in my first year as a junior, junior art director. The only projects I was getting to do on my own were low-budget, all-type. I mean no budget. No money for photos or illustrations. The type was the visual. So I had to make the type work really, really hard. Make it sing. Give it a personality and style. I had to prove I could make great looking ads with just words and fonts so I could move on to bigger work. I did. Now I work with terrific budgets, and I pass the all-type work projects to the juniors working under me."

Portfolio Process

Collaborate. Advertising is a team sport. Creatives work together on projects. So if you're a writer, team up with a designer/art director. And vice versa. You'll both benefit. And you'll both have some of the same stuff in your books. No problem. That's the way the business is, so don't worry; don't think that you have to be the only one doing the ad. Two brains are better than one. Three is even better. Get help; get feedback from peers and pros you meet along the way.

Work out every day. Every day is a portfolio day. Set aside part of each day to work on your book. There's no magic pill for great work. Just hard work. Quality of work comes from quantity of thinking. Write, sketch, design part of each day.

Find your creative time zone – the times of the day when you think best. It might be early mornings, after 5, late night, late mornings. Discover it and book it for your book. Every day. Get in the zone.

Push out 50 headlines for each ad. Review them. Narrow them down to the ten best. Then write ten new versions of each of the ten. Repeat, repeat, and repeat. Same thing with visuals and layouts.

Even if you nail it on the fourth headline or layout, you won't know it's the one, until you've done 30 more. Quantity begets quality. Don't shortcut yourself.

Walk Around Your Work

Tape or pin up your ideas, headlines, and layouts around your house, apartment, or dorm room. On the fridge, bathroom door, windows, walls, closets – anywhere you walk by often. Ideas look different on paper than on screen, and you'll see them differently in different forms. You'll see patterns and combinations that make for better concepts. Your subconscious will make connections that will amaze you. Amaze creative directors, too. Put it up; give your brain some time the percolate.

Agencies and design studios do it with their work as part of their creative process. Why not you?

Fit & Finish

Creative Directors do not expect expensive, original photos, illustrations, music tracks, and other costly production techniques in student or young creative's portfolios. You barely have enough money for pizza and beer, let alone high end advertising production.

What they do expect and what they want to hire is smart, original thinking. Focus on your ideas. Focus on making your work smart. Sweat the communication details. Make everything on the page or screen count. Use stock photos, clip art, borrowed music tracks, great type – whatever it takes to make your ideas communicate.

Progression Portfolio

Creative Directors are looking at your book to learn how you think. So show them. Show a campaign start to finish. Begin with your initial thumbnails, headlines, and layouts. Show how you edited and refined them leading up to the finished pieces. Share the journey of how you evaluated ideas and executions, tried different approaches, decided what was good and what was better to get to the finished piece.

This tactic works for ad campaigns, logos, design pieces, web designs, videos – any piece in your book. It's one of the best demonstrations of your concepting progression. And as you'll read in the side bar, it's a way to increase your odds of getting hired.

Student Tip: "The creative director was rifling through my portfolio, barely glancing at each page. He just kept mumbling, ' Yeah, yeah, OK, Not bad.' He clearly was not impressed. After the last ad, he noticed some tissues and thumbnails stuffed in the back pocket. He pulled them out and started looking at them, slowly as he said, 'These are interesting. Tell me about them.' I did. He said, 'Come in Monday at 9.' I did."

Boring Risk

Do some of your campaigns make you a little nervous? They should. Safe, boring work is much too comfortable. No risk, no reward. Show the CD that you can "wild it out." Creative Directors want to know that you can push the edges, provoke thought and interest with work that is out there. Why? Because they know they can always pull you back a little. They want to know that you have the capacity to really stretch your work. If you were too safe, you would be a risky hire. At least one of your campaigns should have some edge, some tension to it.

Big Finish - There Isn't Any

There is no big finish for your portfolio. No all-encompassing, super nova, creative, magical secret to success. It's just you. And it's a continuing work in progress. So work it. The secret to great portfolio work is work. Quantity of ideas leads to quality of ideas.

Great portfolios don't come from books about portfolios. They come from you. These points will make your book smarter. But you will make it great. You'll get out of your portfolio exactly what you put into it. Get to work.

Work Steps:

1. **Pick a common product** that you really like, always buy, always use.
2. **Write down why you like, use, prefer it.** How does it make you feel when you buy it? How does it make you feel when you can't get it? Don't worry about spelling, grammar, etc. Just write; get your

thoughts down. Fill at least a page. Read it.

3. **Read the entire package.** If your product has a package, what surprises you? Interests you? Write it down. Read it.

4. **Walk away.** Do something else that gives your brain a chance to percolate.

5. **Reread everything.** Discover the core reason why you like this product.

6. **Write a concise statement of your core reason.**

7. **Start writing headlines**, tag lines that capture that core reason.

8. **Sketch out thumbnails** that relate to that core reason.

9. **Repeat.** Repeat. Repeat.

10. **Don't throw anything away.**

Student Work Shouldn't Look like School Work

Jeffrey Epstein
Founder, Chicago Portfolio School

That's the message at the cleverly named Chicago Portfolio School. We bet you can guess where it is and what it does. However, there may be a few other things that are not quite so obvious. Fortunately, Jeff Epstein, the school's founder, is here to offer some advice that may help clarify a complicated world. And, to offer further assistance in getting you ready for that business world to come, it's in a memo.

From: Jeffrey Epstein jeff@chicagoportfolio.com
To: You
Subject: Have you ever seen the movie *Jerry Maguire*?

Hi,

In the movie, Jerry was a sports agent who wrote a Mission Statement called "The Things We Think But Do Not Say."

This is sort of like that. I am writing down the things that keep me up at night, knowing that people have trusted me/my school with the fantastic responsibility of helping them get the job of their dreams.

Every day, I think how to make our school, our instructors, and our students' portfolios better. (No, I didn't write this at 2 am after eating bad pizza like Jerry.)

So help me help you. Here's what I mean ...

It's about the Work.
How good is good?
Campaigns are Ideas, not lines.
Digital/Social/Ambient.
Not so many opinions.
Attendance.
Side Projects.

It's Always about the Work.

Work is how your portfolio is judged; it's how our school is judged. The purpose of this email is to explain to you how to make your work better, which makes the job of getting a job easier.

You will all profit from setting high standards and trying to live and work to them. For instance, telling people/partners you think something is not good enough or smart enough shouldn't be a choice - it's a responsibility. And it should never be taken personally. It's just about the Work.

Don't Let "Like" or "Good" Get in the Way of "Love" or "Great."

If an instructor or reviewer says they "like" something, they are most likely just being polite. Too polite for your own good. You want them to say they "f'ing love" it! You need them to say "That will win an award!" It has to be so good that the next day they tell folks at their job how great it was. Trust me, that's EXACTLY what happens when they see something great; ask them. You need these kind of Campaign Ideas to make a book.

Campaigns Are Things That Have Ideas.

What's the Idea? What's the Concept? What's the Strategy? These are three ways of asking the same thing...what's the f'ing point? Why should a Brand spend millions of dollars to do what you are proposing?

If I ask, "What's your Idea?" I'm not asking for a description of a visual or a recitation of the tag or a description of the execution. I want to know what about the Campaign Idea makes me think better of the Brand. How it will sell more stuff. How it tells me something I didn't know. How it makes me think the Brand is better and cooler for doing it.

This isn't creative writing, people! We're not making things up. Your Ideas need to be true and relevant. You have to know what you're talking about to find a Big Idea. That means homework/research/brainwork. Every portfolio needs four to six Campaigns based on Ideas that are smart.

If I Hear "It Doesn't Need a Headline" One More Time, I'm Going to Scream.

The visual is one part of the story. A headline is needed to tell the rest. If you can't think of an interesting headline that says something true and relevant about the product, then kill the Idea. Put it out of its misery.

A Tagline Is Not the First or Second...or Even Third... Thing You Think Of

It's the last. Please take the time you would have used thinking of a tag and use it to make more, better executions.

A Significant Portion of Every Portfolio Has to Be Digital, Social, and Ambient.

There are thousands of channels to execute in these days. Your campaign needs to have executions in more than a few, and the ones you choose will be judged for cleverness and appropriateness. This means 30% of the pieces minimum. This isn't new news, it's two-year-old news.

To Make Your Work Better, Stop Asking Everyone for an Opinion.

Just ask one or two people whose work you respect. You need a permanent review committee. Think of it as a Supreme Court of reviewers who will provide continuity and the highest standards in the land.

A Recent Grad Finished Her Portfolio in 14 Months.

She was an Art Director student, and she was offered a few really good jobs including an AD job at a mainstream agency, Designer job at an Interactive agency, and an AD internship at Crispin. She took a job at Digital Kitchen, an internationally known motion graphics design house. I asked her how she finished ahead of schedule, and she wrote me a two-page letter explaining her secrets.

Here are the highlights:
- Treat every assignment like it is going in your book.
- Take extra classes (or alternative classes), and treat those assignments as portfolio pieces, as well.
- Respect your teachers.
- Work on Saturdays. Work on Sundays.
- Set up your site early.
- Nothing is ever truly finished; everything can be made better.
- Give yourself a Side Project.
- Have a blast.

FYI, she rarely missed a class, but when she did, she ALWAYS emailed the instructor ahead of time. And she still did the work assigned.

Go to Every Class. Do Every Assignment.

Students who go to every class and do every assignment get jobs significantly faster than those who don't. It's a fact; we see it every day. Treat this thing like a job, and you will find a great one.

What Is a Side Project?

More and more frequently, portfolios feature samples that aren't exactly marketing communication but are best described as "entrepreneurial spirit meets passion project." For instance, one of our students, Kelly Pratt, started *Stately Sandwiches*, a project to cook, eat, and design posters for sandwiches from all 50 States. Her website is *statelysandwiches.com*. Her posters were blogged by Rachael Ray and picked up by Fab.com. Yes, she sold a lot of posters, but this project will be a very successful campaign in her book. Nice work, Kelly!

Last winter another student, Jake Reilly, decided to forgo all means of modern communication for 3 months. That meant no cell, no e-mail, no internet – just old fashion paper, pen, and landline. He called it *The Amish Project* and journaled throughout. When it was over, he posted his journal and a video. It was picked up by Yahoo News, *Chicago Sun Times*, and TV news shows all over the world.

What a fun and funny idea! I wish I'd thought of that! He immediately booked interviews at a few agencies and was hired the next week at Leo Burnett. Good job, Jake!

Let's Talk about It.

I know you have all invested a lot of time, energy, money, and thought into this tremendous undertaking. Please e-mail me anytime with questions, comments, etc. I want to hear your ideas so we can move ahead quickly with making your work great.

My Inbox is always open.

Thanks, Jeff Epstein
jeff@chicagoporfolio.com

P.S. If I say I like something … I'm not being polite. I really mean it!

Work Steps:

Let's review Jeff's memo and see how you measure up.

1. **Work.** OK, whatcha got? How do you think it measures up?

2. **Think again.** How good is good? Is it as good as the competition? If not, what do you think we can do about it?

3. **Get to the core.** Create ideas, not lines. What's the idea at the core of each of your campaigns? Can you communicate that idea quickly, clearly, and powerfully? What did you do to expand that idea?

4. **Expand.** Digital/Social/Ambient. Do your campaign ideas grow into these categories?

5. **Get the right feedback.** Who has the opinions you really value? What are they?

6. **Attend.** Are you in the habit of taking advantage of every opportunity? If not, why not?

7. **Be comprehensive.** You're the one in charge of making everything better and getting that job. How are you doing? How can you dial it up to the next level?

— — — — — —

Jeffrey Epstein has been a copywriter and a Creative Director for small, medium, and large agencies like Scali, TBWA, and Leo Burnett making radio, TV, and print advertising for clients like Miller, McDonald's, and Nikon. He has won awards, and his work has appeared in Communication Arts *and* One Show. *He started Chicago Portfolio School to be the kind of portfolio school he'd want to go to if he were in your shoes. Because, a million years ago, he was.*

Chicago Portfolio School
Sure, we're a Portfolio School for Advertising, Design, and Web Design. But really we're an Idea School. We believe Concept is King and Content is… King, too.

The Top Ten Mistakes in Portfolio Development

Suzanne Pope
Freelance Copywriter & Creative Director

Her name is Suzanne Pope. She has been writing ads for 20+ years. She started a blog to provide free advice and instruction to young people in advertising. She hopes it helps.

This piece originally appeared on ihaveanidea.org in 2005 and, more recently, on my blog at AdTeachings.com. It's published here in an updated form.

The late film critic Pauline Kael once wrote that she never lost her childlike enthusiasm for movies, even though watching them was her job. Each time the house lights dimmed, she still felt a rush of anticipation over what the next two hours might bring.

Miss Kael did not go on to describe how her feelings would change once the movie started, but I can guess. I'm thinking that nine times out of ten, that happy hopefulness would leak out abruptly, leaving her crumpled in her seat like a soufflé baked in a thunderstorm.

And that is roughly what it's like for most creative directors viewing most portfolios. When they lift the faux-leather cover to expose the first plastic sleeve, they'll never reveal what is in their hearts, but it's there all the same: an unabashed yearning to see greatness. Greatness wrapped in freshness. Greatness delivered with a deft touch that restores their love and hope for this business and all the life-affirming things it can achieve.

And then they see your first ad. The one with the condom. Or perhaps the one with the pun. (Or perhaps, as I saw many years ago, the ad with the condom *and* the pun.)

And that's when the soaring anticipation departs. Yes, in body, the creative director is still flipping the acetate pages, but in soul, he's every bit as dead as Pauline Kael. You have stolen the Shetland pony from his inner child, and by God, you are going to pay.

In some countries, the creative director might punish you with blunt cruelty. I cannot speak authoritatively about this because I live in Canada, where we're much gentler about these things. In Canada, he'll opt instead to make you feel encouraged. He'll murmur appreciatively at anything vaguely approaching an idea. He'll suggest a deletion or two in the kindest possible terms. He'll end the meeting by tousling your hair and urging you to keep pushing.

What he won't say is that you can use his name to get time with other CDs in town. What he won't say is that he's eager to see how your work develops over the next six months, so please stay in touch. And through the things he doesn't say, there's a message you should be getting loud and clear, albeit in Canadian: The quality of your work is buried deeply in the fattest part of the bell curve, and if you don't move it to the desirably thin end of the chart, your ad career will be spent inputting the price points on pizza flyers.

Make no mistake. This brand of kindness is ultimately the most cruel because it leaves the young creative satisfied with a mediocre book that's indistinguishable from the hundreds of other mediocre books floating around town. It is equivalent to letting someone leave the house with spinach in his teeth or a mucosal crouton lodged in one nostril.

To get the job you want, you must differentiate your work from what your peers are presenting. To start, you must avoid the top ten mistakes in portfolio development.

Mistake #10: Failing to Take the Hint When It's Time to Pull an Ad

Sometimes, the hint is obvious. The creative director says, "I think you should take this ad out of your book." If you hear that more than once, please take the advice.

But sometimes the hint is less obvious. The CD will praise an ad mildly or say nothing at all. That kind of lukewarm response tells you that your ad is doing nothing to make your talent stand out, and you should consider replacing it.

I can hear what you're thinking right now: "Wait a minute. I don't have a single ad that's been strongly praised by a creative director. Are you saying I have to replace every single ad in my book?"

Yes.

That is what I am saying.

Maybe not this weekend, but definitely over the next few months. Remember, when a CD describes your work as "solid," it's almost never a compliment.

Mistake #9: Investing More in the Execution Than You Did in the Idea

Several years ago, I saw a junior writer whose portfolio was not good at all. What made our meeting even more uncomfortable was the way he defended every sad page in his book. This guy was particularly intent on arguing the merits of a nonsensical ad that happened to be nicely illustrated. When I suggested that he pull the ad from his book, he got angry and told me he didn't want to because … wait for it … *the illustration had cost him 300 bucks!*

If you have an idea for a portfolio piece, and you think you need more than lunch money to bring it to life, there should be loud warning bells sounding in your head. First of all, the truest test of a great idea is its ability to communicate even when rendered with stick-figure drawings. (Luke Sullivan illustrated this point quite literally in his classic book, *Hey, Whipple, Squeeze This.*)

Secondly, to improve your book substantially, you should get into the mental habit of seeing your ads not as part of a permanent collection, but rather, as disposable and easily replaced with better ads. This trick of the mind will serve you well throughout your career because the most successful ad people are the ones who can return to the well time after time without fearing that it's going to run dry.

Mistake #8: Arguing with the Person Whose Feedback You've Solicited

This one is as puzzling as it is common. Somebody makes an appointment, ostensibly to get advice and criticism that will result in an improved book. But it quickly becomes clear that this person is prepared to hear only good things about his or her work. If you recognize yourself in this description, you need a different way of reacting to criticism, preferably one that involves smiling and nodding and saying, "I see." The fact is, anyone who argues during a portfolio viewing is displaying a personality that is ill suited to the realities of agency life. Our best ideas get rejected every single day, often for reasons that are exasperatingly stupid. Smart ad people don't waste time or energy prolonging the argument. They go back and they dig a little deeper. I think it was Lee Clow who said, "The best revenge is a better ad."

I also believe this argumentativeness often comes not from a passionate belief in our ads but from the secret terror that we won't find any other ideas to replace the lame ones on view. This very isolating malaise is actually shared by more people than you'd think. I'll discuss some solutions in the final section of this article.

Mistake #7: Including Scripts for TV or Radio

It's been said that a play exists only when it's performed. The same goes for a TV or radio commercial. Without the nuances of performance, sound design, editing, and so forth, your script might not even be understood, let alone admired. You'll know what I mean if you've ever tried to figure out an award-winning spot just from the script that's printed in the annual. If all you have is a really great print book, you already have everything you need.

Mistake #6: Failing to Show That You're Comfortable Handling Copy

The past fifteen years have been very kind to us copywriters. We've been able to fit the copy for a year's worth of print on the back of a bar bill, with room left over to calculate the tip. In the era of the visual pun, most of the responsibility for execution has been offloaded to art directors and Photoshop.

But to build an impressive book, you must show that you're able to write more than six words of copy at a time. This is partly because visual puns are now commonly dismissed as lazy and formulaic. More to the point, though, the ad with six words of copy does not reflect the reality of what ad agencies spend most of their time doing.

When you start agency life, you may be surprised at how often you're asked to do sales brochures, web content, retail ads, and so on – all of which will require you to craft paragraphs or pages of copy that is concise, logical, and persuasive. This basic skill could once be taken for granted among copywriters, but it's become so depressingly rare that it must now be demonstrated in your book.

Here are a couple of tips to make the task less daunting. First, remember that writing is almost always improved by editing. So if your art director needs 250 words for the layout, discipline yourself to write at least 400. Then start trimming. As the fat drops away from your sales argument, you will start to see ways to tighten your copy and make it stronger than it would have been had you just stuck to 250 words from the start.

Another tip: Buy yourself a copy of *The National Enquirer* or some other supermarket tabloid. Once you're done parsing evidence of infidelity and liposuction, turn to one of the full-page ads for weight-loss gimmicks, copper bracelets, or psychic guidance. Don't laugh. The people who write these ads know what they're doing. They have to sell 500 Praying Hands figurines every week, and they're sure not going to do it on looks. These guys have figured out how to present a compelling written sales argument – to people who can barely read! You'll never see these writers in Cannes, but you would do well to study their techniques. You will start to get a feel for how to build your copy in such a way that factual logic ("Only 500 of these exquisite plates will be crafted!") works in tandem with emotional logic ("What could be more charming than the sight of a toddler who's collapsed, exhausted, in a basket of dachshund pups? Now imagine having that scene preserved forever on your very own Collectors' Edition plate!"). You will also learn how to take what is essentially one long argument and break it up into digestible bits that allow the reader to feel more in control of her decision. You will see how the subheads that divide up the copy actually deliver a kind of shorthand version of the sales pitch so that the main message is gleaned even by those who won't read the body copy. You'll also see how the core message gets echoed in the little captions accompanying the many copy-warming visuals. If you think these techniques are solely the province of mail-order bottom-feeders, you are mistaken. Your first brochure for Prada or Mercedes-Benz will go a lot more smoothly if you're not too proud to learn from The Franklin Mint. The only differences are in the level of diction and graphic sophistication. That's all.

Mistake #5: Digging Deeper into Annuals Than You Do into Yourself

As a child, hockey great Wayne Gretzky got some brilliant advice from his father: "Don't skate to where the puck has been – skate to where it's going to be."

Many creatives won't sit down to work without a stack of annuals by their side. They are effectively circling places where the puck hasn't been seen for, oh, about five or six years now.

Relying on annuals actually makes it harder to write ads. You may well end up with nothing more than an acute awareness of all the great ideas that can't be used because they've already been done.

No less an authority than Bob Barrie has gone on record as discouraging the use of annuals in creative development. He prefers browsing through stock photography for his inspiration. Clearly, it's worked okay for him.

Mistake #4: Including Ads That Rely on Bad Puns

Everyone who knows enough to visit this blog knows that you're not supposed to have puns in your book. Everyone knows that they're corny and dated and sad. And yet every junior book has at least one. This is because puns are the crack cocaine of advertising. They fill us with the euphoric certainty that nothing has ever been so funny and that this tumescent boil of brilliance deserves to be lanced in public.

But before you succumb to that impulse, please make yourself aware of how high the bar is set and of the risks in attempting to clear it. I offer for your consideration three award-winning puns from that golden age of copywriting, the 1980s. This first headline appeared in an ad for Honda (for the Accord, I believe):

Send in the clones.

This next one promoted a $29 pair of sunglasses:

A shade under $30.

This final line was written to sell tickets for the One Show awards dinner:

Another great evening of whining and dining.

You know what? These are really good headlines. They're funny and clear, and #1 and #3 are actually quite insightful. So I would say that puns are okay as long as you can make them good. And how do you do that? By making sure they kick both ways. When a pun kicks both ways, it makes sense no matter how it's read. So in the One Show example above, we know that wine will be served, and we also know that there will be complaining. Thus, the pun kicks both ways. Now, here's a student headline featuring a pun that most decidedly does not kick both ways:

Striking writers.

The writer wished to communicate that the writing in *The Economist* really grabs people's attention. So far, so good. However, if we interpret the pun the other way, we're being told that *The Economist's* writers are refusing to work – which is just about 180º from the intended message. Thus, the pun is the kind of confusing groaner that should never be in your book.

Mistake #3: Including Any Ad Concerning Spousal Abuse, Sexually Transmitted Diseases, Crystal Meth or Doggie Daycare

The reasons for avoiding these ads actually contradict each other. On one hand, pro-bono and boutique clients are deemed to be more inherently interesting than, say, dishwasher detergent or shaving cream. So the reasoning goes, you're making it too easy on yourself. You're not demonstrating that you know how to create attention for the sorts of clients you're most likely to be serving.

On the other hand, the best work in the pro-bono category shows that it's anything but easy. The bar is set so high that anything falling short will look doubly inept.

Whatever argument you buy, you will have a more impressive book if you avoid this well-trodden turf.

Mistake #2: Failing to Check Spelling

Creative directors aren't typically pedantic, but they sure understand the implications of spelling mistakes in your portfolio. If you're not double-checking your work when you have all the time in the world, how careful will you be when you're scrambling to meet a deadline?

Checking spelling is quite different from using Spell Check. Spell Check cannot clear up any uncertainty you might feel around the following words:

- it's its
- their they're there
- your you're
- whose who's

I could go on, but I'm sensing your fatigue. Let me refresh your spirit with a little story.

Many years ago, I worked with a respected copywriter who managed to misspell a word in the headline of a four-colour ad. The film house (ask your parents) had to do a whole new set of separations for a bunch of different publications. The bill was something like $8,000. The agency chose to compound its embarrassment by asking the client to split the cost. *You approved the final art,* the agency argued, *and so the mistake is partly your fault.* Not surprisingly, the client disagreed. *You presented yourselves as communications professionals,* he said, *and I took you at your word. If your writers can't spell, that's not my problem.*

And so the agency swallowed the write-off, and the writer got treated to a full and frank monologue from our creative director. Some of you will no doubt feel this was unfair, that the writer's serenity should not have been pierced by these petty workaday concerns, that the quality reaming-out should have been reserved for the proofreader in the studio. Maybe you're right. But any time you're involved in an $8,000 write-off, believe me, you'll be invited to share in the blame.

For those of you who remain unconvinced, here's one final thought. The creative director will have an easier time finding money for your raise if you haven't already blown it in write-offs.

Mistake #1: Treating Your Portfolio as a Destination instead of a Journey

This is by far the most common mistake. It afflicts people at every stage of their careers, but it will hurt you most when you are young and unknown.

Putting together a portfolio is exhausting and time-consuming. When you're finally done, you will feel as if you've run a marathon with an anvil strapped to each thigh. Because you are a normal human being, you will feel no desire to experience this pain ever again.

And because you don't wish to feel more pain, you will keep ads in your book longer than you should (Mistake #10). You will quarrel with those who criticize your work (Mistake #8). You will overspend on your ideas so that you have an excuse for hanging on to them (Mistake #9).

And so you'll go, quite convinced of the rightness of your approach, but also quite unemployed.

To get out of this mess – or avoid it in the first place – you must find a way to produce more ideas. To do that, you must find a way to counter the pessimism so common among those who have to be creative on demand. Earlier in this article, I described a mental habit, a trick of the mind, that treats great ideas as being easy to generate. I called it a trick of the mind because everybody knows it's not true. Nobody actually thinks ideas are easy. And so we must find a way to fool ourselves, if only for a while. This is why coaches give pep talks before every game. This is why corporations spend so much money on motivational speakers. Does positive thinking guarantee success? Um, no. But it works a lot better than despair.

There's a book you might find helpful in adopting this trick of the mind. It's *The Artist's Way* by Julia Cameron. I must warn you, though: if touchy-feely New Age rhetoric annoys you, you will find this book remarkably irksome. In fact, you should just skip over the next paragraph right now, because what I'm about to say will make you feel like you're prepping for a colonoscopy. No, seriously. I'll meet you down the page in a minute.

Okay, so here's the deal. Julia Cameron worked in Hollywood for many years as a screenwriter. She suffered from severe writer's block and began drinking heavily with the idea that it would make her more creative. Eventually, she realized that alcohol was actually making things worse, so she entered a twelve-step program. It was there that Cameron began to develop the theory that all forms of creative blockage are, like alcoholism, a disease of the soul and a way of avoiding emotional pain. So, she reasoned, if Alcoholics Anonymous works for drinkers, why not have a similar program for the blocked artist? (To Cameron, the term "artist" can apply equally well to a writer, painter, plumber, or chartered accountant.)

And so she created a twelve-step program to get all of us to believe in our creativity again, or believe in it for the first time in our lives. Central to her ideas is the notion that we must reacquaint ourselves with our natural creativity by subjecting it to a daily workout. Thus, we're asked to keep a journal in which we force ourselves to write daily. The writings can be good, bad, or beyond awful. It doesn't matter, just as long as we keep doing it. As with strength training, what's excruciating at the start eventually becomes almost effortless.

A way of applying this technique directly to advertising is to make yourself write three to five ads every day. There are no rules. Puns are a-okay. Do ads for any client you like – heck, even a condom manufacturer. Then, shove your scribbles in a drawer and don't look at them for a month. The exercise will help you get used to generating creative on demand – something you'll be asked to do daily once you're hired.

To those of you who've rejoined us, a hearty welcome back! There's another technique available for generating ads, and it's one you might find more practical and palatable. It involves approaching your portfolio as you would a musical instrument or a sport. If you sat down at your piano or went to the driving range just three or four times a year, your hopes of excelling would be rightfully modest. Yet people who visit their portfolios that infrequently still think the quality of their work is competitive. As an experiment in terror, why not try "practicing" your book for half an hour every day? You will be surprised at how quickly you improve.

And if you do choose to think of your book as a musical instrument, I have some additional reassurance to offer. I am now in my ninth year of guitar lessons. It's always difficult and sometimes discouraging. A long time ago, my teacher took pity on me and scribbled out a couple of charts to show me how learning music differs from other kinds of learning.

This first chart reflects how most people develop expertise in math or history or macramé. You study, you build on acquired knowledge to gather even more knowledge, and over time, your skills and confidence increase.

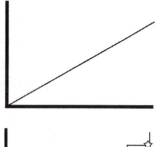

By contrast, the learning curve in music looks more like a broken staircase.

To progress in music, you have to tolerate long periods when you're sure you're not making any progress at all. As a matter of fact, there will even be times (as highlighted by the tiny stars) when you feel your skills are actually in decline. But these are the moments when you

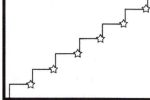

should feel most hopeful, because they typically come right before sudden spurts of new ability. I believe our skill in making ads develops in much the same way. The time you invest in thinking about your portfolio will never go to waste. It may not offer an immediate payoff, but it's still part of what will take you to your next plateau.

To the outsider who wants in, advertising seems as nasty as a high school clique. You're told that you will win or lose based on merit, but no one can tell you exactly how your merit will express itself. It's either in your book or it isn't. But the comforting truth is that improving your book has less to do with talent than it does with tenacity. And pigheaded determination will serve you long after you get your first job. Sometimes, advertising is about taking a good brief and turning it into great ads. More often, though, it's about recognizing small opportunities that twinkle faintly amidst imperfect circumstances. It's about seizing those opportunities and refusing to let go until you've taken them as far as they can possibly go. It's about cultivating the kind of personal initiative that used to be called gumption. That's what advertising is really about. Ask the people who are in it.

They just might quote Pauline Kael: "Where there is a will, there is a way. If there is a chance in a million that you can do something, anything, to keep what you want from ending, do it. Pry the door open or, if need be, wedge your foot in that door and keep it open."

Work Steps:

1. **Check the list:** Suzanne identified ten portfolio mistakes beginners tend to make. Reflect on your portfolio as well as your performance during interviews as you review her list. How many mistakes have you made? Identify them so you can correct them.
2. **Include copy:** For writers, that means you need to have long copy writing sample copy. For art directors, it means you need to be able to show you can design pieces that contain long copy. Yes, this was an issue identified on Suzanne's list, but it's an important one and easily fixable. So fix it.
3. **Check the puns:** Look at all of the ads in your portfolio that contains puns. Do they sell? Are they better than the ones Suzanne showed in the essay? If so, keep. If not, broom them from your book.
4. **Do it daily:** Suzanne mentioned the need to be able to create on demand. It's true. Creating on demand is part of your job description. So get ready for it by trying her exercise every day.
5. **Keep editing:** If you don't get a positive reaction to something, don't keep it in your book (at least as is). No matter how much time or money you spent creating it. It's that simple.

6.   **Follow Suzanne's blog:** It's called adteachings.com, and it's filled with great ideas and advice for young people trying to make a name for themselves in our industry.

— — — — — —

Freelance copywriter and creative director **Suzanne Pope** *is the founder of AdTeachings.com, a website devoted to the training of young creatives. Over the past 25 years, Suzanne's work has been recognized by the One Show,* Communication Arts, *the London International Advertising Awards, and* Lürzer's Archive, *among others.*

Pre-Screen Interviews: How You Can Approach a Pre-Screen Interview with an Advertising Agency

Lena Woo
Manager, Human Resources,
Commonground Marketing

Okay, so the agency has reviewed your portfolio and you've been invited to meet with a creative recruiter. They want to connect you and the work you've done to see if the fit will be right. Now what? Let's find out from the creative recruiter for one of the nation's fastest growing agencies, Commonground Marketing.

Getting ready for the pre-screen can send butterflies into one's stomach. A lot of advertising agencies conduct them over the phone, so it is often met with uncertainty about how to best demonstrate your phone charisma! But, at the same time, it's the first meeting, the first introduction -- stop and give yourself credit for even reaching this point!

Get Smart on the Agency

The best way to prepare for a phone screen is to get smart on the agency. Put less focus on you, since you already know your resumé like the back of your hand. If you crack down on knowing as much as you can about the agency, you will be well-informed. The more you know about the agency, the more you can be a "fan" of it. This can put you on a more level playing field, since both you and the interviewer will share that common interest. The dynamics may even turn favorably into more of a conversation versus an interview.

Craft Your Questions

Once you're well-familiarized with the agency, develop the questions you will ask during the interview. The quality of the questions cannot be underrated. It's about the strategic thoughtfulness that informs the question, providing an opportunity to stand out from other candidates. Infuse your dialogue with that knowledge. Do not do a straight "lift" of the verbiage you may have found on the website, because that is merely regurgitation. Instead, take the information and customize it with your own skills/background. Or use the information to formulate more in-depth questions. By doing so, you can show true rigor and insight.

Agency Information	Standard Question	Thoughtful Question
"Commonground Marketing understands the 'new marketplace' is an exciting and complex world of opportunity for brands and clients that recognize and embrace change."*	"I read on the website about the 'new market-place' and would like to know more about that principle. Can you please expand on that?"	"I have heard about the 'new marketplace' and wondered how you apply this to the everyday regimen when working with clients?"
"We are a culturally and professionally diverse group of opportunity seekers."*	"Can you please talk more about the culture that's described on your website?"	"I enjoy a lot of outdoor activities and team sports and hope that dynamic is something I could add to or help foster at CG. Would that outlook fit well with the current culture?"

* Excerpt from http://discovercg.com/

Honing In on the "Hard" and "Soft" Aspects

When it comes to agencies, the areas to hone in on are the "hard" and "soft" elements. "Hard" would be the factual information (e.g., what is the agency's client roster? What is their media expertise?) The "soft" elements refer to the kinds of leaders who run the agency, the caliber and quality of the employees, the culture -- basically, the aspects of the agency that shape the energy and dynamics of working there. Is it a creatively inspired agency? (e.g., are they more Mac than Microsoft?)

Treat the Interviewer the Way You Would Treat a Client

One of the main soft skills I tend to ascertain within the first five minutes is how well the candidate puts me at ease. This is due to the fact that agencies are in the business of client service, so I need to believe that the candidate has the capability to take care of others. It takes a certain level of ingenuity to have the conversation be about yourself (because it is an interview), but deflect the attention to make it about the agency. This is what client service is about: possessing an opinion, delivering your point of view, but making it about the client and their business.

Show Your Thirst for Knowledge

Another "soft" element to focus on is how you approach the conversation. If nothing else, be inquisitive. Be hungry to learn about the agency because yet again, a client would expect you to have an unquenchable thirst to better their business. If that natural curiosity is evident in the pre-screen, I, as the interviewer, can envision the candidate having that same power to draw in a client and be credible as their agency partner.

Close with Positive Energy

When you come to the end of your interview, it's always recommended to be courteous! The style in which you do that would ideally strike a balance of both professionalism and personable attitudes. Just as you would a client, you would want to leave on a note of positive energy. For example, there's a difference between saying, "I look forward to hearing back from you and your agency once you make a decision moving forward with another round of interviews," vs., "I have really enjoyed talking with you and learning more about the agency, thank you for taking the time." The former statement makes it about you. The latter second statement still manages to accomplish the objective of expressing your interest in hearing back, while positioning it in a way that is complimentary about the interviewer/the agency.

Work Steps:

Getting ready for the interview is as easy as 1, 2, 3 (and 4 and 5).

1. **Review your notes.** Remember when you researched the agencies and marketers back in Section II and started a folder of notes? Now

is the perfect time to crack open that folder and look over the notes so you come across as educated on the market. It's that simple.

2. **Learn more.** Now study the agency's website. Google them to see what the press is saying about them. And you might even want to ask your teachers about the firm (they might know someone there). Another good source: classmates and friends, because some might have even interviewed there).

3. **Ask questions.** What do you want to know? Now is the time to craft your questions. Be sure to make them thoughtful.

4. **Psych up.** You need to believe in yourself to have energy and for the recruiter to believe in you, too.

5. **Say thanks.** If you want to work at the agency, you need to let the recruiter know. And, if not, you need to show that you still appreciate the recruiter's time. After all, it's a small industry, and people talk. You never know who will refer you to another agency.

━ ━ ━ ━ ━ ━

Lena Woo has built her career on a love for talent management and a commitment to playing an integral role in establishing an organizational culture of excellence. Lena is the Director of People & Culture for Chicago-based Commonground Marketing, an agency with a creative spirit that transcends traditional agencies. Lena is responsible for working with agency leadership to drive Commonground's commitment to hire, manage, and retain top talent.

In her years of working with and recruiting exceptional people, Lena has mastered the art of striking a delicate balance between the human connection and the technical aspects of her role in HR. Lena is adept at identifying outstanding people for specific positions within the agency. She is also well versed in creative problem solving, team building, and developing goals that impact the health of the agency.

Before joining Commonground, Lena served as human resources talent manager for DraftFCB where she helped manage talent assessments, rotation, and employee relations for the account management department.

Prior, Lena worked as recruiting manager for Broadpath Healthcare Solutions, managing the full life cycle of recruitment that ultimately improved business productivity and overall profitability, hiring more than 200 employees within one year.

Lena spent more than ten years in account management with agencies including Leo Burnett, DDB, and Ogilvy & Mather where she managed account responsibilities, identified new business opportunities, fostered client partnerships, and provided strategic direction to help guide the creative development, production, and media processes. Over the course of her career in account management, Lena's range of client experience on Sears, Kraft Foods, General Mills, Allstate Insurance, Maytag, and Kellogg's gave her a unique understanding of team dynamics and its impact on work productivity.

Prior to developing her account management expertise, Lena was a buyer for Marshall Field's.

Create Yourself

Dan Balser
Advertising Department Head,
Creative Circus

It seems that no matter how long they've been working or how recently they've been hired, people can't help but talk about change.

Wonder if they're trying to tell us something?

Here, we asked one of the leading Portfolio Schools to give us their take on what it takes in today's marketplace.

Things used to be simpler.

When my peers and I started out as writers and art directors in the early 90s, all we really needed was a portfolio of smart thinking and spec ads that looked real. A portfolio (and I do mean portfolio, all twenty pounds of it) with tight comps and compelling copy was a ticket to employment.

Now, not so much. Now the job of schools like The Creative Circus is more than merely teaching craft. It is now the job of instructors — and subsequently creative directors and mentors — to inspire, enlighten, and motivate a creative to do what it takes, not only to show how you think but also to stand out.

A few years ago a great agency in Portland, Oregon called Wieden + Kennedy started looking at students' books and asking, "What else ya' got?" They wanted to see more than how well a creative did her class assignments; they wanted to see the creative herself. They wanted to see passion, invention, emotion — the stuff of true creativity. After all, the root of the word is, well, *create*.

As usual, W+K was on to something. Today almost every agency wants to see "what else ya' got." They want to know what you'll bring to the party. They want energy, originality and fearlessness.

So if you are committing yourself to the pursuit of a creative career, you are now obligated to see your ideas — even the tiny, throwaway, "dumb" ideas — through to completion. To be successful, you can never utter the words "I ought to." Only say "I'm going to."

Have an idea for a video? Make the video. Have an idea for a T-shirt? Make it. *Do not allow your lack of knowledge about how to make T-shirts stop you.* Otherwise, your idea remains a non-existent, irrelevant wisp.

An idea has no inherent value. But the thing that comes from an idea — now, that's worth something.

I know about following through, because now I consciously, actively, often painfully, do it. But I didn't always.

I vividly remember the day I began executing my ideas instead of merely killing them. It started in a class I was teaching. (This is a whole other story about how much we learn by sharing our knowledge with others, but I digress.)

Anyway, in my classes, I spend the first thirty minutes or so each week passionately talking about career and industry stuff like working with partners, dealing with clients, hitting creative dry spells, horrible kerning in billboards around town, anything and everything both relevant and less-apparently relevant. Those stories are often about my own experiences, sometimes from meetings or issues I've had that week.

One afternoon I stopped mid-rant and asked the class, "Does anyone here care about this at all, or am I just talking to the brick wall?" One student, a talented young designer named Nate Milheim, sat up and said, "No, we love this stuff! We wish all of our teachers would tell us what it's like to actually work in this business!"

That was the moment for me. That was the first time I ever said, "I will" and not "I ought to." I decided right then that I would start an ad-biz podcast. After all, I do like to talk, right? So I would sit down with guests — friends, former bosses, clients, partners, anyone who was willing — to talk with me about their careers. And I would record it and post it online. I would call the show *Don't Get Me Started,* as a reference to my class rants.

That was five years and 125 episodes ago. The podcast has become a valuable asset for The Creative Circus. I have gotten to talk with some pretty big names in advertising, including Dan Wieden himself. And listeners like Nate Milheim can hear, firsthand, what it's like to work in advertising.

Plus — and this is no small thing — the podcast is the only project of significance I have ever worked on in my 25-year career for which I have complete creative control. I am not saying that to boast but to acknowledge the fact that if you are going into a career where you'll be creative for a living, it's not a great idea to rely on your job to scratch your creative itch. It took me a decade to realize that.

At an agency or studio you will answer, rightfully so, to your Creative Director, Account Manager, and Partner. And your agency will answer to its clients. You will be a professional, crafting others' messages with skill. It's fun, a blast actually. But it's never, really, 100% yours.

So pay attention to those flickers of inspiration that appear in your mental periphery. They could lead you somewhere that defines your career or gives you creative control and fulfillment that a job may not be able to provide.

And speaking of jobs, you won't even get one without that one thing that makes you memorable. Strive to be the "guy with the T-shirt company" that a creative department talks about or the woman with that really cool tumblr 3D photo blog that designers forward to each other. You don't have to know where an idea will take you, but you must be willing to discover what it can be.

Which leads me to my final bit of advice to anyone who wants to be relevant in the field of communication arts.

Do stuff. Sign up for things that, at their face value, may not make sense to you.

Doing things like FourSquare, Klout, Viddy, Tout, or Tweekly (and hundreds of other tools, plugins, apps, and services) may be a fool's folly for accountants and lawyers. But as a creative who will be tasked with crafting real messages to real people in a real culture, you need to know how the real world works.

You need to be of your time, and that means being literate, not because you read something in *Fast Company*, but because you actually use Spotify, create your own memes, send JibJab cards, and have six photo apps on your smart phone. You need to use them *to know how it feels to use them*.

It may be clichéd to say that people want you, the younger generation, because you are tech savvy. But since that is often the expectation, you better be prepared to deliver. You need to be the guy in the Cake song who "can access information, make them see that you're the best."

Things used to be simpler. But things now are actually better. It is an incredibly exciting time to begin a creative career. There are more ways to interact, consume, sell, perform, learn, share, create and earn than ever before in human history.

So follow through. On your idea, and on the ideas, experiences, and culture that's being created around you. It's the only way to be relevant, to stand out, and to truly — for lack of a better word — create.

Work Steps:

1. **Show more.** In the words of W+K, what can you show besides a lot of things that look like advertising ideas? How do we meet the interesting person who is you?

2. **Turn your idea into something.** Again, a nice image of that idea sitting in your portfolio is all well and good. But what if you turn it into something that escapes the limits of your portfolio and enters the world? Go for it.

3. **Do stuff.** In creative careers, we learn by doing – not just by thinking stuff up. And, near as we can figure, the more we do, the better we get at thinking stuff up. So… don't just sit there … do something!

- - - - - -

Dan Balser is Advertising Department Head at the Creative Circus in Atlanta. Thanks to the Internet and Dan himself, you can acquire almost as much Balser as you can stand at balserville.com

There you will find Don't Get Me Started, *a biweekly conversation about the industry and the people who populate it.*

Your Other Portfolio

Brendan Watson
Director of Education
The Art Directors Club

*If you want a long career as a creative profes-
sional in advertising or a related field, you truly
need a life beyond it. In the previous essay, Dan
Balser talked about the need for you to go be-
yond your portfolio with side projects that make you memorable. Here,
Brendan Watson talks about the need to continue pursuing your outside
interests – and even wrapping it up into a "second" portfolio.*

So you have a great book, but what else can you show me?

Sadistic as it may sound, this is a question that has become commonplace
in advertising interviews. There once was a time that having a book full of big
ideas executed to near agency quality was a golden ticket to a plush agency gig,
but now it is simply the cost of entry, and a bare minimum at that. More and
more agencies are looking for your "other portfolio," a catchall that speaks to
something that is representative of your interests outside of advertising.

Sure your book looks great, but what fuels your creativity? Don't say advertising, because you'll be running on empty in no time.

Advertising is an all-consuming business. It will take whatever you're
willing to give and then take some more. It demands every waking moment,
and so often we oblige without questioning it. So if the thought of pursuing
something else, even as a hobby, makes you a bit twitchy, you're not alone.

Factories keep track of days passed without an injury, agencies should do
the same for months passed without a day off. The framed pictures adoring
workstations, presumably there to remind people what their families look
like, should be accompanied by photos of paintbrushes, cameras, and other
symbols of creative pursuits long since abandoned.

A common misconception is that to succeed in advertising you must
dedicate your life to it. It's a myth that is perpetuated by the very people who
live it everyday. Sure there are those who have made it to the top by doing just

that, but on the fringes of the limelight you will find many more who burned out along the way with nothing to show for it.

Agencies are looking for creatives with depth and dimension – thankfully, for the sake of your sanity and longevity, this is something you should be looking for in yourself as well. Your other portfolio isn't an exercise in being creative for the sake of being creative – it's a pursuit that will ultimately come back full circle to help with your agency job.

Gone are the days that art directors just art directed and copywriters just wrote. Additionally, creative departments are no longer exclusively made up of those two crafts. Boardrooms and brainstorms are now being shared with creative technologists, developers, and others who not long ago didn't even appear on the agency directory. Creative solutions are no longer the exclusive domain of art directors and writers, so it will be those who can solve a problem three dimensionally that will survive. However, the mental gymnastics required inside the agency are impossible to achieve without challenging your brain outside of the agency.

Think of your other portfolio as a portal to the real world, with regular people. The fact is, while agencies are great places to work, the company you keep rarely represents an accurate cross section of any target market you'd ever find on a creative brief – unless you're working on the agency summer party invite.

Much like your advertising portfolio, there is no magic formula for your other portfolio. In fact, it is even more vague. At least rough guidelines exist for the composition of advertising portfolios, but since your other portfolio is a representation of an interest outside of the business, it could take any number of forms.

Typically it won't even look like a portfolio at all. For some people it's a blog, for others it's a Flickr account. It it might be an album, or a guest column on a culinary website. Fortunately, there are no rules. It just needs to be a concrete answer to the all too important question, so you have a great book, but what else can you show me?

Work Steps:

You want a long career? Start here.

1. **Assemble your stuff.** Make a list of your outside hobbies and projects. All of them. Think back. Are you missing something? What

is a small, insignificant activity to you might actually be the key to setting yourself apart with a prospective employer. Your on-target and taste-inducing Yelp reviews, for instance, might be the key for getting hired as a writer on a fast food account. Or your interest in home repair might just show that you uniquely understand the target audience for Home Depot.

2. **Organize your samples.** What are they? What is the theme that runs through them? Which ones do you consider to be the best examples of your skills and interests? Do they tell a story about your skills, interests, motivations, and abilities? Find the arc of the story and put them in that order. It doesn't have to be in chronological order. It just has to be told in a way that helps people understand you and what you'll bring to your job and career.

3. **Polish this portfolio.** What media best tells your story? It could be printed examples, photos, video, audio, or some combination. It could be "flat" or interactive. If you don't have the skills to bring them alive in these media, get your friends who are skilled in them to help you. After all, these projects just might help them augment their portfolios.

4. **Show it off.** Where should your "second" portfolio live? It could simply live on your blog or be displayed in a printed portfolio or on Pinterest or YouTube – you name it. Just make sure that the medium enables you to easily show it and talk about it during your interview.

— — — — — —

Brendan Watson is inspired on a daily basis and as such feels indebted to the programs he oversees at the Art Directors Club, namely Young Guns and Portfolio Night. He came to the ADC by way of ihaveanidea, which he started working with when it was still referred to as "Canada's Advertising Intellectual Archive." Since then, he balanced his educationally focused position at ihaveanidea with agency jobs as Art Director at Bensimon Byrne, Y&R, and Twist Image. The union of the ADC and ihaveandea presented the irresistible opportunity for Brendan to take his passion for education full-time.

The Secrets of Getting a Job in the Nasty World of Advertising, Design, and Copywriting

Rich Binell
Get Rich Quick,
former Copy Chief, Apple Computer

Editors' Note: This is an article about getting an advertising copywriting job, but actually, the author, Rich Binell, ended up with one of the very best creative writing jobs in collateral – not advertising. He was Copy Chief at Apple Computer's in-house Creative Services department.

Still, this is a great article with useful advice and a good job-hunting strategy, but <u>please</u> take it with at least two grains of salt.

***Grain of salt #1** – understand that the good job you get might not be in "the nasty world of advertising, design, and copywriting." That is where Rich started, but not where he ended up.*

***Grain of salt #2** – Please don't be an obnoxious stalker, despite Rich's passionate good advice. He's absolutely right about the idea of identifying the people you want to work for and learn from. But not every dream is supposed to come true, and not every award-winning writer or designer wants you to camp out on their doorstep. Sometimes you really do have to take no for an answer and move on.*

Rich is a terrific writer. He graduated from Harvard and ended up writing at a small Boston ad agency. There, he did one of the world's best brochures for an early piece of Apple compatible software, and Apple decided he was very compatible.

Rich ended up working for them for quite a few years, where he was the top copywriter at their in-house department.

He is now one of the major "go to" guys in the West Coast world of software and technology, where he delivers his usual smart advice and smart writing for an ever-changing world of software, start-ups, and state-of-the-art secret stuff.

Oh, and one more thing.
Thanks, Rich

I have some secrets to reveal about this, because this is how I actually—accidentally—did it myself.

Be warned. This is not easy. And it is for people with strong constitutions who don't just *want* to do great work.

This is for people who actually would *make serious sacrifices* to learn to do great work.

I had a spec portfolio.

I couldn't get a job with a spec portfolio. I showed my spec portfolio to 40 people. I finally gave up and said, "I'm going to the top. I'm going to talk to the best people in town. I'm going to throw myself at their feet."

It was an accident in my case. I didn't have a crazy person like Rich Binell telling me it would work.

I was desperate, so I did it by accident. I'm begging you not to do it by accident.

The First Secret: You Must Choose Who You Will Work ror, qnd They Must Be 5he Absolute Best People

So, first you must pick these people carefully. You must find your favorite campaigns and find out who did them. Hunt them down. Locate the people who did the work you love.

If you're not sure where to find work you love, start with those big fat design and advertising annuals and awards books.

These reference books will help you get the names of the people who do the work that you respect.

The other way you can do it is to check your own file of the work that you really love—the work that kills you—and hunt down the people who did it. It might take ten phone calls, but you can find them if you try.

If you don't have a file of work you love, then start one today.

Then what do you do.

You decide whether or not you can bear to live in the city where that person works.

It gets pretty cold in places where really good people seem to work: Minneapolis, Chicago, or Boston.

The Second Secret: Do Your Damnedest to Become That Person's Slave, Assistant, or Right Hand Person

Why?

Because write this on your heart: You can learn more in one year from somebody who you respect and who does brilliant work than you can do in the rest of your life from someone from whom you took any old job because it was in front of you.

Guide yourself. Pick the people you want to work for or with and make yourself known to them.

Tell them who you are. Tell them you respect their work. Tell them you think it matters. Tell them you can't wait to get out of the hell hole you're in so that you can come and be a prostitute for them.

They may not give you a job, but if you pester them enough and you're hanging around enough, when they have an opening, you may be the person they call, and that will make your life far different than if you take a job doing paste-ups of PowerPoint presentations for anybody and stop looking.

This is possible.

By the way. I have done paste-ups of PowerPoint presentations for a crappy place.

It sucked.

The Third Secret: You Have to Convince the Person You Choose of Just Two Things

One: That you can do really good work when you must, so you need to have a portfolio that proves that you are capable.

Two: No, it's not optimism. It's passion.

Passion, passion, passion.

You have to want it—bad. You have to want to do great work. You have to want to work with great people. And you have to tell them that you are there to do exactly that.

And that you will stop at nothing to do that.

And that you will start doing anything that they want you to do, that you know better than to go work for some terrible firm in Pocatello when you ought to be working at their—place that does great work—in Chicago.

The Fourth Secret: You Must Make That Person Understand That You Will Not Give Up

You must show up, you must camp out, you must send them a letter every day, you must mail them your work every time you turn out work, and you must cut out their ads and frame them and mail them to them and tell them why you love that work.

You wrack your brain to get in front of that person and make yourself indispensable.

Why?

Because that person will be flattered.

Why?

Because that person may think you're crazy but that you actually want a job really badly doing really great work.

Remember: You are never going to do really great work pasting up PowerPoint presentations. It's not going to happen. You will get no portfolio pieces doing that.

Am I telling you the truth?

Yes.

I got my first job this way.

The Fifth Secret: Offer to Work Cheap

I found the best place in the town I was in, walked in and showed them my portfolio, and said, "I will work for you for my rent money this month."

I told them exactly how much it cost me to rent my house and said, "You pay me that; I will work for you for a month."

Yes. They told me I was nuts.

Four days later they hired me. Two weeks later they put me on staff.

I got to work for the people whose work I most admired—including the most wonderful person I've ever met in my life.

And I worked there for three years.

When I left there, Apple hired me, gave me a huge raise, moved me to California and pretty much cemented my career.

All because I was crazy enough to walk into the best place in town and say, "I will do almost anything to work here, but I can't afford to work for free. You have to pay my rent for me this month."

This is not a secret: This worked for me.

I don't see any reason why it wouldn't work for you.

Work Steps:

Let's give a little more thought to Rich's five "secrets."

1. **Find your ideal.** Who do you want to work for? Have you given it some thought? How would you identify those people and places? How would you find out more?

2. **Strategize.** How would you make an effective approach to that person or place? What are their needs?

3. **Demonstrate that you are the person that they want to hire.** In addition to your portfolio, what pieces or actions can help demonstrate that you are that person?

4. **Be tenacious.** How do you demonstrate that in a good way? Remember, nobody wants a crazy stalker. Hint: Start early. If you're in your junior year and you say that you'd like to work for someone a year from now, that allows for a well-organized, non-threatening communication program. Another point – Rich talks about passion. We want people who care. We don't want people who are crazy.

5. **Create a budget.** Can you afford to do this? If you can get them to like you and appreciate you, there is a chance that you can make at least starvation wages. A chance. Again, by starting as early as possible, you have a better chance of making this work.

Final thoughts on Rich's good advice. This can be an excellent strategy. You identify winners in the marketplace – people who can help you improve your skills, and you focus on getting to know them, finding out what they need, and working to demonstrate that you can meet those needs. Even if this ultimately is not how and where things work out, you will have learned some important things about the marketplace and developed your desirability. Or if you were a total failure on all counts … well, you learned your limits.

- - - - - - - - - - - - -

Rich Binell thinks for a living slightly south of Silicon Valley and way above average.

Section IV:
On the Job

"You will be judged by your worst work."

Larissa Brandao, Senior Designer, Momentum

Even though you probably don't have a job yet, we're going to focus on a few things you'll need to deal with once you cross that threshold.

- We'll launch you with some thoughts from Bart Cleveland of Job Propulsion Laboratories. In "Make or Break. Break or Make," he offers some valuable advice on getting the right start on your career path.

- Next, Clifton Simmons II, a successful survivor of the intern to real job career path, has some advice – though, instead of taking it with a grain of salt, you might want some ice and extra napkins. It's called "Heavy Drinking: What I Learned as an Ad Intern."

- He's back! Frank Blossom of The Polishing Center offers us some "Internship Intel," with tips on how to turn an internship into a full-time job.

- For reasons you will soon realize, this is one of those articles where we went back and forth on – do we keep it or do we pull it? It's by a unique talent – Thomas Kemeny – who went from school and internships into some of the very top creative agencies. We decided that someone like that has something to teach us all. That said, you might want to bring along some extra perspective when you read his piece on, "Your Joyously Short Career."

- Cabell Harris teaches at VCU BrandCenter, one of the top programs in the universe, and he has a company called WORK. Simple. To the point. Cabell offers some spot-on observations about the agency environment – all agency environments. Along the way he offers some more good advice about the work habits that go with a successful career.

- Tim Leake offers some advice we really like. "Don't 'Get' a Job. Create One." This is a business that respects initiative. Tim gets us thinking about some new ways to put new initiatives into that getting-a-job job of yours.
- How good is your work? How do you know? Here, Nancy Tag, author of *Ad Critique: How to Deconstruct Ads in order to Build Better Advertising* gives you an introductory course in these valuable and necessary skills – learning how to make your own work better – and recognizing what's good in other work.
- Sometimes good advice is not good advice all the time. Here, Nancy Vonk, co-author of *Pick Me* (a book you should read), an integral part of "Ask Jancy" on ihaveanidea.org and co-founder of Swim, the creative leadership training lab, takes time from what is obviously a very leisurely schedule, to offer us the very useful and slightly counter-intuitive "Say Yes to No." Read it wisely.
- This book does not have separate doors marked "Men" and "Women," but as you travel your career path, you may find something quite like it. This thought-provoking piece by Karen Mallia sheds some light on some important issues.
- All right, you're almost done with this wonderful book – but not quite. Professor Brett Robbs gives you something more to ponder in "It's About More Than It's About," and then Bruce Bendinger recycles an article that appeared in *CMYK* and on TalentZoo, "The Game behind the Game."
- Speaking of *CMYK* and Talent Zoo, they're both great resources, and we've added them and a few other important resources in an end section we have cleverly titled "Resources."

Make or Break. Break or Make.

Bart Cleveland
Founder, Job Propulsion Labs

We wonder. Can you handle one more essay packed with good advice? We hope so. Because you need it.

Frankly, we weren't quite sure how to handle this one. It's good advice on the habits you'll need to get good enough to get that first job – but it's also good advice on the habits you'll need to keep that first job. We considered printing it twice.

The person who wrote it – Bart Cleveland – is not from there.

He has made a career out of defying the line, "Those who can't, teach." Because he can. And does.

He is one of the reasons that Creative Circus, Miami Ad School, and the VCU Brand Center turn out creatives who get jobs.

These days he runs a place called Job Propulsion Labs. His company has a simple mission: revolutionize the ad industry by empowering its professionals to successfully manage their careers. Welcome to Cleveland.

In the movie *Orange County* actor Jack Black plays a flunky, the older brother of high-schooler Colin Hanks. Hanks's character dreams of attending Stanford University where he will learn how to become a great writer at the feet of an author he worships. Black drives Hanks to Stanford to convince the dean that he should be accepted to the prestigious school. On the way, Black explains to his younger brother how he's going to do something with his life as well. He has all of these great ideas, and he just needs a break.

These two characters are not much different from most young people entering the advertising industry. Both have dreams and passion to achieve something. But Black's character expects success to fall in his lap, while Hanks's character realizes his efforts need guidance if he is to truly achieve something. There are far too many of the former coming into our industry. They see their dreams chopped and pureéd and end up giving up.

Don't think that a graduation ceremony for higher education is the ticket to success in this business. Even the best advertising programs are a foundation and nothing more. If anything it has simply baited a hook, and you, the fledgling, are the worm.

I doubt anyone reading this book has a career goal of obscurity. On the contrary, what makes advertising so alluring is its potential for fame. We crave recognition for our creativity and unique way of thinking. We pride ourselves in being innovative problem solvers. Most of all we want to change the world. Or at least we want to affect culture so significantly we change the conversation. Basically, we want to be relevant.

This is why we admire those who have done such things. When I entered the business, our heroes were men like Bill Bernbach, George Lois, and younger men like Lee Clow, Jeff Goodby, Hal Riney, and a guy named Tom McElligott. Today people are following another generation with the same zeal. But like my heroes, those who will change the rules, the new game changers, do not follow. So if you plan to change the world, you need to start with your career. Or more specifically, your career plan.

Ninety-nine percent. This is not a reference to Occupy Wall Street. It's the odds of you achieving a career of obscurity. I doubt many reading this have heard of me. Yet I've won hundreds of awards, including dozens of awards in admired shows such as The One Show and D&AD. So obscurity isn't about success alone. It's about being known by those that you most need to know you. To be recognized by the right people means being in the position to get the right job and the right opportunities to realize one's potential.

The graphic on the following page represents the first three jobs of an advertising career. Notice what happens after job number two. Job number one can be the wrong job: bad boss, bad work, horrible environment. You survive. You get another job. Job number two can also be the wrong job: more bad work, politics, and drama. You survive. You get another job. But something critical happens.

The Abyss.

At job number two there is a "Y" in the road. Both paths lead to another job: one good, one bad. Between the paths is an abyss that separates the haves from the have-nots. Fame from obscurity. Opportunity from drudgery. The longer you travel down the path of obscurity, the further you are from any hope of success.

Everyone's advertising career path

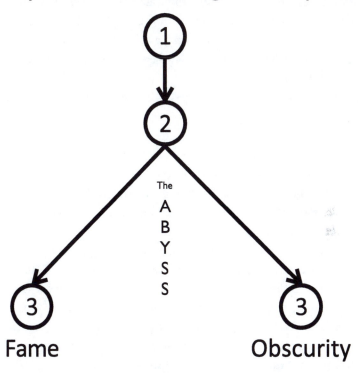

Here's the real scary part. If job number three is bad, you can pretty much kiss your chance to be a one-show-pencil-laden creative goodbye. Here's more bad news: jobs number one and two determine the kind number three will be.

Here's the secret to success: between jobs one and two you can only make one bad choice.

Even though going to the right school is critical, it isn't a failsafe. The only way to ensure you're going to get the shot you deserve is to have a plan. The right plan for you.

To find out if you have the right plan, answer a few questions:

- Name the company where you most wish to work.
- Why? Give me three or four reasons.
- Do those reasons ensure you will succeed there?
- What qualifies you to work there?

More than likely you have the same top three or four names on question number one as 98% of your peers. Think about it. How many of you are going to get hired? Most "hot" places are hiring a handful per year, and they have people lined up that are already working at hot shops. The hot shops love to hire from each other. The logic is that when a person's been vetted by another hot shop, they are less of a risk.

So if you've tried and failed to get into your dream job, answer these questions:

- What *really* kept you from getting a job there?
- Did you ask for a reason?
- If you got one, did you believe it?
- If not, what do you believe is the real reason?

Having trouble with answers? Here are some you can borrow. "My work isn't as good as I thought." "I acted entitled to work there." "They said, I was good but they just didn't have anything, and I believed them."

So you didn't get the dream job. There are other jobs. Jobs that are stepping-stones to the dream job. So you take the job, you play it smart, humbly learning as much as you can. Work hard, be professional, win a few key awards, and your dream agency will take a true interest in you. There are many stepping-stone agencies out there. Most are not in big markets. So broaden your horizon from the usual suspects. Realize that good agencies are almost as tough to get into as the famous shops. Don't overestimate your value to such establishments. They don't need your brilliance as much as you need their opportunities.

Let's say you get a job at a stepping-stone agency. How could you blow it? How have you blown things before? Don't know? Sure you do. Your mother has told you most of your life why you blow it. Your girlfriend or boyfriend told you. Your best friend told you. Your shift manager at McDonald's told you.

You know. You have an Achilles' heel. It may be pride, or laziness, or a lack of discipline. It hasn't cost you a lot in the past. But it will cost you everything if you don't slay the beast. The window of opportunity in this business is narrow. Being fat-headed is a stupid reason for not succeeding.

Failure will not be because they wouldn't give you the chance to shine. Or politics. Or ego. Talent and hard work trumps all of that.

Your only hope is yourself. School is over my friend. You can still win, but it's up to you and only you. Well, not just you. You need mentors. People who can help you see the way and give you a few opportunities. But in the end, success begins and ends with you.

To help you start down the path to Fame, answer one more question. What stands between you and where you want to be? Hint: It could be not being in the right place at the right time. Not having a book that reveals your full potential. It might even be the economy. But, most of the time, it's you. Overestimating yourself and underestimating the difficulty to succeed will put most of you in the position. Whatever it is, have a plan to overcome it.

Here's how:

1. **Get brutally honest assessments of your work.**

    Be forewarned: You are not going to get an honest assessment 98% of the time. Some don't want to be the bearer of bad news. Others believe that if you're not there now, you never will be. And a few don't think you're worth the time.

    Prove them wrong.

2. **After the tears, fix what's wrong.**

    This may take time, so chip away at it every day until you do what it takes to improve your work. Be really nice to people who can help you, and they might continue to nurture you along the way.

3. **Don't blow an interview because you don't understand the company's culture.**

    You may love a company's work. You may idolize people that work there. But until you really know their culture, you won't have a chance of being a part of it.

    Know how they dress, talk, joke, play, sleep, eat, watch TV, go to the bathroom, and, most importantly, work. No matter how much a place says they want unique individuals working for them, they really want people like them.

4. **Play nice.**

    The hardest place to play nice is a place that does play nice. So the best thing you can do for yourself in this regard is to work at a place that doesn't tempt you to do otherwise.

5. **Plan the career you want. Execute it, not yourself.**

    Success doesn't happen by chance. Neither does failure. Advertising isn't a friend. It's a foe that should be conquered and enslaved to serve you. You're in control if you want to be.

You make your own luck. So fire up the boilers and get busy.

Work Steps:

Let's put Bart's advice to work. **Complete this form.**

---

1. **Where:** Name the company where you most wish to work.

   _____

   _____

2. **Why:** (List four reasons.)

   1 _____

   2 _____

   3 _____

   4 _____

   Then answer:

   Do those reasons ensure you will succeed there? (Y / N)

   Why: _____

   _____

3. **What:** (Explain why you're qualified to work there. Be specific):

   _____

   _____

4. **What 2.0:** What is really keeping you from getting a job there?

   _____

   _____

5. **Why Explained:**

   Did you ask for a reason? (Y / N)

   If you got one, do you believe it? (Y / N)

   If not, what do you believe is the real reason? _____

   _____

6. **How:** Identify what you need to do to correct the reason(s) you didn't get the job. _____

   _____

— — — — — —

After a thirty-year career of creating award-winning advertising for companies including Coca-Cola, The Ritz-Carlton, CNN, Cartoon Network, DuPont, and Bloomberg, **Bart Cleveland** founded Job Propulsion Laboratories. The company has a simple mission: revolutionize the ad industry by empowering its professionals to successfully manage their careers.

As a creative leader at agencies such as Saatchi & Saatchi, Falgren, Sawyer Riley Compton, and his own McKee Wallwork Cleveland, Bart mentored dozens of young professionals, guiding them to award-winning careers at hot agencies and companies such as Goodby Silverstein, RPA, Wieden & Kennedy, Mother NY, Crispin Porter + Bogusky, The Martin Agency, Coca-Cola, Cartoon Network, and FedEx. He has been an instructor or guest lecturer at the industry's leading advertising schools and professional organizations including The One Club, VCU Brandcenter, Miami Ad School, Creative Circus, and a myriad of local advertising clubs.

Job Propulsion Laboratories has a simple mission: Revolutionize the ad industry by empowering professionals to successfully manage their careers. The Austin, Texas based company works with people from any location. By designing a comprehensive plan that targets companies that best fit the individual's personality and skills, Job Propulsion Labs helps reshape a career to its maximum potential. Giving control over one's career, whether it be at a premier ad or digital agency, or a leading company such as Google Labs, Apple, or Facebook, has made Job Propulsion Labs a critical tool for success in the rapidly changing advertising industry.

Heavy Drinking:
What I Learned as an Ad Intern

Photo Credit: Michael Durr

Clifton Simmons II
Chicago-area Copywriter and Advertising Blogger

You might have heard that internships are valuable. They're really great "teachers." So if you haven't had one yet, get one. But in the meantime, here are some of the lessons Clifton learned in his internships. (By the way, even if you've completed an internship or two or three, there are still valuable lessons here.) So read on!

Treat internships like potato chips and peanuts – don't stop with just one. In fact, while you're sampling the plain chips, reach for a bag of barbecue. And why stick with peanuts when you can have a bowl of mixed nuts?

So what's this food analogy leading to? Well it's easy to say, "I want to work in advertising." But that's as vague as saying, "I want to be a doctor." What kind of doctor? A pediatrician? Brain surgeon? A vet?

There are many facets of the advertising business – business-to-consumer (b-to-c), business-to-business (b-to-b), event marketing, traditional (TV, radio, print), digital, and the list goes on. How familiar are you with any of them? Everything about advertising will not appeal to everyone. There are people who create TV spots with zero interest in the shopper marketing experience. And I know digital people, for example, who could care less about working on commercials. (Gasp!) Yes, not everyone wants to be Don Draper.

So wouldn't it be great if you had first-hand experience with each marketing field? And wouldn't it be helpful to know what kind of job you're applying for instead of taking any position, only to discover you hate the work? Wouldn't you prefer taking a position, knowing you may have a future there, instead of making a bad decision that leaves you questioning your degree and career choice? Personally, I feel an internship helps dress up a sparse resumé.

Yes, you've demonstrated some enthusiasm by gaining some experience. Internships help you figure out what part of this business you really have a taste for. Plain or Barbecue? While in college (and after), I had six internships, and each one taught me something about where I wanted to be specifically in this business.

Lesson 1: Internships Give You Direction

I actually stumbled into advertising. It was my series of internships that led me to my career choice. In college, I was a journalism major. My goal was to write for a magazine like *Rolling Stone*. So when I accepted my first internship with AAA Michigan, it was with the lofty goal of writing features for their magazine *Michigan Living*. But I didn't write features. I was "stuck" in the classified section, writing headlines and short copy about special events and various things. In other words, I was writing ads, but I didn't understand what a copywriter was at that time. And as an unknowingly budding copywriter, I wrote like a junior writer, making all the beginner mistakes – headlines and copy full of puns, innuendos, and sarcasm. Still, it was my attempt to add some fun to the grunt work.

As a result, I got a lot of compliments about what I was doing. But note: this wasn't an ad agency. Their idea of a good ad was far different from someone in the ad biz (a lesson I'd painfully learn later).

So one day, my supervisor told me that one of my ads was featured on *The Tonight Show* in one of Jay Leno's "Headlines" segments. I panicked and waited to be fired because I thought that part of the show made fun of bad writing and editing. Apparently, the person who sent the clip thought one of my snarky little ads was funny – and so did Leno, I assumed. Unfortunately, I never saw the segment, but I was digging all of the accolades I received from the ad. It even lead to me writing AAA announcer scripts for Detroit radio. (And to this day, I love writing radio ads slightly more than TV.) So by the time I "earned" an assignment to write a magazine article, it felt surprisingly anti-climatic. There was something appealing about this ad business, and I wanted another taste.

Lesson 2: Develop a Thick Skin

My summer internship at D'Arcy Masius Benton & Bowles (DMB&B) was when I started drinking – Pepto Bismol straight from the bottle. I was sure that job was going to give me an ulcer by September. It seemed like I never did anything right. AAA Michigan had mislead me. And for the entire summer, I really thought I didn't have what it took to be in advertising.

I should have known from the interview that this internship expected more from me. That summer, I worked for a creative director (CD) we'll call "Ron." Ron was an import from St. Louis who did some iconic beer campaigns. Naturally, I was in awe – I was learning from a Jedi Master. After reviewing my portfolio, he said he was going to do more than teach me the ways of the word; he also brought me on to prove a point: minorities make good creatives.

Thatt was the summer of 1989. The ad industry had always been criticized for its less diverse hiring practices (and still is today), but I was shocked to actually hear a creative director say that many decision makers firmly believed that many minorities had no business swimming in the talent pool.

Great. So I couldn't be just another intern. I was now Martin Luther Ogilvy, leading creative people of color to the promised land. No pressure there. So I accepted to be part of his social experiment. Why? At my alma mater, Wayne State University in Detroit, I was a member of a scholarship program now known as the Journalism Institute for Media Diversity (JIM), designed to encourage diversity in communication fields. DMB&B were sponsors of the program, giving the university another company to place interns. Plus, DMB&B was a major Detroit agency (Cadillac, Pontiac, FTD), so I'd have been crazy not to take advantage of the learning opportunity.

Immediately, I "learned" that I sucked as a copywriter.

All of the "witty" writing I learned from my first internship was "lazy" and "uninspiring" by Ron's standards. My headlines were too "punny." I wrote radio that made him want to change the station. And if he found a misspelling, well, it wasn't pretty.

Every day my work was criticized. Then I'd sulk away and drown my stomach pains in Pepto. I really wanted to quit, but I felt I owed it to JIM to tough it out.

On the last week of my internship, another CD asked me to work on a new Mr. Goodwrench campaign. I pitched a campaign with the tag line, *"It's not your car, it's your freedom."* Heads nodded around the room. They liked one commercial script in particular, featuring a young man leaving home and Dad getting him off to a good start by getting his son's car checked out by Mr.

Goodwrench. One copywriter told me later that I outdid some of the other creative teams. But when I shared the news with Ron, he said my scripts were "predictable."

Maybe they were, but I didn't realize it at the time. That's when I snapped. There was one week left to my internship, so I didn't care if I got fired. Normally, I'd just take his abuse and drown my anger in Pepto, but this time I defended my work, and I showed him it was on strategy. I wasn't punny. *I was funny.*

That's when Ron smiled.

Strange man.

On my last day, Ron called me into his office. Wearing that same smile, he said he was proud of me. He spent a whole summer trying to "break me," and was proud that I didn't quit. He said he loved my creativity and thinking. But I learned that summer that being creative was not always enough.

"You need a tough skin in this business," he said. Clients can be harsh. Bosses can be difficult. This is a business where you better get used to hearing "no" more than "yes." And a lot of people won't be kind about it. Still, you're expected to take their abuse and face those clients again and again until you've solved the problem.

Although his teaching method was cold, it's probably one of the more valuable lessons I learned as an intern. And no, I didn't lead the revolution of change in hiring practices, but hopefully I opened a few eyes and changed some minds. *"It's not just your car, it's your freedom"* became a campaign for Mr. Goodwrench. And I had my first commercial reel. Not bad for a college sophomore.

Lesson 3: You Don't Have to Work at an Ad Agency to Do Ad Work

When I returned to school in the fall, I found a job at Little Caesar's Enterprises – not slinging pizzas – but as a writer. That's when I discovered in-house advertising.

Many companies do their own marketing. They don't always rely on agencies. Little Caesar's did both. Years ago, Cliff Freeman and Partners was doing some hilarious stuff for them. I got to write the coupon ads – yes, someone actually creates coupon pages.

So if you're narrowing your sites solely on ad agencies for work, you're missing out on big opportunities. Back in the day, ad snobs used to tell me that in-house was for creatives who couldn't cut it at a real agency. That couldn't be further from the truth. TV. Digital. Print. Events. Many companies do it themselves and do it well. On the plus side, you're more likely to get your work produced because, in some cases, you have fewer layers of approvals. On the negative side, you don't work with a variety of clients – just one. (Good thing I loved pizza.)

Remember, corporate communications is not "settling" because you can't get an ad agency job. Depending on the position, it can be an advertising job without the ad agency.

Lesson 4: Internships Get You Hired

Businesses hire their interns, people. They don't hire all of them, so don't take offense if they don't keep you after you've worked your butt off. I was fortunate to get a job offer – twice at the same ad agency.

I took a summer internship at Ross Roy (now known as BBDO) writing ads for Kmart and Chrysler. It was also the summer I was introduced to event marketing working on auto shows. When August rolled around, there was talk about a junior copywriter position opening up. The only thing that prevented me from accepting it was that I was only a junior in college. So I ended up with a consolation prize – they offered me another internship the following summer.

So did the job offer come back after my second Ross Roy internship? It sure did. And I'm not stupid. I accepted, of course. I was graduating in December and was going to start full-time in January.

That was the year I was also introduced to advertising's evil mistress – layoffs. See, for any agency to win an account, meant another agency had to lose it. Ross Roy lost Kmart that year, and people associated with that account lost a job. So that position was gone before I even started.

Lesson 5: Internships Create Contacts Who Keep You Working

People who graduated in the early 1990s know how hard it was to find work during a recession. Granted, it was the *little* recession, but like the circumstances today, you find out companies may not have jobs for you, but they may have work – freelance work.

So I went from a grad with a job to an unemployed grad before the diploma was placed in my hands. But I immediately started freelancing, because my new clients were also my old clients, such as Kmart, Chrysler, and a few others. Many of the contacts I made as an intern were the first to throw projects my way.

Over 20 years later, I'm still in contact with people I've met and worked with as an intern. They've given me job leads, worked with me on projects, and I've done the same for many of them. Your best method to finding a job will always be your ability to network. And who has a better network after graduation than a student with multiple internships under his/her belt?

Lesson 6: Internships Aren't Just for Students. It's Post-Graduate Work

All that tuition money your parents paid or you owe in student loans also bought you college resources you can use after graduation.

Use them.

Call old professors.

Access university employment services.

Do another internship.

Remember, I graduated in 1992 during a recession. No one was hiring. Sound familiar?

I saw that companies didn't have positions to fill, but they had internships. And as I explained in Lesson 4, an internship can lead to a full-time position. So with the assistance of my graduate advisor, I landed my last internship with a non-profit organization, which became my first post-graduation job.

Lesson 7: Four Years of College Is for Suckers

This final lesson could probably get me into trouble with some circles.

It took me 5 1/2 years to get through my undergraduate studies. At first glance, I probably looked like I was on track to becoming a professional student. But I was doing whatever it took to become a *professional*. I started by becoming a *professional intern*.

I saw the importance of scheduling my classes around my internships, because the key to successful internships is your availability. You want the chance to work on something meaningful? Then you have to be able to put in the time to do the job.

An intern who is only available for the minimum requirement of 15 hours per week will not be given the chance to work on great projects. You're not around long enough to complete the assignment. And you certainly won't make any tight deadlines working in the office 2-3 days per week. So unless you can devote more time to the job, get used to the idea that you're doomed to just having an "okay" internship – if you're lucky.

Now an intern who is available 20-plus hours per week is in the position to get a possible shot at the big time (after you've proven yourself doing the grunt work, of course). That's the person who gets the real experience.

So how do you juggle the work and school? For me, it meant taking a lighter class load. It also meant taking more than four years to earn my degree. The extra 18 months gave me true focus about what I really wanted to do with my life. After the first layoff… the second… the third… and even the fourth, I was always determined to have a career in this business.

And without multiple internships, I would have never developed a real understanding about the different disciplines of advertising. Yes, traditional advertising will probably always be the sexiest part of this business, thanks, in part, to *Mad Men*. But look beyond the Don Draper seduction to truly grasp the big picture of opportunities.

Digital. Medical. Business-to-business. Shopper marketing. Experiential. I've done it all. And in their own way, each can be as challenging and fulfilling as traditional advertising.

Work Steps:

Let's get down to business (or at least to internships).

Try these three activities right now.

1. **Apply yourself:** Identify three places where you'd like an internship. Why? Look back at the earlier advice, go on their website to find the contact information, and complete their form, or write them asking for one.
2. **Follow up.** Call in a week to see if you can secure an interview.
3. **Read Clifton's blog:** Filled with practical suggestions and key insights you can use, it's called professoradman.com; check it out right now.

— — — — —

Clifton Simmons is a Chicago copywriter, recently relocated from Detroit. He's written award-winning work for many of the world's biggest brands. Clifton specializes in experiential, digital, events, and promotional marketing.

He owes his career to the many mentors he's had over the years. And in the spirit of "paying it forward," Clifton launched a blog called Professor Ad Man geared toward students and grads interested in advertising careers, mainly on the creative side. Professor Ad Man is a site where readers can get information about building their portfolios, job search and interview tips, and learn industry trends.

Professor Ad Man was recognized as an "Unsung Hero of the Internet" at SXSW in 2010. In 2011, the blog won a Gold Hermes Creative Award.

Class is in session every week at professoradman.com.

Internship Intel

Frank Blossom
Affiliate Professor Grand Valley State University & Coach, The Polishing Center

Internships are becoming as valuable as academics for getting an agency job. This chapter will take you through the ups and downs of an internship and give you tips on turning it into a full time job.

Internships are hard to get, sometimes hard to keep, but they're also often the expressway to a full time job if you really work them.

Think about it. An employer has invited you into their company. They've invested time and training in you. They know you know the people, the processes, the problems, the opportunities, how the phones work, and where the Red Bull, M&Ms, beer, and Sharpies are stored.

Why wouldn't the company give an edge to its interns when a full time job opportunity opens up?

Competitive Sport

Many companies use internships as a proving ground for new hires. They'll bring in five interns and keep three. Or two. Or one. It's a chance for them to see who really wants to work there, who brings real value to the company, and who is the real deal. It's a cliché, but it still holds true. "Past behavior is the best indicator of future behavior."

Here are 14 tips to help you win the competition.

7 Seconds

Start strong. Your co-workers will size you up in the first 7 seconds and start making up their minds about you. First impressions last. And you only get one of them. Make it matter.

So what can you do in those first 7 seconds? What happens, what is noticed in 7 seconds?

- Your eye contact
- Your greeting
- Your hand shake
- Your clothes

What can you control? Your posture, face, voice, appearance. Use them to convey: Energy, Enthusiasm, Professionalism, and Confidence.

Golden Rule

It hasn't failed yet.

Be the Best Report Binder

Interns are the lowest level of the company food chain. And not surprisingly, they are often given low level assignments and responsibilities, like assembling, copying, filing, stapling materials, or binding booklets. Don't look at it as menial, unimportant work. Be a superstar at any task. Be the best stapler in the company. It'll be noticed and appreciated.

And by taking that approach, you'll be demonstrating your professionalism, attention to detail, commitment, and passion for the company.

If you treat the task as beneath you, the company may learn to live without you.

Also, if you treat the task as unimportant, you create an opportunity for another intern to step in and show you up. Remember, internships are a competitive sport.

2 Ears, 1 Mouth and a Pencil (Listen Your Way Up)

Do the math. Listening will take you further in your internship than blabbing on and on and on. You learn more with your ears than your mouth. Synthesize what you hear, and when you open your mouth have an agenda.

When your boss, supervisor or smart coworkers talk – take notes.

> **"Copious ones. Look up copious and any other words that stump you. This is a business of words."**
>
> **Ernie Perich, www.perich.com**

Two neat things happen when you listen and take notes. First, the person talking thinks that they are smarter. Second, they think you are smart.

Twice as Hard

Winning the intern competition is hard work. So work hard, work twice as hard as any other intern. I repeat, twice as hard.

And guess what, by working harder than the others, you'll get to do more and learn more. Plus you won't have to worry any more about learning to say, "Do you want fries with that?"

Do random, anonymous acts of niceness. You won't remain anonymous. Pick up some slacker's crappola left behind in the conference room. Little things make a difference.

Get to Know the Go-To

In every company there are the go-to people. The people other people go to to get stuff done. Especially in crunch times. These go-toers may not be in management or senior positions, but they carry a lot of clout and respect.

Get to know who they are. Build a relationship. Learn from them. Be helpful to them. Become the go-to intern for the go-to person. Your status will improve. Make their job easier, and you'll make your career path easier.

If the rest of the company appreciates and values the go-to person, and you're perceived as the go-to intern – enough said, you get it.

No Down Time

If you run out of things to do, ask for more work. Sometimes it may take a while for your boss to get back to you. Don't camp out waiting. Don't catch up on personal emails or return calls to friends. Don't play Angry Birds at work; you may end up with an angry supervisor. Be cautious and judicious about texting friends at work.

Find something to research or follow up on that's productive and beneficial to the company. Even if it's washing coffee cups, organizing the supply cabinet. Be resourceful.

Criticism – Ask for It

It's a critical business. Get used to it. And use it. Take it with an open mind. Even ask for it. It's how we all get better. Use it to learn, get smarter, and show that you can take it.

When you are criticized, don't blame the client or the account exec, or the production manager. That's considered immature and naïve. Don't be.

Beat Your Boss...

...to work. If your schedule allows, show up for work before your boss or supervisor does. It's a subtle form of respect, a way to beat your competition, and a demonstration of your positive attitude and eagerness to work at the company.

And all it takes is setting your alarm a little earlier.

Leave a Lasting Impression

15 minutes before you head out the door at the end of your time each day, head to your boss, supervisor, or go-to person and ask if they need any help before you leave. Get in the habit of it, and you'll position yourself as more helpful, conscientious, and valuable to the company. Plus you might end up playing a bigger role in a big project.

Bagels & Beer

Go out for beers or coffee when invited. Be part of the team. But don't get sloppy.

Buy bagels (or company snack of choice) every once in a while. Don't be showy; just show you can do your part.

Toxic Gossip

Ask about people in the company. Don't talk about them. Keep your ears open and your mouth shut when it comes to company gossip, snide remarks, catty comments, and dissing. Both inside and outside the company.

There is probably enough gossip in your office without your two cents. The ad business is full of high octane, big ego, and opinionated people, with a lot of competitive spirit for promotions, assignments, and more status. You've seen *Mad Men*. Don't be a conduit for the dissing. Don't add to it, or you might end up the focus of it. Never talk ill of anyone at work. Never. Regardless of how frustrated you might be. It's not a good move. It could undermine a career – yours. And who are you to be making judgments anyway?

Loose Lips

Client business and new business are always private and confidential. So watch what you say out of the office. You never know who's listening in a coffee shop, elevator, or restaurant. Button it up; it's an amazingly small world.

You are a representative of your company, on the job and out and about. In social situations represent your company well. It will serve you well. You never know who may be a potential employer.

Hang Out with Smart

At your internship seek out the smart people, the ones everyone listens to, the ones who always get invited to big meetings. Learn from them. And just like the go-to people, build a relationship with them. Take notes when they talk. Pick their brains and improve yours.

And don't just listen. Ask them about the books, magazines, websites, and blogs they follow. Smart people read a lot. What's on their office shelves? Find out what they read and read it, too.

Be careful in this area. Find the level of eagerness, inquisitiveness, and engagement that is appropriate for you and the company. You don't want to overwhelm someone above you, who could feel a little intimidated.

A Boss's Perspective on a Great Young Intern from the Polishing Center

"I hired her thinking she'd assist me for a maximum of 10 to 12 hours a week. I was wrong. She never worked less than 15 and usually about 30 because she found ways to bring more value to me that I never planned on. She was proactive and took initiative whenever opportunity presented itself.

She was able to take on many tasks and never lose track of them, regardless of how fast I shot the info at her. She would clarify priorities by asking me what I considered to be highest. She took NOTES on everything, so she didn't forget. She paid attention to details so I could focus of other bigger stuff.

And she never talked ill of anyone, regardless of how frustrated she may have felt."

On the Job Training

Now you may find out in your internship that you really don't want to work at the company. That's valuable. And you're better off. So tell them why you are moving on, thank them, and move on.

But these tips are smart habits to get into for any job or other internship you seek and get.

And just because you don't like the company doesn't mean you don't like the people. Ad people move around a lot. You may find them working for a company that you really, really want to work for someday. And how cool would it be if they recommend you for the job.

Then, after you get the job, and you move up the food chain and start hiring interns, give them this list.

Work Steps:

Each point in this article is a "work step."

So maybe you should just read it again.

And when you get an internship, read it again every morning – before you start.

Your Joyously Short Career

Thomas Kemeny
Creative, Mother/New York

Here's an interesting twist on how to build a successful career. Please read it carefully.

If you're tuned in to a bit of irony and sarcasm, you'll uncover some very solid and smart advice.

If, however, you are suffering from one of those things where you take everything much too literally, well, maybe you ought to skip ahead to the next article.

Come to think of it, maybe you should consider an alternate career path.

If I had one piece of advice I could give to young, aspiring advertising students it would be to smoke. Smoke a lot. Each cigarette may take five minutes off of your life, but it gives you five minutes to talk with important members of senior management who also smoke. It's called face-time, and it's crucial to succeeding. If people in the company don't know who you are, then they can't reward you. Cough your way up the corporate ladder.

The benefits of smoking can't be overstated. Creativity experts suggest taking frequent short breaks as part of the creative process, and smoking provides just that. While others are getting into the flow of work, you're outside in the rain mentally recuperating with the other smart people. Also, you'll work more diligently when you are in the office knowing you don't have as long of a life to enjoy your successes.

Additionally, it makes you appear rebellious, which adds to your brooding creative credibility. Obviously some people won't understand, but they'd never understand you anyway. Plus, once they're working for you, their opinions won't matter.

And, of course, it looks awesome with your mustache.

I personally quit smoking many years ago because of the whole emphysema, coughing, heart disease, killing you thing. But you should not make that same mistake.

I wonder sometimes how much further along I would be in my career if I still smoked. I'd roll my breathing apparatus right into that corner office. Later that day I would die in that corner office as the youngest creative executive of the company. My family would weep, but secretly they'd be impressed.

By now I hope I have thoroughly convinced you to smoke. Understandably, though, smoking isn't for everyone. Not all of us have that powerful drive to succeed.

If you don't smoke but still want to succeed, you will need to have tons of great work. It will have to be enough to make up for the fact that nobody knows who you are. It will have to speak for itself. That means stacks of brilliant ideas. Far more great work than any one person should reasonably be expected to come up with without working long hours. So on top of smoking, I also suggest stealing. Original ideas take a lot of time to craft, but taking others' original ideas takes almost no time at all. Really, once you do the math on it, working honestly just doesn't add up.

Sure, some people might whine and complain. They might never work with you again, and in the small industry that is advertising they may not give exactly glowing recommendations when you move on to other agencies. No matter, you'll be dead long before that could happen on account of all the smoking. Besides, if they didn't want their ideas stolen they shouldn't have left them in a locked filing cabinet which one could so easily open with a crowbar and small-grade explosives.

I'm clumsy with explosives, and, as previously stated, I don't smoke, but I think how much better my career would be if I did. I'd swoop in and take people's notebooks, leaving no sign except for the lingering stench of old tobacco. I'd show those freshly borrowed ideas to my smoking bosses as if they were my own. "Brilliant," they'd say. Then we'd share a mighty cough. See how wonderful life could be?

So while I am not able to do these things, you simply must.

What's that? Not a smoker or a thief? You will want to be an asshole. A huge asshole. Let's be clear, I don't mean confident or firm, I mean asshole. Thoroughly abuse those around you emotionally. Never say "thank you." You will know meetings are over because the people around you will be crying. Call everyone else's idea crap instead of coming up with anything better. Lift yourself up by creating a solid base of people you've stomped on. Nobody should want to work with you, but secretly they should feel like they have to prove something to you. Their lack of self-confidence is your windfall. If you do it right, you will rise quickly. Then there will be nothing left to do but celebrate with a warm, delicious cigarette.

Not a smoking, stealing asshole? Really? And you're sure this is the right industry for you? Well, there is one other option. You can be bold enough to talk to the higher ups in your company, even if it scares you. You can do work the right way no matter how long it takes. You can have civility in your interactions even when it's easier to swear. But for that to work, you'll also have to be at a great agency. A place with an open and creative environment. Getting into a place like that is a whole other story. However, my advice on that is a little controversial.

Work Steps:

What could we possibly add to this excellent advice? Except to reread the final pargraph several times. And memorize the advice.

- - - - - -

Thomas Kemeny is a creative at Mother New York. Prior to that he spent five years creating iconic work at Goodby, Silverstein & Partners. He's won awards in the One Show, Cannes Lions, and Andy Awards. He's created ads for ten different Fortune 100 companies. His campaigns have been discussed in the New York Times, NPR, and CNN. He has an equally impressive list of failures.

Work

Cabell Harris
Professor, Creative, VCU Brandcenter; Professor, VCU School of Mass Comm., & Owner, WORK Labs

*One of the major tasks for those looking to establish themselves in a creative career is understanding current professional standards – both the qual-*ity that is demanded and, simply put, how hard you have to work. Cabell Harris has a company called WORK in Richmond, VA. He calls it "an agency for agencies." Cabell has established his credentials with outstanding work and, rumor has it, outstanding work habits. Here are his words to the wise on this important topic.

Let's Roll Up Our Shirtsleeves, Grab Another Cup of Coffee and Get to Work

You are probably well aware that our little agency, WORK, is not counted among the mega-agencies in the modern advertising world. That suits me just fine. I have had the opportunity to work for many of the larger agencies in either a full-time capacity or as a freelance resource. As a result, I have a wealth of valuable insight into what works and what doesn't at the places where you're looking for work.

The good news. My valuable advice is free – or, more accurately, included in the price of this book. The bad news. Free advice is often worth what you pay for it.

Nonetheless, Here Are a Few of My Observations

1. Any agency that does good work or has done good work has a strong Creative Principle who has led by example. Think about it.
2. If you want to see what work is going on in an agency go to the studio. Whether it's new business, research, planning, pitching, or executing it's moving through the studio. The best agencies have well-run studios.

3. Large agencies often are encumbered by internal processes/approvals which make it very difficult to work quickly and efficiently.

4. The business has changed from problem solving to opportunity seeking.

5. The companies that spend the longest amount of time on process do the worst work.

6. Every agency, I believe, has the same process; they just come up with different answers.

    Who are you talking to?
    - The audience

    What do you want to tell them?
    - The strategy

    How do you tell them?
    - The creative

    Where do you tell them?
    - The media

    Was it effective?
    - The results

7. You can find some very talented people in bad agencies. They just may not have the personalities or the opportunities that get them noticed. Or, perhaps, their goodness may be directed elsewhere. Perhaps they are good parents, or they make a truly exceptional vinaigrette dressing.

8. All the great agencies have work that comes out of their doors that would shock you by how bad it is. Well, at least in the early years you may be shocked. Then, sad to say, you are no longer surprised. Disappointed but not surprised.

9. Egos are important for getting the job done. You must believe you can do the work. You must believe you can sell the work. The inexperienced individual will immediately argue and defend their one idea. Why? Because they are not confident they can come up with another. Experienced professionals will do what they can to protect good thinking but know they are capable of many solutions.

By far the most important difference I have found in companies or individuals is "Work Ethic" I have often said that I would rather hire someone with a strong Work Ethic than talent. I have seen too many individuals with talent and potential be surpassed by one who is not easily satisfied and will just keep working.

I was going to stop there but realized I needed to do a bit more work. So here are a few useful thoughts on the topic of work.

It's 5:01pm. Your Boss Is out of Town. You Are still at Your Desk. Why?

OK. This is important. Your real boss isn't the person with the company car. It's the person staring back at you in the mirror each morning. You understand a job isn't what you do but how you do it. Your DNA has a strand dedicated to the work ethic. It's an ingrained code of accountability that can never be instilled through any employee video, seminar, or retreat. You are wired with a commitment to what you know to be true. And your boss is looking over his shoulder.

Your Job Isn't As Important As You Think It Is. Your Work, However, Is an Entirely Different Matter.

You are not defined by a job description. You are not defined by the title on your business card. And you are most certainly not defined by your location on the management chart. No. You are defined by the effort and pride that you put into your work. A job is why the floor gets scrubbed. Work is why it is clean enough to eat off of. Do not confuse your job with your work. It is much too important.

Where Do You Keep Your Work Ethic?

It can be on the end of a mop handle or the end of a scalpel. Work doesn't care. Work only cares about what's important; doing the job the right way. Work doesn't go for fancy slogans. An honest day's work for an honest day's wages is all it needs to hear. Work is hard-nosed. It will not be seated in the latest get-rich-quick seminar. Work doesn't want to be your friend. Work doesn't want to be glad-handed or slapped on the back. Work wants something much more important: your respect.

A Job Will Behave Like a Job Until Told Differently.

What is your job? To sell insurance or paint houses or market pharmaceuticals?

You know better. Do not allow your job description to dictate what you do. Your real job is to challenge the expected. To give the conventional way of thinking a swift kick in the shin. Make your job more than anyone has ever imagined it could be. Too many jobs are content to sit in the easy chair and fall asleep in front of the television. Make today the day you give your job a wake-up call.

Is White-Collar Money More Valuable Than Blue-Collar Money?

Money isn't a true measurement of anything that's important. A $100 bill is a $100 bill. It represents nothing more than its face value. Whether it was earned by someone sitting in a corner office on the 62nd floor in Manhattan or someone repairing railroad track in Wyoming. The true value of money comes from how it was earned. Was it acquired by cutting corners? Or by coming in early and staying late? Money doesn't care. But you do. And that makes all the difference.

Do You Still Work As Hard When No One Is Watching?

How hard you work isn't a function of anyone looking over your shoulder. It is a matter of pride. Knowing that when your job is done, it will be done right. That is the beauty of this responsibility called work. It isn't so much a job as it is a philosophy. A code shared by everyone who has ever dug a ditch, worked on an assembly line, or written a sales report. There is no secret handshake that bonds us. Just a feeling of the right way vs. the half-assed way. You know what camp you're in.

Many Young Men and Women Dream of a Career As a WORK Employee.

WORK is a place where people want to work – and it's a well-earned reputation. WORK's door is always open to those who can meet the test that each one of us had to pass. Those who make the grade can never say: "This is a dull, uninteresting life." WORK is always on the lookout in colleges, universities, and "advertising schools" for young men and women who believe they have what it takes. It is only fair to warn the prospect that a career at WORK is not for those who want an easy, sheltered life, just as the Marine Corps is not a place for anyone who is not ready to fight when called upon to do so.

There is always danger in the pursuit of good advertising. The hours can be long and draining. The code of conduct is stern and demands more than some are willing to give. The rewards often vary between slim and none. But at WORK, good work is its own reward. It's kind of a 24/7 kind of thing.

Being a WORK man or woman has its rewards. We are proud of the, as the French say, *esprit de corps* which exists at WORK. Ours is a closely-knit, "team" organization. Every member has clearly defined duties as well as a personal responsibility to his or her comrades. If you believe you are one of those special few who can make the grade, take some time to send me an e-mail: Cabell@worklabs.com.

Thank you.

OK, everybody. Back to work.

Work Steps:

Here are two key steps. You'll need the answers for your job interview or beyond.

1. **Describe your work ethic.**
2. **List your proof points.** Why should your boss or client believe your claim about your work ethic?

- - - - - -

Both Adweek *and* Winners *magazine have named him one of the top 10 creatives in the nation. Richmond's* Style *magazine declared him Richmond's hottest talent. The Martin Agency made him their youngest VP ever. And today, some of the largest ad agencies and clients in the country, as well as students at VCU Brandcenter, depend on him to solve their problems through creative thinking.*

Cabell Harris began his career with the Martin Agency in Richmond, Virginia in 1981. Quickly moving up to the ranks of VP, Harris played a key role in helping Martin become recognized as Adweek Agency of the Southeast. From Martin, Harris worked at Richmond shop Lawler Ballard. He then worked as a creative director at Hill Holliday of Boston and Chiat/Day, New York, helping these agencies attain Adweek's top honor of Ad Agency of the Year. Along with his advertising accomplishments, in 1989, Harris founded Save The World, a non-profit organization that educated the public on environmental issues and encouraged readers and listeners to become involved in ecological efforts.

And then California called. In 1991, Cabell headed west to become creative director of Livingston and Keye in Los Angeles. There, he focused his energy and talent on television production. A few years later, in 1994, WORK was born.

Harris designed WORK to be an agency for agencies. Agencies that have hired WORK include Ogilvy, Fallon, Chiat/Day, BBDO, and McCann Erickson. Through these agency relationships, WORK has had the opportunity to do projects for name-brand clients such as Exxon, Sears, Hershey's, British Petroleum, and Miller Brewing.

In 1995, Cabell returned to his hometown of Richmond, Virginia, and he brought WORK with him. He expanded his staff and, along with his agency clients, he pursued accounts of his own. Soon, WORK went on to land national accounts like USA Weekend magazine, Kendall-Jackson Winery, The Princeton Review, and Burly Bear Network, a TV network aired nationally on college campuses. In February of 1999, WORK joined Ogilvy & Mather's "Syndicate," a consortium of six of the nation's hottest independent creative shops who assisted Ogilvy with new business pitches as well as campaigns for existing clients.

In 2004, Cabell launched WORK Brands, which takes WORK branded products to market. Examples include WORK beer and WORK apparel. A year later, he started a new product development company called WORK Labs. Today, clients come to WORK Labs for original thinking in a marketplace crowded with copycat ideas, shallow thinking, and poor execution. WORK Labs has produced nine books to date and is presently in the production phase of three others.

Cabell's work has been recognized multiple times in every major industry award show including Cannes, the Clios, the One Show, New York Addys, Art Directors Club, British Design and Art Direction, Effies, and Communication Arts. He's also been the cover story of Graphis magazine.

Don't "Get" a Job. Create One.

Tim Leake
Hyper Island

This article has some profoundly good advice.
Part of a successful creative career is creating a good part of that career. First, you need to create the material that's going to get you that job. And then, Tim's important point, don't stop there. Today's creative environment is full of opportunities waiting to be created.

I had a pretty awesome childhood. But if I could change one thing, I would have been exposed to a more entrepreneurial mindset early on.

My U.S.-public-education-system upbringing led me to believe that the goal was to get a job, do a good job at that job, get promoted, and then retire. Hopefully.

So that's what I did for a long time. And it went okay. I learned a lot. Worked on some big brands and with some smart people. And I got promoted. Hoo-rah.

Then, gradually, over the last few years I realized I didn't have to play the game that way anymore. I could create the job I want. (And, ironically, make myself more desirable to employers at the same time.)

Thing is, with "jobs," you're always at the mercy of other people's definition of what your job is supposed to be. Even when you're in a senior position.

And if you're smart, opinionated, and forward-thinking, this can be immensely frustrating. "Jobs" have particular roles and responsibilities, and most often, companies look to fill those positions with people who have done that role previously.

That's because this is pretty much the only way we have of telling in advance whether someone might be good at what we want them to do.

So suppose you want to do something you haven't done before? Suppose you want to do something *nobody* has done before? How do you get that job?

Try creating it.

By that, I mean just start doing it. There are a couple ways you might accomplish this.

You could start your own company. If you're young, it will likely never get easier to start your own thing than it is right now. (It most certainly is not easier once you have kids and a mortgage.)

You don't need to make much money, so what is there to lose? If you're already unemployed, you really have nothing to lose. If you're successful, then congratulations, you've created a successful company. If you're not, you'll have learned a ton and have the impressive history of having *started a company*. Employers love that.

And thanks to technology, it's easier than ever. Somebody wisely told me once, "all you need to start an ad agency is a client." So don't worry about the rest. Focus on finding some clients and build from there. They don't need to pay much (at first), but they need to be real. (And luckily, there are tons of real clients out there who are happy to not pay much.)

It's intimidating to start your own thing when you don't have much experience yet. But it also means you haven't developed any bad habits yet. And the more work you do, the better you'll get. Starting a company after years of experience makes sense, too, of course. But by then, you'll be used to making money. A dangerous thing when it comes to making bold moves.

(By the way, make sure your company is real. Using a company name on LinkedIn simply to cover a dry spell in your work history is not the same thing as actually starting a company. I've seen way too many people list stuff like "LeakeIdeas, inc." when the proper term was "freelance.")

You could also create a job by adding it to the job you have now. This is a pretty tempting option if you're already employed, since you keep making money. (And the path I took once I had kids and a mortgage.) But it's at least twice the effort, so be prepared to be frustrated that your friends are having lots of fun while you are working your unpaid, self-chosen second job.

But it works.

So if you've been hired to lay out web banners, yet you really want to create iPhone apps; then start pitching iPhone app ideas even though nobody asked you to. Better yet, start actually building some iPhone apps on your own. (Substitute the words "iPhone apps" above with whatever it is you'd actually like to do.)

A third option is to literally pitch your idea for the job you want. Again, this works better if you already have a job. Go to the powers-that-be and pitch what you'd like to do and why it will be valuable to the company. Be creative, passionate, realistic, and well-informed. Even if it can't happen, most will be impressed by the effort.

There are common threads to all three of the options I mentioned: 1) Taking initiative, and 2) Showing what you can do.

At Hyper Island, we often use a metaphor we call "the tennis ball." The harder you throw a ball towards the ground, the exponentially higher it will fly up in the air. And of course, if you just kind of drop it, you won't get much response.

Initiative tends to be prized and rewarded. So it's really up to you. How much effort are you going to put into it?

(A couple "don'ts" when it comes to taking initiative, however: Don't submit unsolicited ideas to an agency you don't work for, and don't offer to work for free. Most ad agencies have rules against this. Try a different tactic.)

No matter what you do, make lots of stuff. More than ever before, people want to SEE what you've done. Not just read about it. The more stuff you make, the better you'll get. And this applies regardless of what you want to do. If it's strategy, make strategic plans and case studies. You have to be able to show more than just talk.

I'm a huge believer in learning-by-doing. There is an unfathomable amount of information out there to us now, mostly for free, which gives us the power to learn almost anything.

Don't know how to code? Google "learn html." Don't know how to start a company? Google "how to start a company."

This was not possible when I started my career. So I got a job. One that already existed.

You don't necessarily have to.

Work Steps:

OK, what if you decided to hire yourself tomorrow – or maybe today – how would we create those opportunities?

1. **Occupy yourself.** What projects do you think you could find to keep yourself occupied?

2. **Hone your skills.** Yes, we know you're busy. But are there some additional skills you think you might need to create a better-than-ever creative you? What are they?

3. **Uncover opportunities.** Here are some areas to consider.

   a. Your school

   b. Local businesses – like your favorite restaurant. (A flyer that goes under a windshield is hard to object to.) Does a friend or relative have a business that needs a poster?

   c. Local non-profits – a church, a charity, a local project – they all need fund-raising.

   d. A local band or club – we always want a new poster and a new T-shirt.

— — — — —

*For over 17 years, **Tim Leake** has leveraged creativity to solve business problems for brands and advertising agencies. Used to be, those solutions were ads. Lately, it's been a lot more interesting than that.*

Now, at Hyper Island, Tim helps brands, ad agencies, and individuals adapt and thrive in an ever-changing digital world.

Before joining Hyper Island full-time, he spent seven years at Saatchi & Saatchi NY, most recently as Creative Director and Director of Creative Innovation.

He got his start in the industry at TBWA/Chiat/Day in Los Angeles and had the privilege of working on world-famous efforts like the Energizer Bunny and Taco Bell Chihuahua campaigns.

Other agencies and brands he has collaborated with (pre-Hyper Island) include Dentsu, Colby & Partners, Digitas, FCB, MSNBC, Toyota, General Mills, JCPenney, American Express, Bally Fitness, Wherehouse Music, Qwest, California Avocado Commission, Disney Channel, Warner Bros., eToys, Mervyn's, Earth Day Network, Suzuki, Unocal 76, and Kinko's.

*For over 15 years **Hyper Island** has been designing learning experiences for students and industry professionals alike, to produce top-level digital talent.*

First established as a school situated on an abandoned prison in Sweden, Hyper Island is now a thriving global presence with two main areas of focus: Student Programs (which immerse young talent in intensive learning experiences from digital art direction to e-Commerce to data strategy) and Executive Programs (which help organizations and individuals boost their understanding of how society and consumer behavior is changing – and what they need to do in order to stay competitive and thrive.)

Not Everyone's A Critic...But They Should Be

Nancy R. Tag
Professor of Advertising, the City College of New York

Want to be a better advertising professional? In the following essay, Nancy Tag will introduce you to a key skill you need to develop. It's rarely discussed, but it will set you far ahead of the pack. So let's jump in right now.

Critique Skills as an Ad Business Basic

"Why do so many ads stink?"

That's the number one question I hear as a professor of advertising. Considering all the money, expertise, and time spent on developing something even as straight-forward as a print ad, it's a very valid question. The answer is almost too obvious: the reason most advertising is bad is because it's really, really hard to produce advertising that's good.

That's the simple truth about a very complex process where so much can go wrong. The collaborative nature of advertising requires many people of very specialized talents to come together at various stages of development. This means there's a potential for disaster at any given moment. However, most individuals are actually pretty good at their area of expertise. Indeed, with an increase in portfolio schools and management programs in colleges across the country, the industry has never been filled with more knowledge-able people. So why aren't all their efforts more successful? Why is advertising still so... stinky? If I had to pinpoint one reason, it would be this: the people who determine whether the advertising lives or dies – such as the brand managers and account strategists – don't truly know how to evaluate the creative product. And the people who create the advertising – such as the art directors and the copywriters – don't know how to explain it to them in language they understand.

This has been the fundamental flaw in the process since Doyle Dane Bernbach ushered in the creative revolution. When creativity drives a campaign idea, it's more difficult for business-minded professionals to judge the work's value. Likewise, art directors and copywriters struggle to translate their creative ideas into marketing terms that management appreciates. This "failure to communicate" is one of the most frustrating aspects of the business. And yet, weak creative judgment almost seems accepted – even lauded – as a defining boundary in the management/creative divide. This is truly unfortunate. Every stakeholder who participates in the process should have the skill to recognize a great idea, judge its effectiveness, and champion its survival in an articulate, meaningful way.

So what IS this skill that bridges the gap between the creative and business professionals? It's called critique. This is the ability to deconstruct a creative product and talk about it meaningfully. To me, the people who are fluent in critique are incredibly valuable to the business. These are the people who are asked into meetings. The ones you want to hang out with. They're the people who end up being associated with the work. They become indispensable to work-based discussions. People who know how to critique advertising are the ones who get to the next level – and more quickly.

Wait a minute. Everyone is a critic of advertising, you might say. However, there's an enormous difference between "critique," in which one deconstructs an ad in order to construct something better, and "criticism," in which one complains about a commercial that's just interrupted his or her favorite TV show. Critiquing an ad or campaign concept is to talk about it meaningfully. Critique pulls the work apart, examines it, and determines if the elements make sense and if the whole comes together. It's discussing whether strategic goals have been creatively and appropriately translated into engaging content. Critique enables constructive dialogue. It's key to the collaboration that defines the art director/copywriter relationship. It's what happens when work is presented up and down the line within the Creative Department. It's what all those creative types do while they're drinking a beer after work and paying more attention to the ads on the TV over the bartender's head than to the hotties at the end of the bar. Critique is, quite simply, how work gets better.

Being good at critique doesn't just make the work better, it's also the reason why seasoned art directors and copywriters have so much to say during creative presentations. They're used to talking about the work and what makes it effective – especially to each other. The other professionals in the room aren't. Sadly, many lower level creatives often aren't good at bridging the divide. That's why clients can be literally speechless after a creative presentation. Imagine how disconcerting it must be for a high-level business person, who is used to being in command at business meetings, to suddenly lack fluency in a marketing matter of such importance. This is not just damaging to the psyche but also to the work. In addition, without an ability to critique the work, there is no real dialogue. It's as though both sides of the table are suddenly speaking different languages. The process becomes less productive. Relationships strain. The work suffers.

In some ways, I consider critique to be the flip side of presentation. As most of us know, the ad industry puts an enormous emphasis on presentation skills – with good reason. Even a great idea can die if it is not compellingly presented. That's why academic institutions dedicate considerable energy to developing presentation skills at all levels of their curricula. Once you've entered the field, presentation workshops top the list of professional development programs. Most of this training, however, treats presentation as a culminating end point and one-way form of communication. That's not always true. Often, presentation is only one half of a dynamic relationship; the other half is critique. Critique makes a presentation interactive and collaborative, turning the audience into participants as much as spectators. Of course, many formal presentations only work well as one-way communication with a person at the podium and the audience at silent attention. But how many presentations will you go to in a day that really work like this? Most are touch points for collaboration and opportunities for dialogue. Yet most people don't truly seize these opportunities – because they don't know what to say. The industry may give a lot of lip service to the importance of collaboration, but how can you truly collaborate when the players have such varying skill levels when it comes to actually talking about the work?

Given its importance, it's a shame that the industry doesn't actively develop critique skills among its own ranks. You'd think it would be the focus of every new employee training seminar, especially for the folks in account management. But it isn't. How about for creatives? Nope. Perhaps it's because common wisdom believes that critique is the natural language of creative people. But it's not. Right now, in cubicles across the land, juniors are doing their best to cultivate it on their own. Want to know what makes a creative team successful? The ability of the art director and copywriter to bounce ideas off each other through meaningful critique. How did they learn how to do that? On their own. By knowing that their survival depends on it.

So if you want to rise quickly in this business, my advice is to improve your critique skills, especially if you're looking to be an art director or a copywriter. The better you are at critique, the better partner you'll be. And the better partner you are, the better your work will be. The better you are at talking about why your work is better, the more likely you'll sell your work. You've got to be able to discuss it meaningfully and convincingly in a way that others understand. That way, you'll not only be able to sell your work to your creative supervisors, but to account managers. And account supervisors. And if you can do that, you'll get invited to meetings with the client. And the client's boss. Then you'll get noticed. And that's how you get ahead. Being good at creating great work isn't enough. You have to be good at articulating why it's great.

Work Steps:

Want to get good at critiquing advertising? (We know you do, because it's a key to becoming a success in the industry.) Then follow these four simple steps:

1. **Read and report.** Nancy suggests that you read 10 magazines each week you normally don't read. Here are her instructions when you're reading those magazines:
    A. Rip out six ads that you think are effective and six that you think are ineffective. Then back into the strategy:
    B. WHAT is the message?
    C. WHO is the ad talking trying to talk to?
    D. Now consider: HOW is the ad delivering the message? Being able to identify and then assess these three basic aspects of an ad is the first step to being good at critique.
2. **Read more.** This weekend, curl up with *The Accidental Masterpiece*

by Michael Kimmelman. Nancy loves this book. As she says, "It's about the importance of slowing down and digesting the world around you. That's when you appreciate that art is all around you. This book will help you teach yourself to get past the superficial and search for deeper meaning."

3. **See a movie.** Another suggestion: "Go to a foreign film with three friends. Afterwards, go out to dinner and spend the entire meal critiquing the film," says Tag. "See how many things you can say about every element: the plot, dialogue, symbolism, acting, cinematography, editing, music, casting, direction, in the context of film history, compared to American films, etc. If you haven't managed to run out of meaningful things to say by dessert, good for you!"

4. **Study Nancy's book.** *Ad Critique: How to Deconstruct Ads in order to Build Better Advertising.* We love this book and believe that it will really help you get ahead in this business.

Nancy R. Tag is a professor of advertising at the City College of New York where she's Chair of the Media & Communication Arts Department and Director of the Master's Degree Program in Branding + Integrated Communication. Prior to coming to CCNY, she taught advertising to potential art directors, copywriters, and design managers at Parsons School of Design where she was twice the recipient of the Henry Wolf Award for Teaching Excellence.

As a partner of Tag/Scordato, Nancy has created work for Shiseido, NARS, and the Grove School of Engineering. She has won industry awards as a creative director at various agencies in New York City and has two TV commercials in the permanent collection on advertising at the Museum of Modern Art.

A graduate of the University of Pennsylvania with a Master's in Media Studies from New School University, Nancy lives in New York City with her husband and son.

How to Keep a Client

Alan Rado
Founder and Owner, Adrado

What's the best way to keep a client? Simple. Keep them happy. If a client is happy, there's less of a chance they'll bolt for (what they may think are) greener pastures. Sounds simple enough. Sometimes it is, and sometimes it isn't. Here are ten things Creative Director, Art Director, and Educator extraordinaire, Alan Rado, has learned along the way to help achieve and maintain that goal.

Step 1. Recognize That It's a Challenge and an Opportunity

When clients come to an agency, they usually have a problem that needs solving. Fair enough. But a more positive way to look at it is that they don't have a problem. Rather, they have a challenge. Problems are negative. Challenges are positive. Better yet, every challenge leads to an opportunity. Better still, when you meet a challenge, it not only builds the client's business, it builds your reputation. So no matter its size, look at each assignment as your most important.

Here's an interesting analogy. Compare what we do to running a restaurant. The most important reason people go to eat at a particular establishment is the food. We keep coming back if we like the food, the value, and the meal experience. If it becomes boring, or unappetizing, or we experience an unhappy meal occasion, we're gone. One bad meal can do it.

Clients are the same way. If they don't see the enthusiasm you have for their business, they will notice it very quickly. If the work is stale and unappetizing, they will simply leave – and they won't leave a tip.

These things are easy to remember during the early days of a client relationship. As time goes by, you need to find ways to keep things fresh. Keep raising your own expectations – whatever those expectations are ... selling things, moving consideration, improving attendance at the trade show, or otherwise pushing the client's numbers. If you can't keep it fresh, you need to reconsider your chosen profession. After all, we're not only selling things, we're building long-term relationships – with customers and with clients.

Step 2. Listen

Are you really listening? Or just waiting to talk? Find out what the client is really saying. If they think you're not listening to them, they're not going to listen to you.

Here's a true story. Bear with me. It was about twenty years ago, and it was a TV shoot for Cadillac – approved the week before. The mission was to prove that, when it came to handling, Cadillac out-performs a Lexus. There were two spots, one for Seville and one for DeVille. In both cases, the solution was a slalom demonstration. Due to budgetary concerns, it made sense to shoot both spots in the same location. The challenge, however, was to make each spot look different.

As we went through the storyboards, frame by frame (the production company had even built a scaled down 3D version of the set), the client was not happy. He was not convinced that the two spots would look different.

He slowly raised his voice: "Are you kidding me guys! They look exactly the same. I'm not paying to have them look the same! No #%$#-ing way!" You could tell he was upset. The director believed it would be achieved in production. The client was incredulous. Both of them dug in their heels, and it went downhill from there. This led to one of the weirdest things I'd ever seen. The client took off one of his shoes and proceeded to bang the table with it. He yelled out: "Are you %$#@#-ing listening to me!" I thought his head would explode.

Well, that got everyone's attention, but maybe not in a good way. The director got up and casually walked out the door. We were dumbfounded.

At that point, I said we should take a break. Meanwhile, I'd scribbled down some ideas during that fiasco. The Creative Director was three time zones away, and it was late. I had only been at the agency for a few months, and it was my first time with the client. But I had listened. Filming was to start the following week.

We all sat down again, and I proceeded to explain my ideas – based on listening to the client's concerns.

First, let's open each spot with completely different shots and angles.

Then, in post-production, finish one with a sepia/gold tone and give the other a blue tone. The client really loved that one. All during my explanation I made sure that the client felt he was part of the process. Most of all I made it seem that I had taken the time and effort to listen to his concerns. I can still remember how I felt when I saw him shaking his head in agreement. He was now confident that the two spots would look and feel different yet still maintain the core message. Success was achieved!

Happy endings. Production went smoothly, and the spots turned out great. The agency won a few awards, and I got a raise to boot. From that point on, my relationship with the client was rock solid. As a matter of fact, for the next five years, I was the main art director on all TV production for Cadillac.

The moral of my story? Listen. Creative legend Bill Bernbach used to keep a piece of paper in his pocket that he would pull out and read to himself in the middle of client meetings. It said: "Maybe he's right." He knew the power of listening.

One more thing. I never used that director again.

Step 3. Focus on What the Client Needs

On a basic level, all clients know what they want – more business, fewer problems. But that doesn't mean they know what they need. Usually, they'll ask for something that they think they want. We need to respect and understand their perspectives.

I use the "yes, and" approach – not "yes, but." We've all heard about the "yes, but," and we know that it means "no." With this approach, the client's request is always respected and acknowledged. First, give the client what they want – what they have requested – and then, as a bonus, because you care about their business, give them what you think is a better option.

This gives you more power to then solve their problem in the way we know they truly need. But if you don't give them what they want, they won't even hear what you say about your ideas.

Here's an example of the "yes, and" approach. One top creative built her career doing wonderful work on M&M's – you've seen it – with little cartoon candies having funny contemporary dialogue. At first, she thought they needed to get rid of the characters – they were shallow and childish – and the business needed to appeal to more of an adult target.

The client – smart and savvy – agreed with the creative team as to the objective – but suggested that perhaps the real challenge was to get those already established advertising properties to work better against the adult target. The result was work that made both clients and creatives happy.

Clients also need to know you care about their brands – and their budgets. Never forget that you're dealing with the client's money.

When presenting your ideas, be armed with great reasoning and strategic backup, and discuss options openly but with a point of view. As they say, "It's hard to read the label when you're inside the bottle." Clients often don't know what makes a compelling ad. They can succumb to the notion that a laundry list of their product attributes – plus a nice big logo – is what it takes. Maybe. But probably not. You need to help them get to their real goal – better business and few problems – as a true partner. Care about the business. Express yourself with conviction, passion, and – most of all – logic.

Then execute the hell out of it. After all, our first job is to meet client expectations. And their first expectation is always professionally executed work.

Step 4. Think Long Term

Long-term relationships are the gold standard of our industry. Your goal is to help their brand succeed and look good, all the time. When you are new on a client's business, it's a temptation to change everything – particularly if business is not all we'd wish. Yet, one of the ways advertising builds power is with cumulative impression.

Step 5. Stay Current

Our industry is ever evolving, combining subjective and objective input. There is room for multiple organizational structures: multinationals, factory production houses, boutique special-interest, mom and pop shops, as well as basement hackers, libertarian artisans, coders, and artists. More important, our audiences are evolving as well.

In today's world the use of social media (as of this writing, close to one billion users on Facebook alone) has become more and more pivotal. Apps for smart phones are being created every day (presently over 700,000). Viral marketing was not even in our lexicon ten years ago. Now it has become a viable solution.

We need to know what's hot. What's now. What's right. What's cool. Go to the movies. Watch programs that you normally wouldn't. Subscribe to

Advertising Age, Adweek, Archive, etc. Check out websites that cater to advertising. Know your applications (Photoshop, Illustrator, InDesign, etc.). You get the picture.

Additionally, we're not clerks in a discount clothing store. We're more like tailors who build reputations on the quality of the cloth and the cut. And, as styles change, we keep things looking good in that new environment. So we need to look for employers and clients that align with our skills. For instance, I got my second job because I worked on similar brands in my first one. However, my second job enabled me to expand my skills, because it gave me the opportunity to work on television spots where my first agency employer had me focusing on print.

Just think: We only succeed when we – the employee, the employer, and the client – work to a common goal – and then keep meeting that goal year after year.

Step 6. Park Your Ego at the Door

I remember working with a creative director who always thought he was right. If the client didn't agree with him then they were the ones that were wrong. His ego was just too big. He was not known for long-term relationships.

Clients know when you're talking down to them. Make them feel smart. It's all about working together to find common ground. And you do share something in common – something very important – the success of your account.

It should always feel like you and your clients are on the same team and that he or she had a part in developing the winning formula.

Step 7. Build Your Own Brand

You're also a brand, too. Even long-term clients come and go. You also need to improve the marketing and reputation of "The Brand Called You." Clients want to work with winners. When you're winning together, this is a good thing. One caveat – even though clients know you work on other business – they usually don't want to hear about it. Which brings us to the next point.

Step 8. Remember That Every Client Is Your Only Client

No matter how many clients you have – and no matter the size of their billings

– never forget that each one is equally important. A client with smaller billings can become one with bigger billings. A quieter client can't be "pushed aside" for one who is louder. And a "tougher" client might be the one who ends up becoming your biggest support. (And it's always good to have a "fan" on the client side.) In many cases, potential employers are more open to hiring a creative who can find that happy balance and sell a client on something cool...thus showing that he or she knows how to deal with the difficult clients.

Step 9. Be Creative

I'm sure you've seen an episode of *Mad Men* or *The Pitch* where they walk into a meeting and present one idea. In my experience, that's a terrible way to go.

Why give the client only one option? It's silly. Not to mention stupid. You've put all your eggs in one basket. What if they hate it? What if there is some legal consideration that makes your strong, simple idea un-usable? It's a dangerous business – don't make it more dangerous than it has to be.

It's fine to have a point of view. Have reasons why one of the approaches is a better bet than the other very good approaches? Fine. But don't look like you only have one idea.

My rule of thumb has always been to go in with at least three solid directions. One you love to death (one that will win tons of awards and give you a huge raise next year) and two others that you can be happy to live with. Always be realistic.

Clients want to see creative work. That's why they hire us. They want the work to be successful, because it reflects on their character. And they're counting on us to do it.

You know something? For them, it's a little scary. They're trusting us to keep them in business. It's up to us to identify the right target and the right solution to the problem. Scratch that. The creative solution that brilliantly meets the challenge.

Step 10. Make Your Client Your Partner

Some of us have client friends for years and years. Once a client finds a creative that solves problems/meets challenges, they stick with them. Do you have any idea how often clients are disappointed by some creative genius with the wrong idea?

When you can have one of those partnerships, it is literally money in the bank. And it can be fun. Times together are more enjoyable when you're winning together – because we all like to play on a winning team.

Can times get tough? You bet. But whenever things get difficult or uncomfortable, if you can honestly and sincerely show that you both have the same goals, very often you can win through.

And if, as can happen in our business, good things come to an end, just remind yourself – if it were easy, they wouldn't need you.

Do your job as best you can, understand their market and business needs, and become a valued extension of their brand team. If you can do this, I predict you will hear "yes" as a regular thing. Good luck.

Work Steps:

Let's get started on building successful, happy, long-lasting client relationships. Try these work steps now – so you can be prepared when you're on the job.

1. **Practice listening.** When you receive feedback on your work, say it back in your own words. Then go beyond the topline comment and try to figure out why he or she said it. Do you agree or disagree? Why? How can you use it even if you disagree? (Remember: You need to have a second skin. Don't take criticism personally. It's about the work, and everyone wants it to be great.) Additionally, are there any patterns emerging from the comments? If so, what can you learn from them?

2. **Set deadlines.** This is a deadline-driven business. Clients want it "done yesterday." So create extra projects with clearly marked deadlines. Then as you're getting close to them, see how you respond. Does the work become better, or do you freeze up? If you freeze up, how can you change that reaction? It's important to know how you react under pressure and to find (healthy) strategies for dealing with it.

3. **Solve an assignment three times.** Just as Rado suggested you give clients three options, create three options – or more – for every portfolio assignment you get. This will give you more flexibility with your portfolio, and you might come up with some unexpected solutions with your third campaign.

4. **Show your passion.** It's important to be driven. But you also need

to love what you do. There are many ups and downs to this business. But if you're passionate, you will survive. See Work Step 3 for a way to show it.

5. **Name your favorite ad campaigns.** You need to know the history of this business. Not just ten but thirty, forty, or even fifty years ago. What are the great campaigns? And what are the taglines that have endured the test of time? Why do you think they have endured? Potential employers will ask during interviews. You need to get you answers now.

6. **Get a game plan.** Think down the road. Where do you want to be in five years? Your plans might – and probably will – change. After all, this is a quickly changing industry, and you need to stay one step ahead. But an answer will help you focus. As the saying goes, "Live in the present but plan for the future."

━ ━ ━ ━ ━

Alan Rado is an experienced/accomplished creative director, who has worked at top advertising agencies including DDB, DMB&B, BBDO, and McCann Worldgroup. Alan has consistently led and developed award-winning campaigns and managed groups along the way.

He has developed and executed a wide range of integrated, cross-channel marketing and promotional campaigns for clients such as Anheuser-Busch, McDonald's, GM, BP, and Humana, to name a few.

Alan continues to consult, create, and strategize with clients across the country. Currently, he's the founder and owner of Adrado, a creative consultancy that helps clients succeed in growing their business.

Also, as an adjunct professor, Alan has taught courses in advertising, graphic, and digital design in Chicago at Columbia College, The International Academy of Design & Technology, and Harrington College of Design.

Saying Yes to "No"

Nancy Vonk
Founding Partner of Swim.

Not all good advice is good advice all the time.

Here, career expert Nancy Vonk, a former co-chief creative officer at Ogilvy, offers some useful perspective on one of those big simple things.

It makes you realize that, sometimes, "as simple as yes or no" isn't simple at all.

Thanks, Nancy.

A two-letter word is more powerful than just about any other tool in the arsenal of the successful advertising professional. It's exceptionally hard to say out loud for most people, especially those who are naturally inclined to want to please others. "No."

Its antonym is far more popular, and sexier. "Yes" is a word to use like a mantra when confronting fear, risk, challenges of all sorts. The emphatic YES is the battle cry of people who go far.

We learn from our earliest years we'll be rewarded for saying yes to new, scary experiences – from that first taste of exotic, vaguely creepy asparagus, to performing in the third grade play.

When we fixed our sights on advertising as a career, saying yes to the near-impossible school exercises of attempting to beat Axe ads, entering global student contests, learning the painstaking craft – was mandatory. YES, I can do it.

In our first jobs, "yes" is a badge of honor. It's a word that will bless you with preferred status; when the seniors know they can turn to you for help at any hour, under any circumstance, you will get all the benefits of working closely with them. "Yes" is the key to the castle.

So what about "no"? The dirty word, the word that brings on conflict, discomfort, prompts anger and "bad attitude"-branding for some who dare say it. They don't tell you about "no" in school – the negative, the dangerous word. With so much focus on "yes," it seems there's no room in the curriculum to explore all the scenarios where "no" is the only shot you'll have to produce great work.

A word so powerful has to be used with skill. Using it recklessly could curse you with the dreaded "whiner" label – someone others avoid and don't take seriously. You can't pull out this big gun any old time, any old way. I have a formula for identifying the right time: it's whenever saying "yes" would conflict with big picture goals for the brand and/or for you. The temptation to say "yes" when you know in your gut it's the wrong thing to do usually happens when focus is on short-term goals – when it may be easy to forget the big picture.

Let's look at a seemingly absurd example to illustrate. A Nike client asks the creative team to create a jingle for the famous tagline. Yeah, wouldn't "Just Do It" be even *more* powerful if sung – that would really stick in people's heads. This is a new, senior client and you're dying inside but afraid to alienate him with a quick "of course not, idiot." And indeed, that would not be the right way to say "no." What to do? A quick ruling on "yes" or "no," in your head, first – short term, a "yes" would make the client happy, and they'd leave the meeting feeling good. But what about the big picture goals of the brand? Is "Just Do It", in a jingle, consistent with the tone of the brand? And if you just do it – create the ad with that jingle – will the long-term result be worth the short-term win? NO. OK, so you know "yes" is not the right answer. But how to be the downer in the room – the one who will say what the client (and maybe nervous account people) do not want to hear? You have two good options. One is to say neither yes or no – suggesting that a decision this important calls for some reflection back at the ranch can buy time to create the best case for sticking with that silent "Just Do It." Option two is to go ahead and tell the client why that jingle is out of alignment with the brand's DNA. If you feel confident that you can articulate the explanation in a way they can hear (rationally, not emotionally), there's nothing like the present to discuss with respect. Yes, no matter how stupid the question may sound to you – it's critical to respond respectfully. If you want to see backs go up instantly and heels dug right into the concrete floor, let them get the slightest whiff of "you idiot."

Or there's this: a senior writer asks you to take on a project that you know very well you don't have capacity to do well – or maybe at all. For fear of looking like you have a bad attitude, you say yes. In the moment, it's a win. The senior is happy, and you avoided conflict (as most humans would prefer to do).

However, you've just set yourself up for failure on at least two fronts. If you blow the deadline, you and the senior responsible for the job will both pay a price. Not much is worse in ad land than missing a deadline. If you deliver – but poorly – you may be mistaken for not being as talented as they thought. Alternatively, your "no" will prompt frowns, but with explanation of workload and authentic concern you will disappoint, the senior can either turn to another or shift around your projects so you can do it. Either way, they will be relieved you were honest and they didn't risk a poor outcome. This is a very common scenario, BTW. You will have many occasions to take a deep breath, ask yourself to consider the big picture, and make the call. Yes or no.

Most of us worry it's a sign of weakness to turn down any request from the boss. But in fact it's a sign of self-respect and maturity when you know your limits. If you burn out because of crushing workload (particularly the sustained variety), you are sabotaging your career. "Yes, I'll do it!" is great, up to a point. Some all-nighters and stretches of long hours are common and unavoidable at most places. But when "yes" is translating to consistently bad work and fatigue-related health issues, it's a sure sign you need "no" to pull out of the downward spiral. Your boss doesn't actually want you to get sick, to burn out. If you're valued, they don't want you to leave, either. The truth is they are probably oblivious to your reality. It's up to you to explain and look to them for solutions. Workload issues are their problem to solve.

Another common scenario: an account person skirts protocol and comes directly to you (instead of going through traffic) for an "emergency." They are panic-stricken, and you feel for them and want to help. But the only right response is "no." Remind them you've promised to adhere to the agency's traffic system, so you have no choice. Take a number, like everyone else.

We'd all have better portfolios if we took the dramatic step of taking work off the table when it's been maimed by research, or the client won't budge on adding that extra content that will sink the idea. How can we ever pull off saying no in that scenario, without catastrophe? Here's the thing – most clients need to believe you believe in your own work. They are looking for your full conviction as an important sign their millions will be spent wisely. Not many will push the green button after hearing these chilling words: "As it now stands, we no longer believe this work can achieve the business objectives we promised." You are almost always better off to kill your own, mangled creation and go back to the well. There are always more ideas, probably even better ones. Some of the most famous work in the industry was born only after clients killed the previous, inferior work.

"No" doesn't get any easier to say as people advance, even into senior positions. Over time, its disuse can have terrible consequences. A mediocre portfolio (= fewer job opportunities, less money, less happiness) can be assured. The "yes-man," though appreciated by some in management as a "team player," doesn't command too much respect from co-workers or the very clients he or she accommodates with idea-killing compromises.

"Yes" has its place – often. But compared to "no," it's easy. Start getting comfortable with the conflict, the difficulty. Used wisely, it will get you out of the deep doo doo and may even make your career. Say it with me. You can do it: rhymes with go, grow, dough...

Work Steps:

As Nancy notes, this is a word that must be used wisely.

Let's think about that for a moment or two...

1. **Discover "the best interests of the brand."** This can be hard to know, but, as a core value, it's a good place to start. If it's not in the best interests of the brand, you probably shouldn't do it.

2. **Go to your boss.** Should you be the one to say it? Most of you reading this book are either low-level creatives, or, if you move up, you'll get to be low-level creatives. Let's face it – they want you to be agreeable. "Jump," they say. You're supposed to say, "How high?" That said, if there's a "no" that needs to be said, is there someone you can talk to who can say it for you. Remember, it may be very important that someone says "no." It may not be important that you are the one who says it.

3. **List some examples where someone should have said "no."** Advertising that damages the brand is one good example. Can we identify things out there in the business world, or the world in general, where someone should have said "no." Let's find an example or two.

▬ ▬ ▬ ▬ ▬ ▬

Nancy Vonk was Co-Chief Creative Officer of Ogilvy Toronto before founding a creative leadership training lab, Swim, with long-time partner

Janet Kestin in 2011.

They have won many top industry awards including Cannes Lions, One Show Pencils, and Clios. They are the creative directors of Dove "Evolution," winner of two Grand Prix at Cannes, and Diamond Shreddies, winner of a Grand Clio.

Nancy has judged many of the world's top advertising awards shows including Cannes, Clios, One Show, and D&AD. In '08 she was the first female chair in the history of the Art Director's Club of New York.

Nancy and Janet's honors include being named to Creativity magazine's Top 50 creative people of '08, advertising Women of the Year at the WIN Awards in LA, and the AWNY Awards in NY in '07, and induction into Canada's Marketing Hall of Legends in '11.

They have a widely read advice column, "Ask Jancy" on ad site ihaveanidea.org. They penned a critically acclaimed Adweek book, Pick Me, *in 2005. It has become a staple in advertising schools from Texas to Turkey. They are currently writing a business book for HarperCollins.*

Nancy is a mentor and frequent lecturer at ad schools including the renowned VCU Brandcenter. She has been on the board of the One Club since '09.

How to Get Ahead in Creative,
Even If You're a "Girl"
(Men: Read This. It'll Do You Good.)

Karen L. Mallia
Associate Professor, University of South Carolina

This is good advice. Some of it may rub you the wrong way or seem terribly politically incorrect. Probably so.

But Karen is presenting some very real facts of life about the "boy's club" atmosphere present in many creative departments.

Some of it is as simple as the competitive nature of the business.

Other aspects are more complex, and, again, Karen provides a useful lens we can all look through – all of us.

Should some of this change? Probably so.

But there are some red meat realities built into the competitive nature of the marketplace that favors the hunters rather than the gatherers.

That said, we'd like to thank Karen for putting this out there. Maybe some day we'll have to get rid of this article because it is so yesterday and the world has changed. Until then … pay attention boys and girls.

It may be hard to believe, but life is not fair. Neither is advertising. You've grown up in a world where life is supposed to be color blind, gender neutral, A.D.A. compliant, and politically correct. Forgive me for bursting your bubble if you're unaware, but honey, we ain't there yet. (In case you didn't notice, that was a dreadfully sexist bit of language – as is my chapter title. Time to start paying more attention – to text and subtext.)

If you survived portfolio school, congratulations. You've demonstrated raw creative talent, resilience, taking direction, building a great portfolio, and perhaps even getting your first creative job. Getting that first job as a writer or art director may be hard, but it's a fair fight – because it's mostly about talent, passion, persistence, and hard work.

Getting your second, third, and other positions, now that's another story. You still need those key skills, but the game changes as you move from junior to more senior positions, whether in the same agency or whether you move out to move up. That's true for men and women. However, pretty much since advertising began, agency creative departments have been playgrounds for ambitious young men, and that has serious implications for ambitious young women. While Adidas reassures us that "nothing is impossible," success in advertising is, like it or not, a very different experience for women than it is for men.

Welcome to the Boys' Club

Despite 50 years of modern feminism, affirmative action, class action lawsuits, and changes everywhere else in business and society, agency creative departments have remained intractably the "Boys' Club." It's not just that there are more guys in creative. It's the culture. It's one of the reasons why there are so few women in creative leadership. If you haven't noticed, chances are it's only because you haven't recognized the signs, or realized the implications.

It's a fact. For years, women have come out of colleges and universities and portfolio schools in equal or greater numbers than men. Women keep getting creative jobs (because they are every bit as talented), but their numbers dwindle as rank rises. Today, fewer than 18% of advertising creative directors are women. You can count the number of female chief creative officers in major agencies on your hands. Literally.

Award shows routinely struggle to attract top women for their juries, knowing the world is watching the ratios. *Creativity* magazine was trashed in 2006 for an issue highlighting "the most influential creative people of the last two decades." Not one of the 50 named was a woman. Not a single one.

Advertising Age's "Women to Watch" profiles 40 women annually. On average, maybe one or two are agency creative women. Some years, there are none.

Deal with It

If there has been any change in creative departments since the *Mad Men* era, it's been a very slow, scarcely perceptible evolution. None of this makes any real sense in a world where women drive nearly 85% of all purchase decisions. You would assume that women creatives would be revered for their insight, but this is not the first thing in life to defy logic and good sense. So for now, you've got to deal with it.

How? Recognize the realities. Despite all our naïve belief in objectivity, and faith that talent and hard work will be always recognized, the world doesn't work that way, especially the world of advertising. That's true even if you're male; it's even truer if you're female. So learn from those who've gone before you, and confront the realities.

Knowing Your Craft Is Only the Beginning

A creative career only starts with enormous talent and tireless hard work. You are one of many thousands of talented people who want a career in advertising. Some will move to the next level, a handful will rise to the top, and thousands will wallow in the middle or lose their way in some layoff. Who goes where? What differentiates the future stars? Success lies not just in knowing the craft, but also in knowing the *business* of advertising (indeed, the business of business), learning how to navigate the labyrinth and having a profound understanding of human nature.

Here are some things you need to know. First, know your agencies inside out. Some are better for women, some worse. Know which is which, before you take a job there. After looking at an agency's creative reputation, study the corporate culture – its personality and values. Who are the leaders? Are there any women in key creative positions or in agency management? How many? What are they like, personally and professionally? Are they people you aspire to emulate, or not?

Creative departments feel like no other microclimate in business. Machismo is rampant. You will see this in the importance of gamesmanship, in the locker room atmosphere, and in the war and sports metaphors that crop up in language every day. Multiple teams working on the same assignment constitutes a "gang bang." And most importantly, the macho culture is one of extreme competitiveness. Does that stimulate your creative juices or make you anxious?

In a highly competitive creative department, some women are power players. Their adrenaline and competitive nature can compare with any man's. They can curse with the best of them. These women have no problem thriving, unless they get too aggressive. (Then, of course, they're bitches.) If you're that personality type, you have an innate advantage over your sisters as long as you don't cross the b-line.

Unfortunately, the majority of women are acculturated to play nice, to be team players, to want others to be happy. Women like that make great agency producers but rarely become big-time creative directors.

Choose your approach based on who you are and where you want to go. Many successful women become "one of the boys." That tactic calls for plenty of cursing, drinking, and carousing. Then there is *The Power of Nice*. In it, Linda Kaplan Thaler and her business partner debunk the prevailing wisdom that only an egotistical ass can win at the ad game. Yet another creative director's route to the top was via the Southern-belle, seductress mode, flattering and manipulating all the men around her. What suits you? Being yourself might not work, if you're too reticent and self-deprecating. Play the part that works for the life story you want to write.

Success Rides on Personal Capital

Personal capital is the perception of what you're worth – the sum total of your talents and traits – like creativity, leadership, charisma, commitment, resilience, and more. It's not what *you* think you are, but more importantly, what *others* believe you're worth. Personal capital plays a crucial role in getting ahead.

It doesn't just happen; you create it. How? By actively building the brand that is you. Begin by cultivating your reputation in the agency through the brilliance of your work and your dedicated work style. Become the person the creative director seeks out when a problem arises that no one else can be depended upon to deliver. That's how you get noticed by your immediate supervisor and the higher ups.

Beware the idea thief. There are egomaniacs out there who "forget" to credit their subordinates as they maneuver up the line. Either passively or actively, they'll claim your ideas for their own. Don't let them. In advertising, ideas are currency.

Generally, women are much more modest about their accomplishments, while men tend to be quite comfortable tooting their own horn. It's one of the key factors leadership scholars blame for the dearth of women leaders. So make sure that people know who you are and what you've done, both inside your agency and in the industry at large. Never *assume* that good work will automatically be noticed or rewarded. It won't.

Advertising industry awards are much maligned for ad people patting themselves on the back, and for the accusation that creatives worry more about winning awards than selling products. Maybe so. However, they are an undeniably important way for creative people to build social capital – and successful careers. If your name is attached to great work, people notice. Recruiters look. Creative managers look at award show credits. So do other creatives. It's how people build reputations, boost their capital, and catapult themselves to bigger jobs and bigger salaries. Should you be fortunate enough to have your agency fund your attendance to the award shows, you rub elbows with the best and the brightest creative people, your next potential partner or boss. (See Networking.)

Personal capital. That is an important part of how you will get your next job. Or not.

Networking ≠ Facebook

Even though you're really consumed by your job, you need to step outside and network with others in the industry. (That's real-life, real-time, interpersonal networking – outside the virtual world of LinkedIn, Facebook, Twitter and the like, though those have their place.) You will continually be amazed at how small the advertising industry is. Join The One Club, The Art Directors Club, AIGA, SoDA, AWNY, your local AAF chapter. (If you don't know what they are, you are already behind your peers.) In those organizations, you will make friendships and foster relationships that will be mutually beneficial throughout your career. You will notice and be noticed by the people in the industry who are serious about advertising and design and digital. You will meet other creatives who will some day be hiring. You may meet media people who will someday build an in-house creative group. You will meet people who will be hiring freelancers, starting shops or becoming tomorrows CEOs. Don't ever claim you're too busy with the job at hand. Get it done, and get out there.

A word about online social networking: It is about reciprocation. Not "what can you do for me," but exchange – like every other human transaction. Remember that. Imagine yourself on the other side of that communication and visualize what it feels like to be a successful professional bombarded with people asking you for favors, advice, and jobs. Yes, good people want to mentor young people and help them get ahead. But why *you*? What can you contribute? Never forget that there are thousands of other talented people out there just like you. So why should somebody bother with *you*?

Politics, Ghettos and Other Ugly Realities

Golf games. Titty bars. (I can't believe I wrote that. But I did.) Foosball. "The guys" going out for beers. Yeah, in the 21st century these issues are still around, and you will confront them. However, media people and account people usually have more opportunities with the first two than creative people. How you deal with them is a whole other chapter that I don't feel like writing. Just be aware.

A bigger, but more subtle, political landmine for women is residence in the Pink Ghetto. Here you live in the gender equivalent of "separate but equal." You're introduced to it when you're given your first assignment for "a woman's product." It can start innocently enough, maybe with hair color or cosmetics. Next thing you know you're the go-to person for baby food, menstrual products, and adult diapers. You wonder why the guy next to you is working on assignments for cars and electronics and winning agency kudos and industry awards. (How many major creative awards have you seen for fem hygiene products? Have you ever said, "I wish I did that ad," about one?)

Beware. Residence in the Pink Ghetto comes with its own set of "golden handcuffs." (You've got to love those agency color metaphors.) It might seem very attractive in the short run. You'll get promoted to ACD and get a huge raise to handle that dishwashing detergent account. Next thing you know, you can never get a job doing anything outside your pretty little niche. And you're the first person to go when the layoffs inevitably come, because you're not an "A-list" creative doing the fabulous work the agency is building its reputation on.

Break out of your comfort zone. Volunteer for assignments in other groups, in every product category. Remember the trite but true aphorism: You're only as good as your last ad.

Let's repeat lesson number one here. Talent and a great book are not enough to sustain a career, just the price of entry. What takes you onward and upward is everything else that you are, say, and do in every working hour. It's interpersonal relationships. It's your communication skills – how you sell your ideas, interact with your peers, how you present to management. It also derives from many things that are probably illegal, usually unspoken, sometimes unconscious, and yet contribute to business success or failure: what you wear, how you laugh, how well you "fit in" with the rest of the group, whether the client likes you, whether your boss is insecure and threatened by you, and a thousand other factors that are equally hazy and subtle. But very real.

Know Thyself

Take your cue from the ancient Greek aphorism inscribed at the Temple of Apollo at Delphi, "Know thyself." Forget what others want and do. Know your ambitions, your desires, what you are willing to sacrifice, and what you must do to be happy.

A job in creative is not a job, it's a lifestyle. In many agencies, creative people are expected to work very long hours, day after day, week after week. That's why years ago people dubbed a certain agency "Chiat Day & Night." In that regard, the whole business has gotten worse over the last twenty years, for everyone, due to tighter budgets, 24/7 access, and demanding clients. Keeping that kind of schedule is doable for a while when you're young and single, but after a decade of paying dues – will you still be expected to work regular late nights and weekends and give up vacations? The level of worka-holism expected will vary from agency to agency, so make sure you know where you're going to be able to be happy and to succeed. Know how much you're willing to give for how long, in order to become successful.

Work-life balance may be mentioned in HR departments, but it is not in the vocabulary of most highly creative agencies (see Chiat Day & Night). In the creative department, where deadlines loom and client demands are met, work isn't put away for tomorrow. Yes, some women who've made a name for themselves in the business are able to cut sweetheart part-time deals or work from home occasionally. But those kinds of policies are unofficial, "under the radar," individually negotiated, and reserved for those who a company values and wants to keep.

Know what *you* want and how *you* define success. Some people are what management gurus call "career primary." That means your job is the single most important thing in your life, and all else is secondary – including your spouse, children, movies, and vacations. These are the people most-likely-to-succeed in advertising. Most of them are male and have stay-at-home wives or a functional equivalent. The women who succeed to the stratosphere are typically childless or have husbands with less demanding careers who can pick up the slack. Or they reside in countries with more family-friendly policies than the US.

Speaking in generalities, smaller markets are more forgiving. Less hot shops are often saner places to work. Sometimes moving up the ranks makes having a personal life easier. Some great creative directors actually do go home at reasonable hours by making sure they're productive every hour they are in the office (i.e. no foosball). Not surprisingly, those are usually women. Or the men who have wives with equally demanding careers.

Start Your Own Agency and Run It Differently

It's no accident you see great creative talent jump ship from agencies when they hit the childbearing years. Once you've established a nice brand that is you, freelancing or starting your own agency is a great option for striking the personal balance you want. Many women have done it, or started other businesses. There's Amazon in San Francisco. Womenkind in New York. Sally Hogshead and her consulting firm, Radical Careering. Alessandra Lariu is pioneering a whole new way of working with her company, Shout. Just be careful you don't get too successful. Linda Kaplan Thaler struck out on her own in 1997 to have more time for family and did such a terrific job building the place that she now works at big agency again.

Some Really Good News

Thanks to an incendiary sexist comment from Neil French a few years ago and the power of social media, the conversation about women in creative has come out of the closet and into the open. Thanks to passionate researchers, more and more studies provide information about the ongoing disparities in gender and race in advertising and help offer solutions. Thanks to an explosion of newer digital shops, there are places to work that are unencumbered by cultures and processes that make it hard for women to succeed. Fewer women are intimidated by digital, and increasing numbers are employed in digital design and copy, user experience, and even SEO. (Coding not so much.) As digital advertising becomes less about IT and engineering and more about content development, that dovetails perfectly with something women are inherently very good at – communicating.

Increased work in social media is blurring the boundaries with public relations – a field historically dominated by women. New companies are being founded by and for women, developing new models for work, and encouraging and empowering creative solutions to an age-old dilemma. More and more clients are questioning the fact that more than 85% of their consumers are women but not nearly enough of their creative directors are.

In the meantime, since we've all lived thus far in a culture that very often suffers from low-grade testosterone poisoning, we're prepared. And thanks to the highly talented women who've come before us, from Helen Resor to Helen Gurley Brown … from Mary Wells to Linda Kaplan Thaler, Caroline Jones and Carol Williams … from Phyllis Robinson and Lois Wyse to Cheryl Berman and Susan Hoffman and Susan Credle, it has slowly dawned on the advertising industry that women have something to offer. Astonishing talent, actually.

Recognize We're All in This Together

Do we have to work a little harder and put up with a bit more? For now, probably.

Cut to the chase – learn from the masters. See how your sheroes made it: read their books, articles, and blogs. Find a mentor. Once you rise in the business, be a mentor. Consider it your moral obligation to help others grow. Study after study shows that two of the things that contribute most to women's success are having great mentors and a supportive environment.

That organizational culture is a bit trickier to impact. (We've lived by traditional male codes for a very long time.) But with more and more men demanding work-life balance, it should get easier for everyone in advertising to have a career *and* a life. Get your male friends on board. Culture is created and sustained by all its participants – so be an agent of change rather than settling in with the status quo. Cue the trusty Gandhi quote: "Be the change you wish to see in the world."

Is a creative career worth it? Watch *Art & Copy*. Feel the adrenaline rush of hitting a great idea. See your first ad online or on TV. Win your first Addy or Pencil or Lion. Having read this, you're at least ten career-years ahead of your peers. Move it!

Work Steps:

Here are some books and articles that Karen thought were worth your attention.

Acker, J. (1990). Hierarchies, jobs and bodies: A theory of gendered organizations. *Gender and Society*, 4(2): 139-58.

Broyles, Sheri J. and Jean M. Grow (2008), "Creative Women in Advertising Agencies: Why So Few 'Babes in Boyland'?" *Journal of Consumer Marketing*, 25 (1), 4-6.

Cadwalladr, Carole (2005), "Focus: Sexism Row: This Advertising Boss Thinks Women Make 'Crap' Executives. It Seems He's Not Alone: Carole Cadwalladr Talks to Neil French About His Comments, and Looks at Why Women Are Blocked From Reaching the Top," *The Observer* (UK), October 23, 19.

Carter, Nancy M. and Christine Silva, (February 2010) Pipeline's Broken Promise. Available online at: http://www.catalyst.org/publication/372/pipelines-broken-promise

Fuegen, Kathleen, Monica Biernat, Elizabeth Haines, and Kay Deaux (2005), "Mothers and Fathers in the Workplace," *The Economist*, 376 (8436), 63-65.

Gill, R. (2002, March). Cool, Creative and Egalitarian? Exploring Gender in Project-Based New Media Work in Europe. *Information, Communication & Society*, 5(1), 70-89.

Harris, Rebecca, "She's the Boss." *Marketing Magazine*, 11964650, 7/31/2006, Vol. 111, Issue 26.

Hartman, John K. (1988), "Assessing Women in the Creative Department: What Creative Directors Think," Paper presented at the Annual Meeting of the Association for Education in Journalism and Mass Communication (71st, Portland, OR, July 2-5).

Ibarra, H. (1992). "Homophily and differential returns: Sex differences in network structure and access in an advertising firm," *Administrative Science Quarterly* 37, September, 422-447.

Mallia, Karen L. and Kasey Windels (2011), Will Changing Media Change the World? An Exploratory Investigation of the Impact of Digital Advertising on Opportunities for Creative Women, *Journal of Interactive Advertising*, 11(2).

Mallia, Karen L. (2009). Rare Birds: Why So Few Women Become Ad Agency Creative Directors. *Advertising & Society Review* (10)3.

Mallia, Karen L. (2008). New century, same story: Women scarce when *Adweek* ranks "Best Spots." *Journal of Advertising Education* (12)1.

Nettleton, Kate (February 29, 2008), "Is the advertising industry sexist?," Close Up-Live Issue, *Campaign* (UK), [http://www.campaignlive.co.uk/news/787634/Close-Up-Live-issue---advertising-industry-sexist/?DCMP=ILC-SEARCH], (accessed on February 29, 2008).

Nixon, S. (2003). *Advertising Cultures: Gender, Commerce, Creativity*. London: Sage.

Olson, Millie (2007, July 10). Where are all the women in this biz? *Advertising Age*. Available online at: http://adage.com/smallagency/article?article_id=119118.

▬ ▬ ▬ ▬ ▬

Karen Mallia is a former copywriter and creative director, teaching creative strategy, copywriting, and integrated campaigns at the University of South Carolina. Before that, she taught advertising at The City College of New York and at FIT/SUNY. Her New York ad agency career spanned two decades and numerous agencies – from Ogilvy to Scali, McCabe, Sloves to TBWA\Chiat\Day and several smaller shops. Her resumé of award-winning work ranges from cars to cosmetics, from Fiberglass to fragrance and financial services. She finds the creative process infinitely fascinating and researches creativity, leadership, and (you guessed it) gender. She fervently hopes to change the world through cause communication and public service advertising.

It's About More Than It's About

Brett Robbs
Associate Professor, University of Colorado

Just when you thought you had all you needed, the game changed again.

This is a story that will keep repeating itself.

Here, industry and education veteran, Brett Robbs, co-author of Idea Industry: How to Crack the Advertising Career Code, *gives you some initial thoughts on cracking that career code.*

So you've put in the hard time it takes to figure out what you want to do. Then you've crushed yourself to master the skills and develop the strategic or creative portfolio you believe will get you where you want to go.

All that's important. Critical, actually. Because nobody is likely to hire you if you don't have the right tools and show you can use them effectively.

But here's something that's easy to overlook in the midst of all those coffee-fueled nights you're putting in: the abilities and ideas you're working so hard to hone may turn out to be the table stakes that get you in the game but may not be enough on their own to win the hand.

That's because it's about more than it's about.

Put another way, advertising is not only about the world of business, but it's also about the world. But just acquiring the necessary skills can be so challenging that it's easy to forget there's more to it than that.

Still you can't simply focus on advertising and figure the life thing will take care of itself; it won't. To explore the world's textures, experience its flavors, and uncover its nuances requires the same conscious effort needed to hone your strategic or creative abilities. And making that effort is critical.

As one advertising executive points out, "Generally the final two or three candidates are all at about the same level." So to decide which person to hire he asks himself this question: "Who do I want to sit next to on a plane from LA to New York?" In short, he hires the person he finds most interesting.

Why should being interesting matter? Danny Gregory, executive creative director at McGarryBowen, explains it this way: "The very best advertising usually doesn't feel like advertising; it feels like life. So make sure you have a life before you try to create an ad." Howard Gossage, the legendary advertising thinker, makes it even clearer: "People read what interests them, and sometimes it's an ad."

You're not likely to develop a strategy or an idea that will catch the consumer's attention if you're simply prattling on about the same old, same old. Instead, you've got to see and experience things in a way nobody else has. Or to borrow a phrase from Dos Equis, you've got to become "the most interesting man or woman in the world."

How do you do that? As Leo Burnett pointed out, the secret is having "curiosity about life in all of its aspects." To be interesting, you have to be interested. So stay curious, my friends. And adventurous.

You won't discover the world's unexplored corners if you continue to stick with the familiar. But pushing yourself out of your comfort zone doesn't mean you need to go skydiving. Maybe you try a new food, go to a restaurant by yourself and see how that feels, take a different path to work, or visit a biker bar or a Nascar event, unless you do that already. A friend who is afraid of birds went to an aviary and told a very funny story about what that was like – the kind of story you'd enjoy hearing on that plane from LA to New York.

If you're in school, use your summers. You can't afford Europe? Why go where everybody else is going anyway? Instead look at your own backyard from a different perspective. If you're wealthy, maybe take a blue-collar job, or if you're not, go work in a yacht club. You'll meet new people, enrich your thinking, and collect stories you can use, not just on that plane but also in your work.

And that's really the point. Agencies hire you not only for the insights and ideas you have today but also for the ones you'll have tomorrow. They know that if you're always fueling your imagination with new experiences and discoveries, you'll continue to be interesting and your work will too. So in the end what wins you a seat on that plane will also give you the work that keeps you in the game.

Of course, to be offered a seat on that plane, you're going to have to get yourself and your ideas in front of the right people. Doing that can be so difficult at times that you may find yourself ignoring everything else. But would the most interesting man in the world do that? Again, it's helpful to remember that the job search is about more than it's about. After all, your larger purpose is not just to find a good job but to create a rewarding life that your job will be a part of.

A recent graduate said to me, "I don't care where I have to go for a job as long as I get one." "So," I replied, "you'd actually be up for that opening in South Dakota" (Yes, I know the Black Hills are beautiful). The point, of course, is that there is life after work.

You want that life to be fulfilling or at least not misery-making. But even if you believe that at this stage of your career it needs to be all about the work, keep this in mind: if you're not happy in the hours after work, no matter how short they may be, you're probably not going to be happy at work. And that will affect your performance.

So before ever starting your job search, spend some time thinking about what makes you happy. Is it, for example, being near friends and family, heading to the mountains on weekends, or being in a great city with art and theater nearby? I was about to take a job at an agency in a California beach town when I noticed that I was the only person on the beach wearing shorts, wingtips, and black socks. It wouldn't have been a good fit. So it's important to figure the place thing out.

And while you're at it, think about what kind of work environment you're looking for. Agency cultures differ widely – some are sweat shops, others are account or creatively driven, and still others can be rough and tumble places filled with sharp elbows.

What's perfect for one person is less so for another. I once found myself in an interview with a woman who midway through our meeting announced, "Here you're known by the people you destroy." I later learned that she was known as the "piranha lady." Had I looked into things more carefully I would have known all of that on the front end and wouldn't have wasted her time or mine. So do your research. Then once you know the kind of city and agency you're looking for, go for it.

When you do, you may want to take a page from Phil Mickelson's book. In getting ready for a tournament, he notes that, "if you focus so much on the result, sometimes you can get in your own way." So he suggests, "try not to think about winning and instead try to enjoy the challenge that lies ahead."

That's especially true when it comes to the job search. If the result is the only thing that makes it worthwhile, then the mountain of nos almost everybody receives along the way becomes even more discouraging. That will come through in interviews and put another obstacle in your path.

The key, as Mickelson says, is finding a way to enjoy the process. And there are lots of ways of doing that. You'll want to find the one that's right for you.

When I finally got out of school and started to look for a job, I visited cities where I thought I might want to work and then set up interviews. Naturally, I got a lot of "we'll get back to you" from people who never did. I'd like to say that, despite all the rejections, exploring different agencies and meeting the people that worked in them made it all worthwhile. It didn't.

But what did was exploring the world around me at the end of those very long days. I hung out with a bunch of panhandlers on Bourbon Street and raked in some cash, bought drinks for an old bluesman in Memphis until my money ran out, and talked with an ancient southern belle at a fading diner in Atlanta.

I was seeing places and people like I'd never seen before. The job search was turning out to be about a lot more than finding a job. That helped keep my spirits up amidst all the challenges and all the nos until that elusive "yes" came my way.

So keep in mind that it's about more than it's about. Not just because that outlook can make for a more successful outcome but because it also makes for a richer, more rewarding life.

Work Steps:

1. **Keep expanding your portfolio.** In addition to your wonderful portfolio, what else is there? Is it interesting and to the point – that screenplay or the novel probably isn't it. So, let's think – what might be it?

2. **Do more.** Leo Burnett looked for "curiosity about life in all its aspects." How are you expanding your horizons while focusing on your book? Does that sound like you're going in two directions at once? You get the idea.

3. **Enjoy the journey.** Sure, you'd like to get to that destination and

start cashing that paycheck. But there's probably going to be a step or two along the way. What are you doing to make the most of it?

4. **Make the most of it.** Once you get the job, don't stop. This is a business that needs people who keep growing.

━ ━ ━ ━ ━ ━

Brett Robbs is an Associate Professor at the University of Colorado.

He joined the faculty after a successful career as a creative group head and creative director at major agencies. Taking his own advice and doing more than just advertising, he also served as administrative director of the Center for Southern Folklore and continues to develop advertising for a variety of organizations in addition to his responsibilities at the University. His research focuses on how changes in the advertising industry should impact the college curriculum. He is co-author (with Deb Morrison of the University of Oregon) of Idea Industry: How to Crack the Career Code *(One Club, 2008) The book provides an inside look at the major areas in an advertising agency and offers practical advice about how to launch an advertising career.*

The Game behind the Game

Bruce Bendinger
Copy Chief, The Copy Workshop

Bruce wrote this a while ago. It's already appeared in CMYK *and the* Talent Zoo *website. But we're guessing you missed it. So here it is again.*
It's advice worth remembering.

Once upon a time, I heard a line about Hollywood that was attributed to F. Scott Fitzgerald. It sort of went like this: *"When people look at Hollywood, they're like an audience watching a ventriloquist act – everyone is fascinated by the dummy."*

Hold that thought.

Next scene. Lunch with a creative legend – a good citizen and a fine person. Happy with the agency. Happy with the work. Then again, a problem account just left. Lunch is over, and the legend goes back on the job. And that's over, too.

One of the things we talked about during that lunch was the limits of what we do. Example. Shoot a commercial with cool models, cool film, cool music, and cool editing. At the end, we super some fairly hip store like Abercrombie or The Gap. Or whoever is cool this week. And the spot is … cool.

Now, let's try it again. Cool models, cool film, cool everything. And at the end of the spot we super the name and the logo of some fairly lame store. Not so cool. And there's probably nothing we can do about it. Not in this lifetime.

Why? Because the business behind the brand doesn't have what it takes – and consumers know it. But my question is – do you?

What are you thinking about as you page through the award books or the latest little *ADWEEK/AdAge* feature on some cool creative? I have my suspicions.

Well, as you might suspect, this is not yet another, "It's about the work/ think the unthunk/good isn't good enough/make the world a better place," speech.

Though I kinda like the "make the world a better place" part.

My advice to you is to put on some X-ray glasses and look past the dazzle of cool headlines, cool graphics, cool awards, and, of course, THE CONCEPT. Stop thinking about ads for just a minute – and start thinking about the business behind the ads. Please.

Insert story here.

Once upon another time, I was down in Atlanta teaching for a week. The class is showing me their work for Jack Daniel's Charcoal. Cool headlines, concepts, etc. I look at the stuff. I gasp. My brain reels. I realize that these bright kids don't have clue one about the charcoal business, which is this high tonnage/low margin business driven by trade deals and end aisle displays at a mall near you.

Hey, a nice four color ad in *Southern Living* – I guess it wouldn't hurt, but if you don't have the distribution and the dealer loader and the promotional event, forget it, even if someone did put the ad up on the refrigerator – or in an award book.

So we talk about the business for a bit, and I see that once these bright young men and women actually understand the business, there are cool posters for parking lot barbecue contests and cool coupons (with cool ad attached) that encouraged customers to buy slightly more expensive cuts of meat in the back of the store, so the supermarket might want to stack that slightly more expensive charcoal in the front of the store.

All of those student ads showed something that most advertising doesn't – an understanding of the business.

Wait a minute, you say. I'm in the real world, and I'm doing ads for consumers, not supermarket managers, and doesn't the creative brief at the agency do that? Well, maybe yes and maybe no. Because the next piece of not-so-good news is most agency folks are still looking at that cute ventriloquist act, thinking the next cool concept in the next clever ad will be the one that makes the difference. Until they come back from work one day and find out they were worrying about the wrong thing.

I think I better repeat this. Too many of those good-looking guys and gals smiling at you from those photos as they pick up their awards are playing the wrong game.

And the speeches. I swear some agency people seem to think that if they just say the word "brand" often enough, clients will quiver in delight, and all problems will be solved. Shut up. And stop looking at the dummy.

Instead, do these three things:

Career Tip #1. Ask about the business. Clients are sick and tired of agency people who are more interested in the advertising than in the business that pays the bills. Ask the client about the business – not the ads. For practice, ask the account execs. Show that you care about their business – not your advertising. You will immediately differentiate yourself from virtually every other creative that client has ever met. And, along the way, some may become friends. This is a good thing.

Career Tip #2. Work on businesses that work – even if some of them ain't all that glamorous. If the One-Show Wannabee part of you isn't satisfied, dig up a little pro bono. There's still lots of Elmer's Minnows* swimming around out there. Just don't confuse 'em with the big fish. Once you see how it works when people do it right, it will be very clarifying for you for the rest of your career, which I hope is a long one.

Career Tip #3. Make at least one business-oriented magazine part of your reading list. *Wired*, for starters, *Business Week*, *Fortune*, the Marketplace page in *Wall Street Journal*. Whatever you can stand. Read something by Peter Drucker. Stop paging through the award books. Get the story behind the story. Or get ready for a nasty surprise after lunch someday – instead of dessert, I guess.

Finally, as a reward for reading this far, here's a bonus tip.

If your fate is working on one of those don't-quite-have-what-it-takes-brands, tell yourself that you're in luck.

First, you get a chance to find out firsthand what makes businesses not work, which will make you even more appreciative of the ones that do. And maybe – just maybe –you'll be the one who figures out how to take a dead-in-the-water business and give it new life. It can happen. But trust me, it will take more than a ventriloquist's trick. Or a One-Show Pencil.

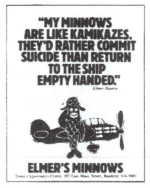

"MY MINNOWS ARE LIKE KAMIKAZES. THEY'D RATHER COMMIT SUICIDE THAN RETURN TO THE SHIP EMPTY HANDED."
Elmer Hamre

ELMER'S MINNOWS
Elmer's Sportsmen's Center, 107 East Main Street, Baudette, 634-9589

---

* Elmer's Minnows was a little bait shop in Minnesota. Tom McEligott wrote award-winning ads for them – and turned Elmer's into a little bait shop with award-winning ads. These ads also helped establish Tom's talent, also a useful business objective.

So good luck. And start paying attention to some of the folks who don't seem to be moving their lips.

Work Steps:

1. **Read up.** Did you read any business articles today? Hey, it's okay to read *Ad Age* and/or *Adweek,* and Stuart Elliott in the *New York Times* is good – he'll send his weekly article to your e-mail box. But what else? *The Economist*? *Business Week*? Read one a week and find the one you like best.

2. **Create a new business.** You're probably working on your portfolio – do you have a hot new business in your book? Why not try to track one down from the business press – or *Wired*. A hot start-up idea that nobody has ever seen an ad for. Nice.

3. **Find a problem business.** Might as well find a business with problems. Think. How would you solve this company's problems? First, think about solving the real problem of that business. Then, do an ad about it.

4. **Ask a small business to let you do their advertising.** For the business of your career, this might be a very good thing.

Resources

This book is just the beginning of what should be a growing library of resources to make you better and better.

First, there's a list of books you might want to read. If some of the authors seem familiar, they are – because you already read something they wrote, and that means you've been paying attention. Good.

Each of them have quite a bit more to say, and you should treat the piece in this book as a step in the right direction – find out what else they have to offer.

Next, thanks to the publishers of *CA*, *CMYK*, and the One Show publications. Each of them, in their own way, is providing valuable resources to help you stay current in a fast-changing world. Month-by-month. Quarter-by-quarter. And year-by-year. We've also included some blogs and websites that can help you stay current, an ever-going odyssey for everyone in the industry – including a few curated by people in the book.

Finally, we've listed a few awards show annuals you should read, so you know what's winning awards. (But please don't read them right when you need to create a solution – or your work could end up being very derivative.)

Combined, these resources should continue to help you succeed in the three key areas of your career – your portfolio (as I tell my students, it's never really done until the day you decide you want your employer to "retire you," although you might be able to coast for a few months after), your job search (again, it's never really done), and your everyday experience on the job.

Magazines

CMYK Magazine
150 West 76th Street, #5B
New York, NY 10023
www.cmykmag.com

Communication Arts (*CA*)
Coyne & Blanchard, Inc
410 Sherman Avenue
Palo Alto, CA 94306
www.commarts.com

Luerzer's Archive
American Showcase
915 Broadway Avenue
New York, NY 10010
www.luerzersarchives.com

One. A Magazine
The One Club
260 5th Avenue
New York, NY 10001
www.oneclub.org

Websites

New websites are getting launched daily – so keep an eye out for them – but here are a few that should get you started:

adbuzz.com
adsoftheworld.com
adteachings.com
adverbox.com
adwomen.org
agencycompile.com
creativity-online.com
ihaveanidea.org
hbr.org
professoradman.com
talentzoo.com

Advertising Annuals

There are many awards shows and awards in annuals in advertising. Read as many of them as possible. At least the latest ones. The following annuals are probably the best as well as the easiest to find:

Art Directors Annual
The Art Directors Club
106 West 29th Street
New York, NY 10001
212-643-1440
www.adcglobal.org
The annual is published by RotoVision SA in Switzerland

Communication Arts
(They produce advertising, interactive, design, illustration, and typography annuals.)
Coyne & Blanchard, Inc
410 Sherman Avenue
Palo Alto, CA 94306
www.commarts.com
(CA also produces annuals in interactive, design, illustration, and typography.)

Creativity International Awards
2410 Frankfort Avenue
Louisville, KY 40206
www.creativityawards.com
The annual is published by Collins Design (Harper Collins).

The One Show Annual
(They produce four annual professional award competitions: Advertising, Design, Entertainment, and Interactive as well as a student competition that covers these areas.)
One Show Publishing
The One Club
260 5th Avenue
New York, NY 10001
www.oneclub.org

Books

Aitchison, Jim, *Cutting Edge Advertising Third Edition: How to Create the World's Best Print for Brand in the 21st Century*, Singapore: Prentice Hall 2008.

—, *Cutting Edge Radio: How to Create the World's Best Radio Ads for the 21st Century*, New Jersey: Prentice Hall, 2003.

—, *Cutting Edge Commercials: How to Create the World's Best TV Ads for the 21st Century*, New Jersey: Prentice Hall, 2001.

Arden, Paul, *It's Not How Good You Are, It's How Good You Want To Be*, London: Phaidon, 2003.

—, Whatever You Think, Think the Opposite, London: Phaidon, 2006.

Armstrong, J. Scott, *Persuasive Advertising: Evidence-based Principles*, London: Palgrave Macmillan, 2010

Avery, Jim, *Advertising Campaigns Planning: Developing an Advertising-based Marketing Plan 4th Edition*, Chicago: The Copy Workshop, 2010

Azzaro, Marian, Dan Binder, Robb Clawson, Mary Alice Shaver, & Olaf Werder, *Strategic Media Decisions: Understanding the Business End of the Advertising Business 2nd Edition*, Chicago: The Copy Workshop, 2008.

Barletta, Martha, *Marketing to Women: How to Understand, Reach, and Increase Your Share of the World's Largest Market Segment 2nd Edition*, New York: Kaplan, 2011.

—, PrimeTime Women: How to Win the Hearts, Minds, and Business of Boomers Big Spenders, New York: Kaplan, 2007

Bendinger, Bruce, *The Copy Workshop Workbook 4th Edition*, Chicago: The Copy Workshop, 2009.

Bolles, Richard Nelson, *What Color is Your Parachute: A Practical Manual for Job Hunters and Career Changers*, Berkeley, CA: Ten Speed Press, published annually.

Caples, John (Revised by Fred Hahn), *Tested Advertising Methods 5th Edition*, Paramus, NJ: Prentice Hall, 1997.

Cialdini, Robert, *Influence 4th Edition*, Needham Heights, MA: Allyn & Bacon, 2001.

Crispin Porter + Bogusky (text by Warren Berger), *Hoopla*, New York: powerHouse Books, 2006.

Crow, David, *Visible Signs: An Introduction to Semiotics*, Switzerland: AVA Publishing SA, 2003.

The Designers and Art Directors of the United Kingdom, *The Copy Book: How 32 of the World's Best Advertising Writers Write Their Advertising*, Switzerland: RotoVision SA, 1995.

Dru, Jean-Marie, *Disruption: Overturning Conventions and Shaking Up the Marketplace*, New York: An Adweek Book – John Wiley and Sons, 1997.

Duffy, Joe, *Brand Apart: Insights on the Art of Creating a Distinctive Brand Voice*, New York: One Club Publishing, 2005.

Dzamic, Lazar, *No-Copy Advertising*, Switzerland: RotoVision SA, 2001.

Fisher, Roger, William Ury, and Bruce Patton, *Getting to Yes: Negotiating Agreement Without Giving In 2nd Edition*, New York: Penguin Books, 1991.

Fortini-Campbell, Lisa, *Hitting the Sweet Spot: How Consumer Insight Can Inspire Better Marketing and Advertising*, Chicago: The Copy Workshop, 2001.

Foote, Cameron S., The Business Side of Creativity: The Complete Guide to Running a Small Graphic Design or Communications Business, Third Updated Edition, New York: W. W. Norton, 2006.

—, The Creative Business Guide to Marketing: Selling and Branding Design, Advertising, Interactive, and Editorial Services, New York: W. W. Norton, 2012.

Gladwell, Malcom, *Blink: The Power of Thinking Without Thinking*, New York: Little, Brown and Company, 2005.

—, *The Tipping Point: How Little Things Can Make a Big Difference*, New York: Little, Brown and Company, 2000.

Gossage, Howard Luck, *The Book of Gossage*, Chicago: The Copy Workshop, 2006.

Handley, Ann & C.C. Chapman, *Content Rules: How to Create Killer Blogs, Podcasts, Videos, Ebooks, Webinars (and More) that Engage Customers and Ignite Your Business*, Hoboken, New Jersey: John Wiley & Sons, 2011.

Hanlon, Patrick, *Primal Branding: Create Zealots for Your Brand, Your Company, and Your Future*, New York: Free Press, 2006.

Higgins, Denis, *The Art of Writing Advertising: Conversations with Masters of the Craft (David Ogilvy, William Bernbach, Leo Burnett, Rosser Reeves)*, New York: McGraw-Hill, 2003.

Hogshead, Sally, *Radical Careering: 100 Truths to Jumpstart Your Job, Your Career, and Your Life*, New York: Gotham Books, 2005.

Johnson, Michael, *Problem Solved: A Primer in Design and Communication*, London: Phaidon, 2002.

Kabani, Shama Hyder, *The Zen of Social Media Marketing: An Easier Way to Build Credibility, Generate Buzz, and Increase Revenue*, Dallas, Texas: BenBella Books, 2010

Kaplan, Morton H., *When You Speak, Do They Listen: A Sixty-Minute Guide to Public Speaking and Persuasive Presentations*, Chicago: Columbia College Chicago, 2005.

Kaplan Thaler, Linda, Robin Koval, with Delia Marshall, *Bang: Getting Your Message Heard in a Noisy World*, New York: Currency Doubleday, 2003.

Kirshenbaum, Richard and Jonathon Bond, *Under the Radar: Talking to Today's Cynical Consumer*, New York: Adweek Books – John Wiley & Sons, 1998.

Lamott, Anne, *Bird by Bird: Some Instructions in Writing and Life*, New York: Pantheon, 1994.

Landa, Robin, *Advertising by Design: Generating and Designing Ideas Across Media 2nd Edition*, New York: John Wiley & Sons, 2010.

—, *Designing Brand Experiences*, Clifton Park, NJ: Thomson Delmar Learning, 2006.

—, Graphic Design Solutions 4th Edition, New York: Wadsworth Publishing, 2010.

Levinson, Bob, *Bill Bernbach's Book*, New York: Villard Books, 1987.

Lidwell, William, Kristina Holden, and Jill Butler, *Universal Principles of Design: 100 Ways to Enhance Usability, Influence Perception, Increase Appeal, Make Better Design Decisions, and Teach Through Design*, Gloucester, MA: Rockport Publishers, 2003.

Lorin, Philippe, *5 Giants of Advertising*, New York: Assouline, 2001.

Lois, George, *Damn Good Advice (for People with Talent): How to Unleash Your Creative Potential by America's Master Communicator*, London: Phaidon, 2012

MacKenzie, Gordon, *Orbiting the Giant Hairball: A Corporate Fool's Guide to Surviving with Grace*, New York: Viking, 1996.

Mathieson, Rick, *The On-Demand Brand: 10 Rules for Digital Marketing Success in an Anytime, Everywhere World*, New York: AMACOM, 2010

—, *Branding Unbound: The Future of Advertising, Sales, and the Brand Experience in the Wireless Age*, New York: AMACOM, 2005

Mayer, Martin, *Madison Avenue U.S.A.*, Lincolnwood, IL: NTC Business Books, 1992.

—, *Whatever Happened to Madison Avenue?* New York: Little, Brown and Company, 1991.

Mickelson, Pamela L., *Brand Builder Workbook*, Chicago: The Copy Workshop, 2012

Minsky, Laurence, *How to Succeed in Advertising When All You Have Is Talent Second Edition*, Chicago: Copy Workshop, 2007

Monahan, Tom, *The Do-It-Yourself Lobotomy: Open Your Mind to Greater Creative Thinking*, New York: Adweek Books – John Wiley & Sons, 2002.

Myerson, Jeremy, *Rewind: Forty Years of Design & Advertising*, London: Phaidon Press, 2002.

Neumeier, Marty, *The Brand Gap: How to Bridge the Distance Between Strategy and Design*, Berkeley, CA: AIGA / New Riders, 2003.

—, *Zag: The #1 Strategy of High Performance Brands*, Berkeley, CA: AIGA / New Riders, 2006.

Oakner, Larry, *And Now a Few Laughs from Our Sponsor: The Best of Fifty Years of Radio Commercials*, New York: Adweek Books – John Wiley & Sons, 2002.

Ogilvy, David, *Confessions of an Advertising Man*, New York: Atheneum, 1985.

—, *Ogilvy on Advertising*, New York: Vintage Books, 1983.

—, *The Unpublished David Ogilvy*, edited by Joel Raphaelson, New York: Crown Publishers, Inc., 1986.

Paetro, Maxine, *How To Put Your Book Together and Get a Job in Advertising, Newly Revised*, New York: W. W. Norton, 2010.

Peppers, Don, *Life's a Pitch: Then You Buy*, New York: Doubleday, 1995.

Peterson, Bryan L., *Design Basics for Creative Results*, Cincinnati, OH: HOW Design Books, 2003.

Phillips, Andrea, *A Creator's Guide to Transmedia Storytelling: How to Capture and Engage Audiences Across Multiple Platforms*, New York: McGraw Hill, 2012.

Pope, Suzanne, *How to Train Ideas to Come When They're Called: Notes and Advise for Young People in Advertising*, Montreal, Canada: IHAVEANIDEA, 2011 (available at blurb.com).

Pricken, Mario, *Creative Advertising: New Edition Ideas and Techniques from the World's Best Campaigns*, New York: Thames and Hudson, 2008.

Reeves, Rosser. *Reality in Advertising*, New York: Alfred A. Knopf, 1961.

Richards, Stan, *The Peaceable Kingdom: Building a Company Without Factionism, Fiefdoms, Fear and Other Staples of Modern Business*, New York: Adweek Books – John Wiley & Sons, 2001.

Ries, Al and Jack Trout, *Positioning: The Battle for Your Mind, 20th Anniversary Edition*, New York: McGraw-Hill, 2001.

Robbs, Brett and Deborah Morrison, *Idea Industry: How to Crack the Advertising Career Code*, New York: One Club Publishing, 2008

Roberts, Kevin, *Lovemarks: The Future Beyond Brands*, New York: power-House Books, 2004.

Roman, Kenneth and Jane Maas (with Martin Nisenholtz), *How to Advertise: Building Brands and Business in the New Marketing World*, New York: Thomas Dunne Books, 2003.

Schaefer, Mark W., *Return on Influence: The Revolutionary Power of Klout, Social Scoring, and Influence Marketing*, New York: McGraw Hill, 2012.

Schmetterer, Bob, *Leap: A Revolution in Creative Business Strategy*, New York: Adweek Books – John Wiley & Sons, 2003.

Schultz, Don and Heidi Schultz, *Brand Babble: Sense and Nonsense About Branding*, Mason, OH: Thomson South-Western, 2004.

Schultz, Don E., Stanley I. Tannenbaum, and Robert F. Lauterborn, *Integrated Marketing Communications: Putting It Together & Making It Work*, New York: McGraw-Hill, 1993.

Sharp, Bill, *How to be Black and Get a Job in the Advertising Agency Business Anyway*, Atlanta: Sharp Advertising, 1969.

Shaver, Mary Alice & Tom Reichert, *Make the Sale!: How to Sell Media with Marketing*, Chicago: The Copy Workshop, 2003,

Soloman, Robert, *The Art of Client Service*, Chicago: Dearborn, 2003.

Spence, Edward and Brett Van Heekeren, *Advertising Ethics*, Upper Saddle River, NJ: Pearson Education, 2005.

Spencer, William Burks, Breaking In: Over 100 Advertising Insiders Reveal How to Build a Portfolio That Will Get You Hired, Seattle, Washington, Tuk Tuk Press, 2011

Steel, John, *Truth, Lies, and Advertising: The Art of Account Planning*, New York: Adweek Books – John Wiley & Sons, 1998.

Strunk, William, Jr. and E. B. White, *The Elements of Style Fourth Edition*, White Plains, NY: Longman, 2000.

Sullivan, Luke, *Hey, Whipple, Squeeze This: The Classic Guide to Creating Ads*, New Jersey: John Wiley & Sons, 2012

Tag, Nancy, *Ad Critique: How to Deconstruct Ads in Order to Build Better Advertising*, Los Angeles: Sage, 2012.

Tellis, Gerard J., *Effective Advertising: Understanding When, How, and Why Advertising Works*, London: Sage, 2004.

Twitchell, James, *Adcult USA: The Triumph of Advertising in American Culture*, New York: Columbia University Press, 1996.

—, *Twenty Ads that Shook the World*, New York: Three Rivers Press, 2000.

Underhill, Paco, *Why We Buy: The Science of Shopping*, New York, Simon & Schuster, 1999.

Vonk, Nancy and Janet Kestin, *Pick Me: Breaking Into Advertising and Staying There*, New York: Adweek Books – John Wiley & Sons, 2005.

Wells, Mary, *A Big Life (in Advertising)*, New York: Alfred A. Knopf, 2002.

Wells, William D., *Planning for ROI: Effective Advertising Strategy*, Englewood Cliffs, NJ: Prentice Hall, 1989.

Wilde, Judith and Richard Wilde, *Visual Literacy: A Conceptual Approach to Graphic Problem Solving*, New York: Watson-Guptill Publications, 1991.

Williams, Tim, *Take a Stand for Your Brand: Building a Great Agency from the Inside Out*, Chicago: The Copy Workshop, 2005.

Wunderman, Lester, *Being Direct: Making Advertising Pay*, New York: Random House, 1996.

Young, James Webb, *A Technique for Producing Ideas*, New York: McGraw-Hill, 2003.

Zinsser, William, *On Writing Well, 30th Anniversary: The Classic Guide to Writing Nonfiction*, New York: HarperCollins, 2006.

Art Directors Club

The Art Directors Club is the first organization of its kind and one of the most concentrated groups of creative talent in the world. For more than ninety years ADC members have funded programs to Connect, Provoke, and Elevate creative professionals in all aspects of visual communications around the world.

Young Professional memberships are available at the discounted rate of $100. The Art Directors Club offers numerous career-altering programs for its Young Professional Members such as:

ADC Young Guns

The industry's only international, cross-disciplinary, portfolio-based awards competition. Art Directors, Designers, Photographers, Directors, Motion-Designers, and other creatives age 30 and under who have been working for at least two years, full-time or freelance are encouraged to enter every spring. Visit adcyoungguns.org.

Portfolio Night

Every May the world's top Creative Directors meet with advertising students and juniors in cities on every continent for the world's only simultaneous portfolio review and recruitment event. For many aspiring creatives this is a once in a lifetime opportunity to meet with this calibre of Executive at the same time, in the same place. Visit portfolionight.com.

National Student Portfolio Review

Each May, 300 of the country's most promising creative students descend upon The Art Directors Club for an intense session of portfolio reviews. Students benefit from the feedback and encouragement from the foremost art directors, creative directors, designers, and creative recruiters in the NYC area. Visit adcglobal.org.

For more information on the benefits of becoming an ADC Young Professional Member, visit adcglobal.org.

The One Club for Art & Copy

Members of The One Club are part of an international community that stands behind their mission to champion excellence in creative advertising and design in all its forms.

The organization is greatly beneficial in providing educational events and networking opportunities for people in advertising and design. One Club members enjoy free or discounted admission as well as priority on exclusive events and opportunities with limited availability (i.e. volunteer during Creative Week and have access to the world's most amazing Creatives and events, free of charge).

They support creative endeavors by providing an online display of work in the Portfolio section of their website and feature member work in their bimonthly newsletter (circulation over 40K) and social media outlets to provide international exposure for their members.

One of the biggest perks for student and junior professional members, is their virtual "members only portfolio review" where top Creatives provide young members with one-on-one feedback on their work. Many of these reviews end in job opportunities or established mentor relationships.

Other membership benefits include:

- Complimentary One Show, One Show Design or One Show Interactive annual with printed list of members.
- Free subscription to *one. a magazine*, a journal written by creative people about the creative process
- A 10% discount in the online store, including orders of additional Pencils and Merit Awards Certificates.
- Discounted tickets to all One Club award shows and industry events, including The One Show and Creative Week Passes.
- Free or discounted admission to various other One Club events throughout the year.

For more information email membership@oneclub.org or visit oneclub.org/oc/membership. Get a 10% discount with the voucher code JOBWORKSHOP. THE ONE CLUB

Communication Arts

CMYK

CMYK is a quarterly magazine that features the best in student work. You should get it.

Go to the *CMYK* website (www.cmykmag.com) and either buy single issues in their store or click on Subscribe – that will take you to https://www.themagstore.com/ and you'll know what to do.

You might also connect with *CMYK* on Facebook. It's a great resource for seeing what your fellow students are doing.

Luerzer's Archive

Subscribe to Luerzer's Int'l Archive at a discounted student subscription rate - only $39 for 6 issues of Luerzer's Int'l Archive. Or get one-year print (6 PRINT issues) + 1-FULL year Digital access (PC/MAC, mobile and Tablet) for only $99. This offer can be found on our website: www.luerzersarchive.us.

Acknowledgments: The Part Where I Thank Everybody except the Dog

Laurence Minsky
Executive Editor

Suzanne Pope in her excellent blog, adteachings. com (check it out), posted a graphic by Mary Ellen Tribby showing the difference between successful and unsuccessful people. It included the observation that successful people have a sense of gratitude while others have a sense of entitlement. I believe this to be true, and I certainly recognize I was not "entitled" to receive such great essays to produce another book.

I recognize that everyone who contributed essays and other elements of the book did so out of the kindess of their hearts and a burning desire to help the next generation of creative people succeed. And I hope you are as grateful to them as I am since they've helped me realize my goal of producing another book; I hope they're helping you realize your goals as well.

First of all, I want to thank Bruce Bendinger for seeing the possibilities and enabling me to bring the book concept to life. I also want to thank Lorelei Bendinger-Davis, Pat Aylward, Aaron Mitter, Eugina Velazquez, Stefanie Crawford, and the rest of the Copy Workshop team for their thoughts, en-thusiasm, energy, support, brain cells, ideas, lunch conversation, and more (the true list would be book length). Plus, I want to give a special shout out to Frank Blossom for all of his time, energy, thoughts, advice, and insights that went into shaping this book.

Of course, thank yous go to Dan Balser, Rich Binell, Frank Blossom, Bart Cleveland, Katarzyna Dragovic, Mary Ryan Djurovic, Jeffrey Epstein, Colleen Fahey, Kelley Fead, Cabell Harris, Thomas Kemeny, Wendy Lalli, Robin Landa, Tim Leake, Rick Mathieson, Cal McAllister, Karen L. Mallia, Erik McKinney, Thomas McManus, Ignacio Oreamuno, Andrea Phillips, Suzanne Pope, Alan Rado, Stan Richards, Brett Robbs, William Rosen, Ron Seichrist, Robin Shaprio, Cliftin Simmons II, Ethan Smith, Luke Sullivan, Nancy Tag, Kara Taylor, Nancy Vonk, Aubrey Walker III, Brendan Watson,

Mike Williams, and Lena Woo for donating their outstanding essays as well as to Larissa Brandao, Angela Marton, and Allison Sullivan, for contributing their thoughts. And I want to thank Richard Greb, Katherine Fisher, and Sandra Allen for their help and advice.

And, since people are known to judge books by their covers (at least initially), I want to thank everyone at Commonground Marketing for contributing such a fine "billboard" for the book; I believe it captures the spirit of the contents. So, thank you, Lena Woo, Director of People & Culture, for arranging it; Sherman Wright, Co-Founder and Managing Partner, for agreeing to it; Stephanie Breese and Amy Blahnik, Project Managers, for ensuring a smooth development process; and Kristi Pagoulatos, Associate Creative Director, for producing such an attractive piece of art.

I also wish to thank Warick Carter, Louise Love, Doreen Bartoni, Alton Miller, Robin Barger, Mirella Shannon, Margaret Sullivan, Tom Hamilton, and Herbert Allen of Columbia College Chicago for creating the supportive atmosphere that enabled me to complete the manuscript. And thanks to my academic collegues – especially Shanita Akintonde, Sandra Allen, Hyunjung Bae, Kevin Christophersen, Dave Gordon, Sandra Kumorowski, Sherlene McCoy, Peg Murphy, Craig Sigele, Mike Swidler, Margot Wallace, and Cornell Wright – for contributing to that atmosphere. And I want to thank all of my clients and students. After all, I learned so much from all of them.

Most of all, I wish to thank my wife, Rhonda, and my daughter, Jorie, for their support, encouragement, understanding, and acceptance of a large pile of notes in our home office.

As for the dog, well ... While loyal and paitent, I have to draw the line somewhere. She brings much to my life, as does the cat. But they really didn't ... On second thought, perhaps ...